Language and Antiracism

NEW PERSPECTIVES ON LANGUAGE AND EDUCATION

Founding Editor: Viv Edwards, *University of Reading, UK*
Series Editors: Phan Le Ha, *University of Hawaii at Manoa, USA* and Joel Windle, *Monash University, Australia.*

Two decades of research and development in language and literacy education have yielded a broad, multidisciplinary focus. Yet education systems face constant economic and technological change, with attendant issues of identity and power, community and culture. What are the implications for language education of new 'semiotic economies' and communications technologies? Of complex blendings of cultural and linguistic diversity in communities and institutions? Of new cultural, regional and national identities and practices? The New Perspectives on Language and Education series will feature critical and interpretive, disciplinary and multidisciplinary perspectives on teaching and learning, language and literacy in new times. New proposals, particularly for edited volumes, are expected to acknowledge and include perspectives from the Global South. Contributions from scholars from the Global South will be particularly sought out and welcomed, as well as those from marginalized communities within the Global North.

All books in this series are externally peer-reviewed.

Full details of all the books in this series and of all our other publications can be found on http://www.multilingual-matters.com, or by writing to Multilingual Matters, St Nicholas House, 31-34 High Street, Bristol, BS1 2AW, UK.

NEW PERSPECTIVES ON LANGUAGE AND EDUCATION: 114

Language and Antiracism

An Antiracist Approach to Teaching (Spanish) Language in the USA

José L. Magro

MULTILINGUAL MATTERS
Bristol • Jackson

Thandi...siempre

DOI https://doi.org/10.21832/MAGRO0442
Library of Congress Cataloging in Publication Data
A catalog record for this book is available from the Library of Congress.
Names: Magro, José L., author.
Title: Language and Antiracism: An Antiracist Approach to Teaching (Spanish) Language in the USA/José L. Magro.
Description: Bristol; Jackson: Multilingual Matters, [2023] | Series: New Perspectives on Language and Education: 114 | Includes bibliographical references and index. | Summary: "Beginning from the premise that being non-racist - and other 'neutral' positions - are inadequate in the face of a racist society and institutions, this book provides language educators with theoretical knowledge and practical tools to implement antiracist pedagogy in their classrooms"— Provided by publisher.
Identifiers: LCCN 2022061528 (print) | LCCN 2022061529 (ebook) | ISBN 9781800410442 (hardback) | ISBN 9781800410435 (paperback) | ISBN 9781800410466 (epub) | ISBN 9781800410459 (pdf)
Subjects: LCSH: Spanish language—Study and teaching (Higher)—English speakers. | Spanish language—Study and teaching (Higher)—Social aspects—United States. | Racism in higher education—United States. | Critical pedagogy—United States. | Anti-racism—United States. | Whites—United States—Race identity.
Classification: LCC PC4068.U5 M34 2023 (print) | LCC PC4068.U5 (ebook) | DDC 468.0071/073—dc23/eng/20230315
LC record available at https://lccn.loc.gov/2022061528
LC ebook record available at https://lccn.loc.gov/2022061529

British Library Cataloguing in Publication Data
A catalogue entry for this book is available from the British Library.

ISBN-13: 978-1-80041-044-2 (hbk)
ISBN-13: 978-1-80041-043-5 (pbk)

Multilingual Matters
UK: St Nicholas House, 31-34 High Street, Bristol, BS1 2AW, UK.
USA: Ingram, Jackson, TN, USA.

Website: https://www.multilingual-matters.com
Twitter: Multi_Ling_Mat
Facebook: https://www.facebook.com/multilingualmatters
Blog: https://www.channelviewpublications.wordpress.com

Typeset by Deanta Global Publishing Services, Chennai, India

Contents

Introduction: Antiracist Pedagogy Works!

I.1 Contextualizing This Book

'Why are we having all these people from shithole countries come here?' With these words, US President-elect Donald Trump referred to US immigrants from El Salvador, Haiti and African countries when arguing with lawmakers about their protected status. The 45th president, an overt racist and a symptom of a history of racism, could have been the subject of an entire monograph dedicated to the racist comments he made during his presidency. However, this is not the goal of this manuscript. Addressed to educators, this book aims to tackle racism in (Spanish) language classes by understanding and implementing antiracist practices aimed at decolonizing the curriculum. Nevertheless, 45's presidency is important for contextualizing this text, which I started writing in 2019. I am aware that the following words may sound harsh and strongly worded for readers who did not live in the United States under this presidency (and now, under its sequels and an uncertain future) like I did/do. But for those who, like me, had to experience it from a sociopolitical locus similar to mine, my tone may sound somewhat modest and nuanced.

Despite Trump's failure in the 2020 election, after four years of what I suffered during a bizarre far-right presidency (exacerbated by the COVID-19 crisis), many of us live under the impression that overt xenophobia and racism have become accepted and normalized by almost half of the voting population in the United States. One only needs to drive out of the main US urban centers and enter the realm of White suburban and rural America to see overtly racist messages posted on roads, cars and homes all over the country – yes, I consider that signs supporting Trump are overt racism because he is an overt racist. This is not an opinion; the data demonstrate that anti-immigrant sentiment, racism and sexism are much more strongly related to support for Trump than, for instance, educational level (Schaffner *et al.*, 2018). Trump did especially well with White people who express sexist views about women and who deny racism exists. At best, these racist attitudes and behavior have been

1

criticized from a passive, distant, disassociated perspective by a 'liberal' segment of mainstream society. At the same time, we wonder how we ended up going back to an America in which overt racism is not only justified and displayed but also promoted from the United States' highest office of power, which has also exported it to global far-right political organizations.

The answer to this question is evident. America never stopped being racist; it just adopted, for a long time, another type of racism, what Bonilla-Silva (2003) described as a racist society without racists. Moreover, after Barack Obama was elected president, some believed that we now lived in what some called a 'post-racial America', despite the profound inequalities reflected in housing, banking, employment, health care, education and criminal justice, or the fact that Black and Latino youth are being brutally massacred by White supremacists (including the police) across the country. Some of these actors are the very same people who attacked the US Capitol with impunity on 6 January 2021. While I reflect on the political context when I first started writing this introduction and how the situation evolved, I cannot avoid shaking my head off.

On 8 November 2016, the *collejón* – the term used in Madrid *barrios* for a hard slap in the back of your neck – arrived, (un)expectedly, merciless, sharp, waking some people up, lifting masks and hoods for many others, showing the ugliest face of overt racism in the United States. The phenomenon propagated around the world due to the globalized nature of today's politics, in which think tanks and conferences such as the Conservative Political Action Conference (popularly known as the CPAC, an annual political conference attended by conservative activists and elected officials from all over the world) discuss and promote media and political strategies to promote the success of neo-nationalist/populist far-right political parties with aggressive neoliberal agendas. It must be noted that although the outward relationship between neoliberalism and neo-nationalism is generally presented as antagonistic, they share much common ground and interests in areas such as immigration, as Felman (2011: 25) argues. In the words of Giorgio Agamben (2009, cited in Felman, 2011: 25), what public opinion, at least in the US context, refers to as 'the Right and the Left, which today alternate in the management of power, have for this reason very little to do with the political sphere in which they originated. They are simply the names of two poles – the first point without scruples to desubjectification, the second wanting instead to hide behind the hypocritical mask of the good democratic citizen – of the same governmental machine'. Besides, it is arguably questionable to label as 'the Left' any political party with a neoliberal orientation. I would consider both poles on the right of the left–right political spectrum. Outside the United States, similar neo-nationalist parties include the Belgian People's Party (Belgium), the British National Party (United Kingdom), the French National Front (France), the German NPD

(Germany), One Nation (Australia), the Social Liberal Party (Brazil), the Swedish Sweden Democrats (Sweden), the Swiss People's Party (Switzerland) and Vox (Spain).

Suddenly, that strange enigma associated with the problem of racism that Albert Memmi (2000) talks about – 'no one, or almost no one, wishes to see themselves as racist' – became obsolete. Those recent times when Whites, shielded by what Bonilla-Silva (2003) calls 'color blindness', enunciated positions that safeguarded their racial interests without sounding 'racist' are long gone. Although many Whites still reject overt racism, in a growing range of social, political and geographical landscapes there is no more need for 'color blindness' to express resentment toward minorities and criticize their morality, values or work ethic or to even claim to be the victims of 'reverse racism', or even more surrealistically, claim to be part of some sort of freedom resistance movement. For some, being a racist far-right militant has turned into being anti-system, a kind of freedom fighter. The appeal of being transgressively racist and politically incorrect has driven many Whites to be part of a bizarre resistance movement that internalizes a need to fight for White privilege, perceived as being in danger of extinction. At the same time, it is the economic elites who benefit most from this rhetoric. But this new rhetoric has consequences. Counties that hosted a 2016 Trump rally saw a 226% increase in hate crimes, such as the 2019 racially motivated mass shootings in Texas and Ohio (Feinberg *et al.*, 2019). However, media outlets keep portraying these racist terrorists as 'lone-wolf losers', rare exceptions that have nothing to do with a current racist political climate that feeds from both overt and covert racism. And yet, a mob of these 'lone-wolf losers' took over the Capitol, and as I write this, only 13 of them have been charged, despite being captured on camera and identified. After all, what could happen to them? Several months earlier, on 25 May 2020, George Floyd had been publicly executed by police. The three officers involved were released on bail, waiting for their trial to take place in March 2021.

However, after George Floyd's execution, many people realized that simply being non-racist is not an option: antiracism is the only approach acceptable to fighting racism. Being non-racist – along with other positions of so-called neutrality – is not valid in the fight against this scourge; being non-racist equals racism. Antiracist scholars and/or educators now have an opening, and talk of antiracist workshops, classes, university programs, school curricula and even corporate interventions has started to propagate. But racism is rooted in capitalism and neoliberal policies, and antiracism demands a systemic change, which many are unwilling to even consider. General consent for neoliberal and/or neo-nationalist ideologies, and the implicit or explicit rejection of possible better and more just socioeconomic systems, are deeply rooted in society. It is in this sociopolitical context that this book is written.

I.2 Direct Action, a Direct Approach, a Direct Unapologetic Tone

A great part of the pedagogical proposal I introduce in this book is based on the tradition of direct action passed by historic figures such as anarchist Louise Michel (1830–1905) or human rights leader Malcolm X (1925–1965). That is, freedom cannot be granted by the oppressor: it must be taken by the oppressed by any means necessary. This influence is necessarily going to translate into a very direct approach in my antiracist pedagogical approach as well as into, sometimes, the use of a virulent and direct unapologetic tone throughout the book, such as the one used in some of the previous assertions in this introduction. This tone may produce some pushback, and I run the risk of losing some readers along these pages. While I would like to reach as many readers as possible, it is not the purpose of this book to become a mainstream source of knowledge or merely a tool to help people feel better about themselves. The goal is not to make the reader feel bad, either. Similar to my approach in the classroom, in which I aim to reach as many students as possible, it is not always possible to reach everyone. I acknowledge that some potential White allies may feel uncomfortable with some passages of this book and may feel inclined to stop reading before they get to the practice-oriented second part of this book. It is not my intention to create a dogmatic pedagogical approach or push away potential allies, but rather to approach language and racism in a direct and explicit manner without sugar-coating it. I intend to spark discussion and help to engage and develop antiracist educators and approaches and improve or create new materials. In order to do that, sometimes my tone and content may generate some cognitive dissonance. The intention of generating this dissonance is to push toward reflection, self-criticism and critique and direct action, not to be taken as a reproach or a personal attack.

I also want to emphasize that my approach to antiracist language teaching should be taken as one proposal among others. My intention is far from creating 'the correct path to follow' to be an antiracist educator, but rather to introduce what I have been doing with the hope that this can be of some help to you, as it has been to me and others. My proposal is based on research intersected by my experience and its (historic, sociopolitical, economic) context, which does not make my approach better or worse than others, but more importantly, should not be read as an either/or approach. Moreover, as you will see, some of my proposals may seem innovative, while others are based on basic critical pedagogic principles. More often, it is a combination of both.

I.3 What Do I Refer to When I Talk about Racism?

When I refer to racism in this book, I refer to White racism in the United States. I will explain further in Chapters 1 and 3, but I would like to anticipate some possible critiques. Some readers may argue that

I generalize when I use the term White to refer to a very diverse population that comes from many different (geographical, ethnic, religious, sociopolitical, etc.) backgrounds. But in accordance with critical race theory (CRT), the heterogeneity of Whiteness dissipates in juxtaposition to those racial groups constructed as racialized others in a similar way that our own intradiversity within each racialized minority constructed as a racial group dissipates in juxtaposition to Whiteness. And note that I use the first-person plural when referring to racialized minorities, which offers a good opportunity to introduce myself. The following reflection about my own identity(s) – intentionally a bit messy and confusing, as identities are in nature – is important because, as we will see in this book, the educators' own experiences and the reflection on these experiences are crucial when developing/implementing antiracist pedagogies.

I.4 'What Are You?': A Reflection on the Identity of the Author of This Book

An infamous question that racially ambiguous individuals often hear in the New York City streets is, 'What are you?' As you can imagine, this question may be interpreted in multiple ways, but those familiar with the multiethnoraciality of this city know what this question really means: you are not White, but I cannot really tell what (race, ethnicity) you are. I will try my best to reflect on my identity(s) and imagine that while riding the A train in Brooklyn and being casually asked this question, I – for once – have the opportunity to expand on it.

Dr Jesus Valverde, one of my favorite professors during my psychology *licenciatura* back in the 1990s, told us something I never forgot: 'Nunca podemos ser objetivos porque no somos objetos, somos sujetos' (we can never be objective because we are not objects but subjects). Since then, positionality has been a key issue in my research, scholarship and even artistic practice. I am not afraid to show my true colors – *al contrario*, I embrace them. Thus, during my following attempt to try to identify myself, I may be able to shed some light on how I understand identities, in plural, as multifaceted, dynamic, always open to appropriation, reappropriation and transformation, in constant evolution, always depending on the sociopolitical and historical context, who performs them and who is the audience, something that will be discussed in more depth in Chapter 3. As Eric Buyssens (1970) argued, the study of identities is the study of communication processes; that is, the means used to influence others and recognized as such by the others in question.

Hybridity and identity always go hand in hand. I am a father, husband, son, brother, graffiti artist, MC, music producer, water polo coach and player, from the hood (from *Alkorcón*), working-class, scholar, educator, male, heterosexual, antiracist, immigrant, feminist, non-religious, Hispanic, non-White and bilingual, but one of my identities that intersects all of them is Hip-Hop: I am Hip-Hop. Moreover, I am not only Hip-Hop but also *soy Hip-Hop* (phonetically [xip xop]), that is, my Hip-Hop identity was developed first in Spanish. I proudly carry the stigma associated with being a Hip-Hop scholar who is a *real* Hip-Hop head who started as a graffiti artist and became a well-recognized MC in the Spanish-speaking world. This also has an influence on the pedagogical tools that I propose. They are intersected by Hip-Hop because that identity is a central component of my identity(s). But, anticipating critiques, and due to the high presence of Hip-Hop throughout this book, let me explain what I understand by Hip-Hop.

Hybridity is at the core of Hip-Hop. The way I understand Hip-Hop implies using whatever is within one's reach to create. When Hip-Hop started, resources were limited, very limited. Hip-Hop emerged from a situation of precariousness and lack of opportunities. Hip-Hop heads brought into the mix any available technological devices, tools and cultural artifacts within their reach to create. This creative framework permeates the way I develop my pedagogical approach because most of the time, resources for developing antiracist curricula are scarce, and you have to work with what you have in a similar way we are accustomed to in Hip-Hop culture.

Although many outsiders may associate Hip-Hop with misogyny and violence due to mainstream media and its exploitation and promotion of Hip-Hop based on those topics, for many insiders like me, that is not what we refer to when we refer to Hip-Hop. I do not doubt that many hegemonic ideologies penetrate Hip-Hop in a detrimental way (especially detrimental for the people who originated it), and the artistic result of these ideologies, particularly in rap music, is exploited in mainstream outlets to monetize and demote youth's critical thinking. However, as I argue (Magro, 2016b), since its origins, especially in the case of rap (but also in graffiti, DJing and breakdance), there has existed both a collective and individual consciousness that has distinguished between real Hip-Hop artists and 'sell-outs' (those who drop out and betray the ideological values of Hip-Hop because of business goals, whether or not they are met). Already in 1979, the Sugarhill Gang appropriated and sold the popular raps written by renowned MCs from the emergent Hip-Hop scene of the Bronx, such as Grand Master Caz, to record them and turn them into the prefabricated commercial success that was *Rapper's Delight*.

Although the festive and popular elements have also been constant themes in Hip-Hop culture since the beginning, Hip-Hop has had a vindictive element of political and social commitment. In the late 1970s, the Universal Zulu Nation organization made this element explicit, calling for unity, peace and love as a form of resistance to the racism and marginalization suffered by young people from underprivileged neighborhoods in NYC. Many other artists, especially in the late 1980s and early

1990s, proposed more aggressive models of social activism and resistance in their productions. Regardless of the style or political position taken by the Hip-Hop artist, authenticity is the main concept that awards credibility to Hip-Hop productions. An important aspect of this authenticity is the socioeconomic background of the artist. In this sense, the Hip-Hop locus of origin and production is undoubtedly located in underprivileged neighborhoods, regardless of the contradictions that may arise in its artistic content.

Thus, credibility and authenticity, what we call in Hip-Hop culture 'keepin' it real', are key tenets of Hip-Hop (Androutsopoulos, 2010), at least for those who understand Hip-Hop in a manner like I do. I live by these tenets. We never fake it. Consequently, as Hip-Hop, I perform the realest identity that I can, but notice how I still use the verb *to perform*, which has to do with Goffman (1956) and his theory of identity as theatrical performance, which will be explained in Chapter 3. Ultimately, as unfair as this may sound, it is the audience who will grant me my identity.

My wife used to say that rappers in the 1990s, when they appeared in films and TV shows, were not able to act. And I agree because they didn't need to. They played roles that were very similar to their lives. Hip-Hop and acting mix poorly. Recently, my good friend Dr Eddie Paulino – who, despite being a Dominican from New York City's Lower East Side Housing Projects, keeps me up to date on all the shenanigans related to Spain – sent me an article about actor Javier Bardem talking about discrimination against Spaniards in Hollywood after being criticized for taking a role playing a Cuban. The online comments on this article were fantastic, but I wanna highlight two of them. One said that all he had to say was that he is an actor and 'it is called acting, the art form of stepping into someone else's shoes. I've played writers, murderers & psychics. Here is a list of my training as an actor as well as my credits'. The other said, 'Spaniards are not White only *cuando les conviene*' (when it is in their own interest). I agree. Whether you are or are not White, it has to be *a las duras y a las maduras* (through thick and thin). For us Hip-Hop heads, it is not ethical to play on both sides of the fence.

I grew up in a drug-infested working-class neighborhood in the periphery of Spain's biggest city, Madrid, where the daughters and sons of national and international migrant parents learned how to run or fight older, but still young, drug addicts at an early age. Thus, I still hold a strong consciousness and pride in my working-class/*barrio* identity. I am a first-generation university student. Although in Spain going to college was almost free when compared to the outrageous costs of US universities, only a very few of us in my surroundings went to college. It was still very expensive for us, 'los de las casas baratas' (the ones from the cheap houses), as one of my coaches used to call us, and most of us would be 'filtered out' by the system or not even consider the university a realistic possibility or path to making a living.

I am a migrant son of migrants. My father grew up in a cave (literally) and could not finish elementary school because he started working at the age of 10 when he moved from La Mancha's countryside to Madrid. My mother, a migrant from Argentina, was otherized because of her South American accent. My paternal grandfather was incarcerated for political reasons after the Spanish Civil War by Franco's regime and survived a death sentence, thus my early antifascist sentiment. In contrast, my maternal grandfather had to emigrate to South America with his family for economic reasons despite fighting on Franco's side, the winners of the coup d'état that ended up in a civil war – which led to the current democracy that never judged the coup supporters and, instead, positioned them and their descendants in the current government spheres.

Growing up, my working-class identity was central, but race was important too, especially for those around me who were racialized. I witnessed racism against family and friends, which was more salient for those of African descent. I even suffered that racism when I was racialized as a Latino immigrant in Spain, and therefore as gang affiliated (public speech in mainstream outlets constantly iconize Latin American youth in Spain as gang affiliated), by police who misinterpreted my Hip-Hop aesthetics as being a Latin American migrant. Notice that being *latino* in Spain has a different connotation to being Latino in the United States. Through a process of otherization, people of Latin American descent living in Spain are racially constructed as a different social group in opposition to what some consider 'real' Spaniards, whatever that may be.

Although I had introductory experiences of being racialized at a young age in Switzerland and the United Kingdom, I was not truly impacted by my racialization until I migrated to the United States, mainly because I was here to stay. This was not a shock for me, as it is for many other Spaniards whose experiences with racial discrimination are from the oppressor's point of view and who try to pass for White and desperately claim Whiteness with more or less success. These Spaniards usually carry with them a sociopolitical view in which there is a tendency to align with whitewashing ideologies and a narrative of Europeanizing Spain (and 'Spanish from Spain', which is basically a center-north peninsular variety of Spanish titled 'European Spanish' by streaming services such as Netflix). This is done through speech and marketing campaigns that aim to emulate the reproduction of otherness, an 'us' vs. 'them' similar to how it is constructed in the United States. But despite not being shocked about my racialization or the racial privileges that a lighter skin tone grants me when compared to Hispanic migrants of African or Native American descent, racial profiling was no less frustrating or dangerous.

I have been living for more than 23 years in the United States, where, despite coming from a country in which people are constantly struggling to index themselves as White, I became racialized as a Hispanic/Latino. I went through the hardships of being an undocumented immigrant until

I regularized my situation through marriage. This period of my life was particularly tough and helps me be aware of the tremendous advantages and privileges offered by this change of status. I have been stopped and frisked numerous times in the street or in airports, even assaulted at gunpoint twice by the police, without any apparent reason other than my 'looks', that is, being a Hispanic/Latino male where I was not supposed to be. During those incidents, neither my companions nor I (all Hispanic men) went up to the officers' faces and showed hostility toward them, as John McWhorter, a strong critic of antiracism, points out as the real reason for police brutality in what he considers a post-racial society.[1] Some of you are fortunate enough to not understand that fear; others do and live constantly under it. I still do.

Moreover, my national identity is as meaningless to me as nationalism is, that is, *ser español me la suda* (I could not care less about being a Spaniard). This lack of nationalist sentiment and my aversion toward patriotism may be, in a way, a political privilege if we see it from a Spanish context perspective. If we think about immigrants in Spain who struggle to regularize their migrant status and, thus, become Spaniards, my anti-patriotism may be considered a privilege. However, lacking a sense of nationalistic patriotism in the US context is definitely not a privilege. All of us who do not stand up for racist national anthems understand the social and peer pressure of not doing so. I do not believe in the idea of nation-states, especially those based on neoliberal market logics. I have witnessed the violence produced by the neoliberal market logics in New York's *hoods* where I lived and worked, kids surviving on chips and soda passing by fancy restaurants on their way to their underserved schools. Most of these kids are Black and Latino and, supposedly, live in a prosperous nation (prosperous for whom?).

But racism not only has a direct impact on me and those around me but also on those who I love the most. I am the husband of an African American woman whose mother is a Jamaican migrant and whose father survived one of the roughest neighborhoods in Brooklyn, NY, to become a lawyer, both awesome human beings. I am also the father of two multilingual, translingual, multiracial, multiethnic kids. I belong to a family that is antagonistic to the logics of the ideology of homogenization.

So, when facing the dilemma of filling out forms with demographic data (or answering the infamous question of 'what are you?'), I always check Latino/Hispano, because that is how 'they' see me. However, although my hispanicity is uncontestable, my *latinidad*, since I was born in Spain, could be contested by some Latinos, who understand being Latino as being of Latin American descent. Many of you readers in the United States, especially those living in the Washington, DC, Metro Area, may be used to middle-class students, teachers, professors and professionals (especially from the banking sector) from Spain who probably influenced your archetype of a Spanish identity – that is, your imagined idea of what being from Spain means. In part, this reflection exercise about my identity is oriented to help you reimagine and contest precisely that image: I am a scholar, I am a professor, I am from Spain, I am from the hood, and I am *not* White, *a las duras y a las maduras*. Probably, it could be easier to claim that my mom is Argentinian, but why? Curiously, she has light eyes and fair skin, and besides, many Argentinians claim to be proud of being 'the most European Latin American country'. My father is the dark one, the one who was called '*moro*' (moor) by my mother's parents when they advised her not to marry him because of his physical features (they are still happily married). *Mi padre* passed on to me his African DNA, which many Spanish people share, as much as they have rejected it. But claiming to be Black would be a long stretch and almost as ridiculous as those racial impostors like NAACP chapter leader Rachel Dolezal, who claimed to be Black for personal profit. As GURU (1961–2010), one of my favorite MCs, said, that wouldn't be 'keepin' it real, that would be keepin' it wrong'.

To add more complexity to the issue, depending on the agency collecting this data, some categorizations will allow me to check my race as Hispanic/Latino, while others would consider this category an ethnicity and ask me to check a box for a race with which I do not identify (sometimes I can escape this conflict when a 'multiracial' or 'other' box is offered). Nonetheless, I am aware of how those Latinos and Latinas of uncontestably African descent, regardless of their social class, cultural affiliations and/or aesthetics tend to be discriminated against by many of 'them' and by many of 'us' at higher rates than people who phenotypically look like me – more Mediterranean, as some people would say – especially if their social class, cultural affiliations and/or aesthetics align closer with Whiteness (not my case). The one thing that I am sure of regarding race in the United States is that I am not White, and I do not have any intention to try passing as White, neither assimilating nor sharing any privilege that Whiteness could grant in a similar manner as it does to those groups that historically were not considered White in the United States but, after long struggles, are now considered as such (e.g. Italians, Jewish).

All of these affiliations and experiences that have preceded me as a scholar have forged my (stigmatized) identities. These identities are necessarily going to permeate my production and guide and influence my scholarly practice, which, framed within a critical paradigm, necessarily denies notions of value-free research.

I.5 Motivations to Write This Book

Reflecting on the intersection of my ethnoracial identity with class and cultural affiliations drives me to reflect on my motivations for writing this book. I am not in a tenure-track position, so academic pressures are not at the forefront of my motivations. A few months ago, I was invited as a keynote speaker to a sociolinguistics conference at a prestigious US university. One of the questions they asked me was how my research on identity and language to develop antiracist pedagogies can contribute or give back to the community. My answer, closely tied to my motivations for writing this book, started by explaining that when I talk about *the community*, I refer to *my community*, since I still feel part of it and never cut my ties to it.

Keeping these ties to my community has to do with the acknowledgment of how fortunate I am to have entered the well-guarded gates of academia, something that I owe in part to great mentors, two of whom were my dissertation directors (a big shout out to Dr José del Valle and Dra Bea Lado), another two from my hood in Brooklyn (a big shout out to Dra Zaire Dinzey-Flores and Dr Eddie Paulino). But being, or rather feeling, fortunate is not the same as being privileged, since privilege is inherited, and entering academia is something that I earned through hard work and many sacrifices. Nonetheless, most of the people I grew up with never had a chance; most of them barely graduated from high school. For many of them, academia was not even a path that crossed their minds. Others tried and never made it. Even for me, it is somehow still shocking that I was able to make it through these gates when I think about where I come from and how this idea of becoming a doctor seemed something reserved for privileged minds with the economic, cultural and social capital to back them up.

However, I do not attribute my success to some sort of individual characteristics or superior intellect, not even solely to hard work and sacrifice, but rather to a combination of factors that helped me, a kid from the *barrio*, to earn a doctorate. When I think about why many of us don't enter the world of academia, I reflect on what could have made the difference in my case. Aside from many circumstances and those apparently low-impact random life events that could have made a difference, I had what many did not – that is, the loving support of two parents who always encouraged me to study, parents who always provided food and the safety of a home. They always covered my basic needs. They contributed to the development of my self-esteem and confidence. They encouraged me to practice sports, which definitely helped me develop self-discipline and physical and mental endurance. Many of my peers who were 'left behind' did not have someone to provide them with this safety net and these developmental tools. This may seem trivial at first glance, but, at least in my case, it made a real difference.

Also, I acknowledge the potential privilege attached to sharing a wonderful partnership with a woman who supports me. Being heterosexual and married also grants me certain privileges that others do not have (e.g. monoparental or same-gender families). Simultaneously, it makes me an outsider to questions related to gender, sexual orientation and marital status different from mine. Although this makes me cautious, it does not prevent me from trying to understand and be an ally.

Thus, not only due to my existing links to those less fortunate than me but also because I feel that it is my moral duty to help uplift as many of us as possible and help to imagine a more just world, my work always has in mind those who are still out there suffering the consequences of a greedy and racist system that turns many lives into a living hell. In consequence, my research is motivated by, and intertwined with, my practice, which is oriented to integrate, in the core, not in the margins or piled up in one single month (like Black history month does in US schools), those voices historically excluded from academia as well as the diverse formats in which those voices travel.

I.6 My Own Privileges

But despite all my claims to oppressed identities, I am not privilege-free. I already mentioned how being a heterosexual male and my marital status are forms of privilege, but another privilege I acknowledge is, ironically, how my stigmatized identities grant me a critical awareness of power dynamics and systems of oppression while allowing me to be an insider in the fight against these systems.

Whenever I work with my racialized students, this is something that I notice, and which I point out to them, with the subsequent empowering effect. I notice and recognize their generally higher awareness threshold at the time they enter my courses when compared to their White counterparts regarding many of the issues this book attempts to address. Racialized individuals live with many of these issues and are forced to think about them, while for Whites, this is something optional.

Some Whites, and recently more and more, enter my courses with critical awareness as well, because they have read about topics related to antiracism on their own, or they have been fortunate enough to receive classes in which these topics were addressed. However, as you may be imagining, those Whites who enter my courses with a very low awareness of these issues may feel uncomfortable at first. But an antiracist educator should be able to provide a safe space for all to learn and not make possible allies feel rejected or attacked. Nonetheless, I believe there is nothing wrong with that discomfort. The racist world we share is not a comfortable place, especially for those suffering from racism, and this discomfort is caused, in great part, by those with a lack of awareness regarding these 'uncomfortable' topics. My book attempts to raise critical antiracist awareness regardless of the base level of awareness of the readers or their race, as I do in my classes. To do so, it starts from a necessarily critical epistemological perspective in which language is understood as a sociopolitical construct. Within this understanding, I anchor and deploy most of the articulations of language, power and identities that I will discuss.

This work is also informed by the idea of otherness constructed in different ways, depending on the socioeconomic, political and historical landscape. This is true of the construction of the racialized other. However, antiblack racism and colorism are a constant in almost all societies, but without any doubt in the United States and within all its intracultures. Not being Black grants me privileges that I acknowledge, as much as being a Hispanic immigrant denies me others. My understanding of the Black experience is not going to be the same as the understanding of a Black person. This is a fact that never prevented me from hearing, reading, learning and connecting/contrasting those experiences to mine. This is a fact that does not prevent me from fighting against antiblack racism – with Black people, not for Black people. Although the discussion of antiblack racism appears in this book, it is not my goal to be a so-called savior of Black people, like John McWhorter (2021), an African American linguist widely criticized for his reactionary tendencies, would put it. This is mainly because my antiracist approach acknowledges but does not focus solely on antiblack racism. Neither am I trying to become a moral compass of what is right and wrong, but rather helping to stop racism, not progressively, not from a moderate position, but radically and now because I believe racism is detrimental and unjust, and, factually, it exists. And, nope, not all radicalisms are the same. McWhorter (2021), who despite his ultraconservative views considers himself a radical moderate, claims that 'systemic racism is not Black people's main problem' and antiracism is a patronizing and infantilizing stance toward oppressed and non-majority communities. Furthermore, he argues that Black people are considered to be the only social group 'in the whole history of homosapiens [sic]' who can reach true success (whatever this means for him) through the utopian idea of a sociopsychological revolution. I completely disagree with McWhorter. I believe that inequity in the United States is not only a racial issue but a systemic one in which racism is rooted. Moreover, 'in the whole history of homosapiens', we know that any significant transformation achieved by any social group has been achieved through revolution, and revolutions are radical by nature.

There is a current feeling of urgency to fight racism. In my case, this urgency did not start after May 2020, with the public execution of George Floyd, but much earlier – I would say in the early 1990s when I started fighting neo-Nazis as a South Madrid youth. Although I still do not reject any acts to stop racism, I believe that education is the best tool to prevent and stop it. During my youth, there was not much theory available to us; it was mainly praxis. This reflection on my early beginnings made me notice a key issue when I thought about how to fight racism in the language classroom: the disconnection between theory and practice, the disconnection between the talking and 'walking the talking'.

I.7 The Disconnection Between Theory and Practice

This book's twofold goal integrates theory and praxis in an attempt to decolonize the curriculum. On the one hand, these pages aim to inform about theoretical aspects of racism and how it manifests in language programs. In this sense, this book is interested in establishing a conversation about topics that may help educators reflect on an antiracist approach to language teaching while providing the fundamental concepts necessary to be familiar with before attempting to implement it. On the other hand, from a more practical approach 'concerned with the functional process of how the process of decolonization might happen' (Ade-ojo, 2021: 1), this book aims to provide a theory-based pedagogical rationale and strategy to fight racism in the language classroom through instruction that integrates research-based contents related to the sociopolitical dimension of language (also referred to as sociopolitical contents [SPCs]) aiming to raise critical linguistic awareness (CLA) in relation to racism. The purpose of this book, then, is to combat racism within one institution that has historically perpetuated it: the university.

In *Ebony and Ivy*, C.S. Wilder (2013) points out the connection between the physical manifestation of colleges and universities around the United States and the supporting funding, curricular structure and purposes of early institutions. In doing so, Wilder describes the connection between slavery and universities during early colonial times (e.g. George Washington University, University of Georgia). But this is not the only thread linking racist theories to contemporary universities. As Squire *et al.* (2018) argue through the concept of 'plantation politics', parallel organizational and cultural norms remain in place between contemporary higher education institutions and slave plantations. Thus, 'old ideologies and tools for oppressing and marginalizing people of color are connected to newer strategies of repression and policing within universities' (Squire *et al.*, 2018: 2).

US educational institutions – and their educators – have the moral duty to transmit ethical beliefs framed within the national, or rather a-national, self-concept of a pluralistic, democratic, egalitarian ideology, as well as the knowledge and skills necessary to thrive, or at least survive, physically, psychologically and socially in our society and across societies in this globalized world. It is our duty as educators to break a system that echoes beliefs such as, quoting Princeton President Woodrow Wilson, '[T]he college is not for the majority who carry forward the common labor of the world [but] it is for the minority who plan, who conceive, who superintend' (Veysey, 1970: 245, cited in Cabrera *et al.*, 2017).

However, we should be cautious about the racist–antiracist binary presented here and the idea of reconciling institutions. As Kubota (2020) discusses, many educational institutions may produce discourses of diversity and antiracism to display a positive institutional image from the neoliberal capitalist discourse that valorizes human diversity in order to maximize profit. This approach, known as neoliberal multicultural-ism (Kubota, 2016; Kymlicka, 2013, cited in Kubota, 2020), is becoming difficult to distinguish from critical approaches to difference based on anti-hegemonic critiques such as the one I propose. In neoliberal multi-culturalism discourse, 'anti-hegemonic engagements such as antiracism become softened and converted into non-performativity of antiracism – an uncommitted speech act of the promotion of diversity' (Ahmed, 2012, cited in Kubota, 2020: 167). As Kubota (2020) continues, 'spoken and written statements about institutional commitments to diversity and antiracism may give the impression that that is what the institutions are doing. But in fact, these documents create nonperformative speech acts, thus becoming a substitute for action' and 'evidence that we have "done it"' (Ahmed, 2012: 101, cited in Kubota, 2020). Moreover, 'organiza-tional pride and the self-perception of being good block the recognition of racism' (Ahmed, 2012: 111, cited in Kubota, 2020). The main focus of my proposal is on performativity – that is, walking the talking.

Two reports by the Modern Language Association (MLA) in 2007 and 2009 informed about the need for a multicultural and transcul-tural approach to responding to the needs of new millennium students. However, critical pedagogists such as Michael Apple (2004) go further, arguing for not just multicultural approaches but specifically antiracist education. Despite these recommendations, (US) society at large, from the Oval Office to elementary schools, perpetuate and spread inhumane, unjust, racist ideologies, standards and norms. This is done explicitly or implicitly, but always in complicity with racism whenever individu-als claim not to be racist but do not act on racism. The present book demands educators, scholars, students and any individual to have a proactive attitude toward racism, to denounce and combat it. It is not enough to question how social systems work, so this book urges the reader to expose how these systems privilege and oppress various groups while benefiting others – to resist and fight the ideologies that support these asymmetric power relationships. This is the approach this book takes, with a firm belief that a better world can be imagined, envisioned and, therefore, built through antiracist praxis.

However, I feel that it is necessary to specify that although I am aware that intersectionality is crucial, I prioritize racial identities over other identities in my materials. Race is at the core of my research and practice because race, in the United States, plays a primary role in injus-tice. This does not imply that there exists a hierarchy of identities, but, as I will discuss, race cannot be put at the same level of relevance as other identities, an approach that in education has been called multicul-tural pedagogy – an approach that experience has proven does not work (Apple, 2004). Otherwise, we would not be where we are now. Race intersects other identities in ways that create unique experiences (e.g. it is not the same to be a Black man as a Black woman, it is not the same to be a White woman as a Black woman, it is different to be a Hispanic immigrant and transgender than a White US citizen and transgender, etc.). However, many of the activities proposed in this book are based on the intersection of race with class, gender and migration. While issues of class and migration are closely familiar to me, I live in a male body. Despite my attempt to include issues of gender and sex in my proposed activities, living in a male body is a privilege that may pose a limitation to be taken into consideration if or when educators reading this manuscript attempt to implement or improve on my pedagogical approach by substituting and/or adding materials. The focus of my pedagogical approach on racism does not mean that connections to sexism or other forms of oppression cannot be made, developed or integrated. Many of these forms of oppression intersect with many of the materials I present in this manuscript. Many more could be developed.

This book is informed by proposals aiming to decolonize the curriculum. These proposals appear to have been built around the notion of multiplicity of voices in its design and implementation by 'creating spaces and resources for a dialogue among all members of the university on how to imagine and envision all cultures and knowledge systems in the curriculum, and with respect to what is being taught and how it frames the world' (Charles, 2019, as cited in Ade-ojo, 2021: 2). However, these proposals have been overtheorized. Welton *et al.* (2018: 1) argue that 'anti-racism research is more so ideological and theoretical and does not operationalize specifically how to take action against racism'. As a result, educators have difficulty implementing them into their programs (Dávila, 2011, as cited in Welton *et al.*, 2018). Thus, although this manuscript covers fundamental theoretical aspects of antiracist pedagogies to provide resources and open dialogues about envisioning an alternative approach to what is being taught and how, and argues its benefits in the language classroom, it will do so with the purpose of informing antiracist praxis with concrete pedagogical proposals. In other words, attending to this lack of operationalization of antiracism, this monograph provides examples of how to put it into practice through theory-based practical tools designed for educators, with the hope that these will enable them to combat racism in the language classroom and beyond. I do this from an interdisciplinary perspective in which critical applied linguistics (CALx) intersects with sociolinguistics (which I call critical applied sociolinguistics), language ideologies, second language acquisition (SLA), literacy, Hip-Hop pedagogy, social psychology, sociology and CRT.

This link between theory and praxis is crucial for my scholarship to the point that whenever I am offered to teach basic-level language classes, I do it with pleasure, because I believe that basic-level language classes are the arena where most of the battles are fought and for which I developed some (more or less imperfect) pedagogical weapons. I am also against separating manual and intellectual labor, which in the university language departments may be translated as the distinction between higher-level classes (i.e. linguistics, literature, cultural studies, etc.) and preparing students to take these higher-level classes in a language other than English in the busier, more mechanical, less prestigious lower-level classes (i.e. basic, intermediate language classes). Architects should know how to drive a nail and share in that work, and construction workers should be able to draw blueprints, but this is a longer discussion for another manuscript.

I.8 The Role of Research and Researchers in Imagining a Better World

The disconnection between theory and practice brings me to another point in this introduction: the role of research and researchers in imagining a better world.

I believe that our role as educators is to articulate our knowledge, walk the talk and aim to educate our students in antiracism so that when they leave our classrooms, they can be well-informed and have enough tools to fight racism. This goal emerged somehow after some of my colleagues who were interested in promoting a significant change in their daily teaching, particularly in language classes, came to me for help and/or advice after I offered presentations and workshops based on my research. More recently, in an effort by my current university's department of Spanish to integrate antiracist pedagogies into the classroom, we realized the urgent need to instruct instructors in antiracist practices and the issues this instruction poses (Lacorte & Magro, 2022). Thus, this book attempts to help you figure out how to utilize in your daily practice the available theoretical knowledge from CRT, critical sociolinguistics and language ideologies by providing concrete examples and activities.

However, the approach that I propose is not easy to implement. It will require you to maneuver in creative ways, both inside and outside the classroom, both academically and administratively, both individually and in creating alliances with key university players who share your belief in a better world. My antiracist pedagogical activities feed from courses that I designed, as well as from micro activities that I developed within the cracks of existing syllabi, guerrilla-style, at macro and micro levels. They required patience, effort and endurance, but I was always motivated because I am aware that providing tools to identify, analyze and dismantle racism is something that has a direct impact on my life experience, on those who I love, those who I teach and society at large. As educators, we are frequently bullied into believing that our only mission is to provide students with marketable skills in pursuit of success measured as economic growth or hegemonic institutional prestige. The push from university administrators is toward a market logic of profit, while leaving aside helping to build, or at least visualize, a more just world for all.

I.9 Antiracism as a Trend, Antiracism as a Religion

I would like to address two other issues in this introduction. The first is the risk of antiracism turning into a trend – antiracism as an unloaded term used by individuals, corporations and universities to save face without having any intention of dismantling or even looking critically at the system that produces racism and in which it is embedded. The second is what John McWhorter (2021) calls antiracism as a religion.

Many corporations and universities working within a neoliberal system that promotes inequalities at multiple levels are offering seminars and workshops about antiracism. Yet, they tend to be acritical of a system still embedded in White privilege that has underpaid people of color (especially women), if they are employed in those companies at all. As limiting as it may sound, what I propose in this book is just a patch that hopefully will spark real change in fighting racism. But we will never end racism without tackling the system that produces it, a system based on nation-states, neoliberalism and an autocratic system dressed as democracy that promotes patriotism as a form of political control encouraging and convincing the oppressed to 'throw rocks on their own roof'. My approach aims to help develop strategies to deconstruct such a system and stop its reproduction from a pragmatic perspective, not to merely save face by overtheorizing and not doing much about it or by proclaiming bombastic but empty statements without their corresponding putting into action.

This recent trend toward antiracism has dissenting voices. One of the loudest and most articulated is John McWhorter's. McWhorter (2021) defines antiracism as a religion: 'I do not mean that these people's ideology is "like" a religion. I seek no rhetorical snap in this comparison. I mean that it actually is a religion [...] An anthropologist would see no difference in type between Pentecostalism and this new form of antiracism'. While McWhorter (2021) points out that the situation in regard to racism has improved since the 1960s and that you cannot treat racism without taking into consideration social class and education, the statistics still speak for themselves: racialized groups in the United States are still at an economic, educational, social, legal and housing disadvantage when compared with White people (Bonilla-Silva, 2003). Furthermore, hate crimes targeting people of color have increased in recent years, as recent mass shootings show. According to the FBI, about 64.9% of the 8,052 reported hate crime incidents during 2020 were based on race, ethnicity or ancestry bias. According to the same source, within that category, Black Americans made up more than half of the victims (Burch & Ploeg, 2022). Although I agree with McWhorter that race cannot be examined without looking at its intersection with social class and education, these aspects may attenuate racist attitudes against racialized individuals with higher socioeconomic status and education. However, regardless of class or education, racialized groups still suffer from racism. The purpose of antiracism, at least in this book, is not to leave 'millions of innocent people scared to pieces' to say or do the 'wrong thing' (McWhorter, 2021), but to raise critical awareness regarding how those 'wrong things' impact on individuals and inequity, including its fractal recursivity within and between racialized groups, and how to, at least, visualize a more just world.

McWhorter (2021) also argues that 'we need to start reconsidering our sense of racial classifications'. McWhorter (2021: 119), the father of two mixed-race daughters (White and Black), writes, 'If we really believe that race is a fiction, we need to let racially indeterminate people make the case for that', rather than doubling down on racial categorization as a primary mode of identification. This argument is flawed because although race is a fiction from a biological standpoint – not a belief, as McWhorter puts it – race is as real as the higher rates of stop and frisk or police brutality for Blacks and Hispanics in the United States (regardless of class and education). In other words, what McWhorter fails to see is that while, for example, god is a belief as much as race is a social construct, religions and racism are facts. Also, despite our agency to influence how others see us, following Goffman (1956) (as we will see in Chapter 3), it is the audience who ultimately decides the identity of the social actor.

Nonetheless, while I would like to encourage everyone to embark on the path of antiracist education, regardless of your own personal experience and identities, I also want to encourage you to be critical and not take antiracism as a dogma in which certain attitudes and behaviors border on the absurd (e.g. self-censoring language in a linguistics class to avoid referring to a racial slur, as if pronouncing such a word would bring about some sort of magic spell, or intentionally making White students feel bad just for being White). Yes, it is my personal belief, not a fact, that the path toward antiracism is the path to a better world. Nonetheless, the antiracist pedagogies that I propose in this book are research-based and, therefore, fact-based. They are neither perfect nor closed-ended but in constant development and adjustment. What I propose is not a religion, and it should not be thought of as such. Antiracist pedagogy is not an easy road, for sure, but a position of neutrality in or out of the classroom – that is, being non-racist – does not exist; either you are racist or you are antiracist (or at least, you are on your path toward antiracism). I acknowledge that for some readers, this either/or framing may result in pushback, because nobody wants to be called a racist, as Bonilla-Silva (2003) puts it. I hope this book motivates you to do something about it if you feel pushed back.

I.10 Organization of This Book

With this section, I end the introduction to this book, which is organized into seven chapters divided into two parts. Part 1 includes the first four chapters and focuses on foundational theoretical aspects of race, racism and antiracism in the language classroom. Part 2, consisting of the remaining three chapters, focuses on the articulation of this theory into praxis. The reason it is organized in this way is to lure the reader without assuming their level of knowledge about this pedagogical approach and its theoretical aspects, thus facilitating a deeper understanding of the proposed activities in the second part of the manuscript. Chapter 1 introduces some fundamental concepts that will inform an antiracist approach to language teaching. Chapter 2 offers an overview and an ethnographic-based account of the context in which I conducted the research that informed this book. This chapter analyzes general racist trends within the United States higher education institutional context, paying particular attention to common racist language practices within a Spanish language department, the context in which many of us work and aim to implement antiracist pedagogies. Here, I expose these practices and suggest that, despite the lack of research about this topic, based on an ethnographic account, many of the practices in this program are not an exception but an example of what goes on in many (fortunately not all) Spanish departments in the United States. I discuss disjunctions in class, race and national background: first, among the instructors and professors, who come from a diverse array of backgrounds and differ in class, race, national origin, time of arrival and citizen status, among other variables such as their motivations to teach, and second, among the students, who in the setting of my investigation were a homogeneous sample, primarily Anglo-Americans from similar socioeconomic backgrounds, but also included a few cases that were different and became salient in such a homogeneous context. Third, I attend to issues of positionality, the readers I have in mind – who are those educators motivated to take action against racism in the language classroom – and issues of ideology and curriculum on a day-to-day basis. Chapter 3 discusses the (pedagogical) rationale behind the integration of SPCs in a language curriculum. It reviews the dominant linguistic ideologies and representations of Latina populations and other racialized groups while attending to issues of erasure and iconization. Chapter 4 reviews the pedagogical foundations of the materials proposed and, thus, serves as a gateway to the second part of this book, which focuses on the practical implementation of an antiracist pedagogy in the language classroom and attends to practical aspects such as when, where and how to carry it out. Chapter 5 provides 14 pedagogical units that integrate contents related to the sociopolitical nature of language designed to raise CLA focused on antiracism in content-based intermediate/advanced levels of Spanish language classes. Chapter 6 proposes ways for integrating antiracist materials in two different academic settings: lower-level Spanish language classes and an interdisciplinary general education class. Chapter 7 discusses six case studies of students who participated in a CLAp-based Spanish class; the book ends with testimonials from students who participated in a general education language and racism class.

Note

(1) See Shermer with John McWhorter – 'Neoracists Posing as Antiracists & Their Threat to Progressive America', 16 March 2021, https://youtu.be/V54aL5LRTrg.

Part 1
Race, Racism and Antiracism in the Language Classroom

1 Introduction to Foundational Concepts for an Antiracist Approach to Language Teaching

1.1 Racism and Its Remapping from Biology onto Language

In order to determine what antiracist pedagogies are, it is first necessary to explain what is meant by racism in this book because, as Rebollo-Gil and Moras (2006: 381) argue, the term racism, as it is used in US society, is very elastic. The definition of racism used in this book is a traditional one. Based on the field of critical race theory developed by scholars, lawyers, educators and other professionals in the early 1970s, and following Bidol (1972: 1), 'racism is racial prejudice (the belief that one's own race is superior to another race) combined with the power to enforce this bias'. I am leaving out the last part of this definition of racism, 'throughout the institutions and culture of a society', for reasons that align with Kendi's (2019) idea of 'powerless defense'. I will develop this point after further examining the implications of this definition of racism.

One of the implications of this definition is that ideas commonly propagated by White supremacist organizations, such as 'inverse racism', are not valid, despite their unfortunate popularization and normalization. This does not mean that a person without the power to enforce racism cannot be prejudiced. To say so would be dehumanizing and racist. But prejudice and racism are not the same. The point is that without access to power, in the United States, inferiorized groups are incapable of enforcing any prejudices they may have against Whites and, therefore, by definition, be racist against Whites. But notice my emphasis on 'against Whites'. This emphasis seeks to specify that, as Kendi (2019) states, racialized others can also be racist toward other people of color in situations in which, despite holding enough power to dismantle, resist or at least stall racist policies, attitudes or behaviors, they keep enforcing and implementing them.

Moreover, it could be argued that in the event of a power reversal, such as when the symbolic market change and power are reversed, people of color could be racist toward Whites. Let us see an example that I frequently use to discuss this point with my students. In the cultural domain of Hip-Hop, in which Blacks and Latinxs hold most positions of creative power, it could be argued that racialized individuals could be racist toward Whites. Nonetheless, this idea is arguable because it is my understanding that these prejudices function as a defense mechanism to protect the culture from appropriation by the racial group in power within the larger racist society where Hip-Hop is embedded. Sharing, granting and eventually losing this power would mean losing this community's capacity to resist racial inequities through Hip-Hop within the wider racist society in which it exists. Aggravatingly, but not surprisingly, during recent years, many of us witnessed in dismay White far-right militants using rap as a vehicle to express their racist and xenophobic views on social media.

What Kendi (2019) calls 'the powerless defense' acts rather like a shield for people of color from charges of racism when they are reproducing and justifying, working under the same racist ideas, the very same racist policies as the White people they often call racist articulate against them. This happens most of the time for political profit (Kendi, 2019: 57). As Kendi explains, the powerless defense would not take into consideration racialized others who attained power, such as policymakers like the numerous racialized politicians, the executives who have the power to institute and eliminate racist and antiracist policies, judges, police chiefs and officers and the middle managers empowered to execute or withhold racist and antiracist policies, like education administrators, curriculum developers, educators or any other individual. This is so because every individual has the power to be racist or antiracist, to fight racist policies or, at least, to stall them. The powerless defense argument is racist because it overestimates White supremacy, disempowers racialized people and cages the power to resist (Kendi, 2019). Racialized assimilationists strive to gain power and become part of the system or, as Freire (1970) explained, attempt to get rid of the oppressor to become the new oppressor, and that is not antiracism; it is racism.

Thus, the term *racism* in this book is used to refer to a large spectrum of covert, overt, personal, group and institutional/structural acts in a context where Whiteness only has meaning when it exists in opposition to the racial other. And this is a pivotal idea. According to Richard Dyer (as cited in Wise, 2002), White Americans see themselves as just people; it is others who are racialized. This idea concurs with James Baldwin's statement that 'being White means never having to think about it', an existential state of normalcy that does not need any self-reflection on the part of the White subject to explain it (Rothenberg, 2005). In this sense, I agree with Rebollo-Gil and Moras (2006: 1): 'Whiteness is taken in this country at face value'. These personal and institutional acts of racism integrate a system of White privilege in which White students are deeply invested. As McIntosh (1997) explains, this system provides them with opportunities and benefits based on their skin color and, I should add, the language varieties that index those racial attributes. Most importantly, this system denies the reality of this privilege or rather, as I observed as an educator, conceals it and protects these students from even questioning the existence of this privilege.

Traditionally, however, the burden of racism (and antiracism) has been placed on racialized subjects and otherized oppressed groups, making these racialized persons the source of the problem instead of Whiteness being the problem. As W.E.B. Du Bois reflected over a century ago, whenever a racial issue arose, he was asked how it felt to be the problem (Chun & Feagin, 2020). Scholars have focused on developing and implementing pedagogies to empower racialized others and provide them with strategies to fight racism (e.g. Alim & Baugh, 2007; Del Valle, 2014; Leeman *et al.*, 2011; Leeman & Serafini, 2016; Martínez, 2003; Pennycook, 2007). As I will argue in Chapter 2, I believe this is a necessary approach but far from enough. A fundamental challenge presented to us as educators is to discuss oppression in ways that make the importance and immediacy of anti-oppressive measures outweigh the benefit of privilege. The only path to this is by placing the burden and accountability of racism on Whites. However, despite the newest efforts (e.g. Cabrera, 2019; Chun & Feagin, 2020), the lack of research on White antiracism is remarkable. Warren (2010: xi, cited in Cabrera, 2019) observed, 'White studies of white racism could fill a small library, the studies of white anti-racism, if you will, could fit in a small bookshelf'.

To this lack of research, we find an additional problem. As Iowa State University Professor Robert Reason objected in 2014, antiracism has become an identity and not a description of action. According to Chun and Feagin (2020), the analytical focus should be on examining actions and whether they challenge racism instead of asking what a person thinks of themselves regarding allyship. For example, antiracism is when a White person tries to stop a racist assault in the subway; watching Drake's, Beyoncé's or any other Black pop-rap artist's new video is not. Thus, 'the primary focus needs to be on observable actions as opposed to what White college students think about themselves' (Chun & Feagin, 2020: 101).

For a long time now, scholars have argued that we must make Whiteness strange, moving beyond our 'heroes and holidays' approach to multiculturalism toward explicit antiracist practices (Lee *et al.*, 1998). More than ever, the message to White people in the US – or to any other power groups in any given society for that matter – is clear: either you are part of the solution or *you are* the problem. This perspective on who should carry the burden of antiracism (i.e. Whites) determined the context in which I conducted the PhD dissertation research that, in turn, informed part of this book. This does not mean that the pedagogical proposals in this book are targeted only at Whites. However, they seriously consider a pedagogical approach oriented not only to racialized students/educators but also to students/educators identifying as the racializing group. This adds an innovative dimension to the present book.

Moreover – and this is a key point for this book – racism has been remapped from biology onto language. While the so-called post-racial society of the early 21st century – especially during the pre-Trump Obama era – generally viewed as politically incorrect and sometimes even sanctioned remarks about bodies – such as skin color, noses, hair or lips – derogatory comments about racialized groups' language use have become normalized and acceptable. Comments such as 'I don't like them because they speak weird' or 'I don't like when people speak Spanish around me' don't mean anything other than *I don't like them because they're different from us, they are not what we understand as normal in our society, and I don't want them around us.* Thus, unlike with biological aspects of race, these racist individuals believe that speakers should change their linguistic behavior or be held accountable for it, which reveals that language has become central to understanding and fighting racism. Not surprisingly, the field of raciolinguistics is thriving (see Alim *et al.*, 2016; Flores & Rosa, 2015; Ramjattan, 2019; Rosa, 2019).

And thus, a challenge lies ahead. How to forge antiracist pedagogies in the language classroom directed to both racialized individuals and White people, but not coopted by the latter, in a way that does not recreate other forms of oppression while collectively struggling for a more socially just future? Answering this question is one of the main goals of the pedagogical approach proposed in these pages. Therefore, let us next define this pedagogical approach.

1.2 Antiracist Pedagogies

In order to define antiracist pedagogies, it is necessary to define antiracism first. Several definitions of antiracism include a pivotal idea: that being non-racist is not enough to be antiracist. Resonating with the words of Desmond Tutu (as cited in Brown, 1984: 19), 'if you are neutral in situations of injustice, you have chosen the side of the oppressor', I would like to make this point even more clear: a passive attitude toward racism is racist; neutrality does not exist.

Feagin and Vera (2002) defined antiracist Whites as those who had 'participated in at least one anti-racist protest event', thus defined and delimited by public or social action. Bonilla-Silva (2003) goes further. His definition involves the idea of a life-altering component that one cannot readily assume to be present in people who have simply attended antiracist events and encompasses both intellectual and emotional understanding as well as social practice:

> Being an anti-racist begins with understanding the institutional nature of racial matters and accepting that all actors in a racialized society are affected materially (receive benefits or disadvantages) and ideologically

by the racial structure. This stand implies taking responsibility for your unwilling participation in these practices and beginning a new life committed to the goal of achieving real racial equality. (Bonilla-Silva, 2003: 15)

Therefore, participation in protests does not necessarily guarantee that the person fully understands the institutional and all-encompassing character of racist oppression. Besides, we must be careful. Antiracism is not the same as 'racial progressives', a term used by Bonilla-Silva to refer to Whites who, for example, support affirmative action, have no problem with inter-racial marriage and are capable of recognizing the significance of discrimination in the United States.

Although encompassing all the aspects proposed by Bonilla-Silva in his view of antiracism, the definition proposed by the present book goes further. Antiracism is also a proactive attitude accompanied by behavior that aims to resist and erase racism and the subjacent ideologies that promote and normalize it and any of its manifestations, at micro and macro levels; denouncing it, fighting it, strategizing against it, teaching and informing about the process and learning from it.

In that sense, the definition proposed in this book aligns better with Gooden *et al.* (2018), who define antiracism through four central nonlinear stages: (1) gaining/integrating knowledge, (2) examining self, (3) (re)envisioning the world and finally (4) taking antiracist action. It also aligns with Ford and Orlandella's (2015) definition of a White ally:

[A] person who consciously commits, attitudinally and behaviorally, to an ongoing, purposeful engagement with and active challenging of White privilege, overt and subtle racism, and systemic racial inequalities for the purpose of becoming an agent of change in collaboration with, not for, people of color. (Ford & Orlandella, 2015: 288)

In agreement with DiAngelo (2011), I believe the final goal of antiracism is to dismantle institutionalized racism. To do so, antiracism must be aware of and fight those processes of commodification of diversity and racial struggle that leave White supremacist and capitalist relations of power intact. In order to fight racism, one must be ready to fight the system that, for some scholars, produces racism, and for others, the system on which it is based. Flores (2017) calls this system neoliberalism because, as Omi and Winant (1994) argue, besides a political and economic process:

neoliberalism is also a racial project that politically incorporates the demands of the US Civil Rights Movement and other global struggles against White supremacy that emerged in the post-World War II context in ways that 'insulated the racial state from revolutionary transformation

and absorbed anti-racist movements in a reform-oriented transition.'
(Winant, 2004, as cited in Flores, 2017: 112)

Thus, going back to Paulo Freire's philosophy, antiracism's goal
is not to fight or collaborate with the oppressor group in order for an
oppressed group to share that power. Antiracism aims to destroy this
structure of power so it cannot be reproduced over any group. This more
demanding notion of antiracism can be exemplified when we compare
Martin Luther King, Jr's (MLK) approach toward racism in the civil
rights movement versus Malcolm X's approach in the struggle for liberation. These differences have explanatory power about why the former
has been constructed as a glorified iconic figure in the fight against racism
(especially, but not only, by and for White people), and the latter erased
or, at best, relegated to the background while iconized as violent, dangerous and antiwhite. Although MLK was open-minded toward Marxism, had anti-capitalistic feelings (Boswell, 2019) and was hated and
considered a threat to White supremacy, his goals have been constructed
by mainstream culture as those of a civil rights activist aiming to stop
racism while sharing the power with his oppressors within a capitalist
system (which oppresses others within and without its borders) without
dismantling this system or being a threat to it. Let me be clear about this:
this is how mainstream America has constructed MLK's goals through a
process of appropriation and commodification of his figure. Nonetheless,
this construction matches the views of his contemporary radicals against
racism, such as advocates of the Black Power Movement, for whom
'[MLK] remained a staid, unexciting figure, the ineffectual exponent of
an outdated brand of liberalism [...] he never seemed to wander very
far from the political mainstream' (Fairclough, 1983: 1). As Fairclough
(1983: 1) argues, 'although an eloquent and courageous crusader for
racial justice, his ultimate vision – as expressed for example in his famous
"I Have A Dream" oration – seemed to be the integration of the Negro
into the existing structure of society; capitalism was not an issue'.

On the other hand, Malcolm X's goals were aimed at fighting that
power so it could not oppress others, and he documented these in his
autobiography. This idea is pivotal to understanding Malcolm X's popularity among revolutionary groups worldwide, its influence in counter-
cultural youth movements such as Hip-Hop, and the role his approach
toward antiracism plays (X, 1966). Fighting racism is fighting the power.
Fighting racism to substitute a group in power for another one, or to
become part of that power while sharing the privileges that still benefit
some social groups at the expense of others, is not antiracism because
oppression remains and an unjust system prevails. These types of practices, which vernacularly are known as *quítate tú para ponerme yo* (get
out so I can replace you), or approaches such as 'I want a piece of the
pie' are not antiracism. Paulo Freire warned us about these practices and

called for liberation instead. The goal is not to fight your oppressor in order to become the new oppressor.

However, everything being discussed so far in this section is a positionality issue that will lead educators to look with antiracist eyes 'at what we teach, how we position what we teach in its context, and how we are positioned as teachers and learners, especially in relation to others who may not share this position and privilege' (Learning and Teaching Hub @ Bath, 2020: 1, as cited in Ade-ojo, 2021). According to Ade-ojo (2021), while this underpinning positionality is as laudable as it is necessary, it does not provide a process of practical engagement. This leaves curricular decisions, as Ade-ojo (2021: 2) puts it, 'in the hands of the powerful'. This book aims to tackle this issue through its practical proposals.

Now that we know what this book understands antiracism to mean, let us see what antiracist pedagogies are. In general, antiracist pedagogies are the teaching and practice of antiracism (Stanley, 2017). Stanley adds that these pedagogies recognize historical narratives and challenge these assumptions to allow for counterstories to these majoritarian narratives. Antiracist educators should 'clearly understand the history of racism and race relations and its influence on culture and society today' (Seidl, 2007, as cited in Davila, 2011: 41). Before attempting to facilitate critical thinking and change, educators must first examine their beliefs, views and assumptions regarding racialized others (Davila, 2011).

Focused on antiracist pedagogies in the language classroom, this book aligns with the views on critical pedagogy by authors such as Leeman *et al.* (2011) and Norton (2012). These pedagogies examine the role of language in (re)producing, maintaining, challenging and transforming asymmetric power relationships, discrimination, inequality, social injustice and hegemony in relation to race and ethnicity. Antiracist pedagogies in the language classroom aim to break these asymmetric power dynamics through an understanding and pedagogical application of the central idea that the very articulation of power, identity and resistance is expressed in and through language, which is intertwined with social and political structures.

Antiracist pedagogies constantly deal with issues of language and identity. Within a second language acquisition (SLA) framework, Norton (2012) explains that these pedagogies are concerned with which relations of power, within classrooms and communities, promote or constrain the process of language learning. Thus, from a social perspective on SLA, the extent to which the learner is valued in any given institution or community influences the learner's performance and the extent to which a learner speaks or is silent (or writes, reads or resists). In this regard, social processes marked by inequities of race, ethnicity, class, gender and sexual orientation aiming to inferiorize particular social groups may serve to position learners in ways that silence and exclude them, hence blocking their learning process, something that an antiracist pedagogy attends to.

In this way, an antiracist language curriculum understands language not only as a system of signs acquired through different stages through this or that methodology but as a social practice that has the potential to inform us about how experiences are organized and identities negotiated while exposing asymmetric relationships of power between dominant and subordinated social groups. The goal of an antiracist pedagogy in the language classroom is to capitalize on this information to raise critical linguistic awareness (CLA) in order to promote social change, first through understanding, then through action. I will delve into the rationale behind the focus on race in Chapter 3 and into antiracist pedagogies and resistance to antiracism in Chapter 4.

1.3 Language and Identity in the Classroom

During the last two decades, there has been a growing interest in the study of identity in the SLA field due to recent changes in how the individual, language and learning are understood. This change has produced a departure from predominantly traditional psycholinguistic perspectives to approaches focusing on the social and anthropological dimensions of learning, particularly regarding sociocultural, poststructural and critical theory. Even within cognitive linguistics, there has been a turn toward social justice (Ortega, 2019). This turn aligns with my views on language learning and language because it advocates for a multilingual approach to language acquisition and moves away from understandings of language as an object that is bounded and fixed. I agree with Ortega (2019: 28) that conceptualizations of language as something that can be learned to completeness – as if there was a finish line – 'reflect essentialist ontologies of language, including Chomskyan and structuralist ones, both explicitly or implicitly espoused by much linguistic-cognitive SLA'. But multilingualism still names and counts languages. Hence, I prefer to engage with the concept of *translanguaging*, which, in contrast, understands language as 'a dynamic and fluid linguistic repertoire that draws from a unitary system instead of the named languages of nation states' (García & Tupas, 2019: 390).

As a researcher interested in individual differences that relate more to the social than the cognitive aspects of language, I consider it necessary to move the focus from issues that have to do with language acquisition from a traditional psycholinguistics point of view to the relationships between the language learner and the larger social world. Therefore, affective factors such as identity should be understood as socially constructed and dynamic; that is, as changing over time and space, coexisting, sometimes in contradictory ways, within the same individual depending on the context. Theoretical conceptualizations of identity, which will be examined in Chapter 3, are pivotal for antiracist educators.

This position toward individual differences theoretically justifies a need to analyze the diverse social, historical and cultural contexts

– including questions related to race, ethnicity, class, resistance, inequality and iconization of different linguistic varieties and behaviors – in which language learning will take place, so that students negotiate – even resist – the diverse positions that these contexts offer.

1.4 Dimension of Racism in Language

As I already mentioned, racism has a strong linguistic component, especially due to the recent remapping of racism in the United States from being based on biology to being based on language. Racists – and this is nothing new – believe that their language, and their culture in general, is superior to those spoken by inferiorized races. On behalf of the 'improvement' of the situation of these less fortunate peoples, and sustained by a political position of power, racists employ this linguistic ideology to impose diverse doctrines, attitudes and policies on subordinated racial groups, either overtly or covertly (see Rosa, 2019; Zentella, 2016).

Moreover, the linguistic sign is used to index and iconize race to perpetuate power asymmetries between different social groups. For example, let us focus on the particular language varieties used by different characters in Disney animated films. As Lippi-Green (1997) explains, when those animated characters (animals or humanoids) are the heroes or princesses, characters with strongly positive actions and motivations, they speak socially mainstream US English varieties (or what is commonly known as White American English). In contrast, those characters with strongly negative actions and motivations speak language varieties associated with specific national origins, ethnicities and races in non-factual and sometimes overtly discriminatory ways (e.g. the hyenas in *The Lion King*).

This book's pedagogical approach questions purist and standard language ideologies in the language classroom because reducing language to purist normative monolingual linguistic practices – i.e. what White, educated, middle-class elites use (and this is what textbooks, dictionaries and corpora rely on) – has detrimental consequences on the racial identity, ethnocultural affiliations and linguistic insecurity of translingual speakers as well as monolingual speakers belonging to racialized, and therefore otherized, groups (Alim, 2014; Del Valle, 2014; Leeman, 2019; Rosa, 2019; Zentella, 2016). Rejecting and stigmatizing students' linguistic practices is to reject and stigmatize their identities. It is not about being bi- or translingual; it is about who *is*. These ideologies dictate whose linguistic practices – and consequently, the social groups that perform them – are legitimate, praised and supported and which linguistic practices are a problem and should be feared, invisibilized, eradicated, incarcerated and deported. These ideologies perpetuate systemic racism and injustice. Nevertheless, many traditional cognitive linguists in the SLA field, educators, policymakers and even those suffering from or (unconsciously) privileged by these ideologies do not seem to question them.

Racism is inseparable from its linguistic component; racism is based on its linguistic component. The linguistic component of racism is one of the fundamental tools for expressing racism. Therefore, the linguistic dimension of racism provides excellent input to analyze, understand and combat racism.

1.5 A Research-Based Pedagogical Approach

This book is informed by research that I conducted in a US private university's Spanish language program (Magro, 2016a). The study investigated whether integrating content related to the sociopolitical nature of language (sociopolitical content or SPC) influences CLA, motivation and linguistic proficiency in an advanced Spanish-as-a-second-language course. In this section, I will briefly explain the design of that study and how its results support the pedagogical approach suggested in this book. However, I will not present an in-depth analysis and discussion of the research findings (see Magro [2016a] for an in-depth analysis and discussion). On the one hand, I aim to provide a panorama of the pedagogical context where I put into practice the integration of SPC, its underpinning theory and how I obtained and analyzed the data as a result of the integration of these materials. On the other hand, I aim to provide an example of how to design and conduct mixed-method quasi-experimental research in the natural context of the language classroom for those unfamiliar with this type of methodology.

I conducted this quasi-experimental longitudinal study during the spring semester of 2015. It included qualitative and quantitative components within two sections of an advanced Spanish class that followed a content-based instruction model (CBI). In CBI, the integration of a particular content with language teaching is directed simultaneously at learning an academic subject and developing linguistic proficiency in a second language (L2); the target language is the vehicle through which subject matter content is learned, rather than the immediate object of study (Brinton *et al.*, 1989).

The participants in this study were assigned to an experimental group (the group that received SPC) and to a control group (the group that did not receive SPC). The prefix *quasi* is due to the small sample size and the impossibility of controlling all the variables because the investigation was conducted in a natural context. This method allowed me to compare the reaction to the materials of both groups at the beginning, during and at the end of the semester. In this way, I had the opportunity to observe the influence of the integration of SPC in the instruction of Spanish as an L2 in three areas: CLA, motivation and linguistic competence. This was done within the aforementioned interdisciplinary perspective, where the field of critical applied linguistics (CALx) established relationships with critical pedagogy, sociolinguistics, linguistic ideologies, social psychology and SLA.

This study was conducted in an advanced Spanish course at a private university in an East Coast city in the United States, which I will refer to as X University (XU).[1] In this college, the Spanish program (from basic to advanced levels) was highly structured, integrated and standardized. The two courses at the advanced level (Advanced Spanish I and Advanced Spanish II) followed the CBI model. This, and the relative homogeneity of its students – middle-class White youth between 19 and 23 years of age who had acquired Spanish as an L2 an academic environment and whose first language was English – facilitated the control of a large number of variables when comparing an experimental group with a control group. In addition, the enormous volume of integrated performance assessments (IPA) in this program to measure linguistic proficiency in the three modes (interpretative, interpersonal and presentational) provided me with abundant quantitative data to assess the development of the students' linguistic proficiency.

In terms of the characteristics of the participants, and specifically, regarding their homogeneity, the design of my research took into account suggestions made from the study of communication and social organization: cultural or social distance plays a fundamental role in the learning and acquisition of L2s. Schwartz (2014) suggests that Spanish courses for English monolinguals tied to an 'American' identity present two types of otherness. This type of student – representing most of the participants in my investigation – comes from the middle or upper class, identifies as White, has English as a first language and has generally been raised in highly homogeneous communities that share these socioeconomic, ethnic and cultural traits. On the one hand, this type of monolingual student builds an otherness that lives outside of the US borders, an exotic otherness. On the other hand, this otherness is constructed differently than what is found within our borders (Hispanics within the United States). This second otherness lives segregated behind what Schwartz calls the third border. This border is both psychological and social as well as physical; the cause and consequence are that this otherness is very often racialized and considered intrusive and threatening. Likewise, this stigma indexically links their cultural practices to dangerousness and disorganization and negatively stereotypes Hispanics, including, of course, their linguistic practices. These students tend to perceive US Hispanics as illegitimate, 'bad' speakers of Spanish as well as speakers of 'bad' Spanish (Flores, 2017; Magro, 2016a; Rosa, 2019), in opposition to those Spanish speakers who they idealistically consider native – with all the political implications the term native entails (see Flubacher & Del Percio, 2017, for a critical discussion about the term native).

Based on the critical approach of my investigation, the fact that these students yearn to go outside the United States to study in a Spanish-speaking country, legitimizing the linguistic practices of these countries, and ignore taking advantage of the situations that are presented to them within the United States to speak and get in touch with Hispanic culture(s) and language(s), responds to a series of hegemonic and racist attitudes and ideologies that delegitimize US Hispanics. These ideologies and attitudes do not consider US Hispanics to be either authentic Spanish speakers or speakers of authentic Spanish (whatever authentic Spanish may be) (Magro, 2016a). These ideologies are linked to certain linguistic practices and the social groups that they indexically link. Damen (1987) argues that this *us–them* positionality is responsible for these ideologies, which points to broader ideological orientations of power and privilege that oppose difference. In other words, they are hegemonic ideas of normalcy that are not explicitly mentioned, but Spanish courses and their students often work under these premises. Damen proposes that acculturative processes – also known as cultural shock processes – that bridge these differences affect this learning/acquisition. In this sense, I aimed to observe how the inclusion of this sociopolitical language content that deals with these issues of practices/uses, attitudes and linguistic ideologies influences the awakening of CLA, motivation and learning/acquisition of an L2.

Considering what I have explained so far, and based on the observations of critical pedagogy scholars such as Michael W. Apple (2004) on educational curriculum development in the United States, in order to integrate SPC into the syllabus of the Spanish course that was the object of my investigation, I took into account the ideology behind the type of knowledge taught and how it is taught. These considerations were addressed with the purpose of influencing the development of critical citizenship. Rather than following the recommendations of the MLA (2007, 2009) reports about the use of a multicultural and transcultural approach for responding to the needs of the new millennium student (which respond to neoliberal market logics, as Flores [2017] argues), I focus on those proposed by critical pedagogues about the use of specifically antiracist materials (Apple, 2004: 179). Thus, my intention was to fulfill an educational agenda that helps to produce a critical change in my students. This was done by building on the critical perspective in which this research is framed. This critical perspective is also proposed by authors such as Leeman (2018), Leeman *et al.* (2011), Pennycook (2007) and Talmy (2010).

These materials (in-class presentations, texts, audiovisual cultural materials and interactive activities) were designed to stimulate critical reflection on the social and political dimension of language and to, thus, observe how it influences students' CLA (defined as the 'conscious awareness' of a person about the nature of language and sensitivity to its forms and functions [Carter, 2003; Malmberg, 2001, as cited in Griva *et al.*, 2011]). Hence, I integrated into the syllabus contents related to the sociopolitical dimension of language in terms of its use (language function). Language function is used to indexicalize and symbolize race – as well as other intersectional social constructs such as socioeconomic status, ethnicity, nationality and gender – with certain linguistic features (language form). This is done to perpetuate a relationship of power imbalance between different social groups (language function). This definition of CLA also aligns with Norman Fairclough's (1992: 14–15) as an awareness of the ways in which ideas become naturalized or taken for granted as 'truths' about the natural and social world and how these 'truths' are tied up with the language in use.

Likewise, I was aware of the importance of the affective dimension in learning since authors such as Ehrman (1996) and Stevick (1980) noticed that it becomes increasingly evident that the goal of learning in the classroom is not limited to transmitting content information. These authors argue the need to instill in language teaching a concern for achieving deeper vital goals, not only specific linguistic goals. Thus, I recognize the relationship between affectivity and language teaching as bi-directional, because a concern for affectivity can improve both language learning and teaching. The language classroom can contribute significantly, in turn, to educating the students in an affective way. Both directions must be taken into account to achieve better results.

However, integrating SPC in language classes to raise CLA is not something new. As Lacorte and Magro (2022) explain, critical linguistic awareness pedagogies (CLAp) were first proposed in the United States as an educational model for speakers of stigmatized varieties of English, with a primary focus on African American Vernacular English (AAVE) (see Lanehart, 1998). Explicit antiracist proposals emerged from these first studies. These proposals aim to eradicate from the curriculum racist approaches that empower prestige language varieties and inferiorize others (e.g. Inoue, 2015; Paris & Alim, 2017). Due to the widespread circulation of negative discourses surrounding Spanish and the stigmatization of varieties of English that show signs of contact with Spanish and vice versa (Del Valle, 2014; Leeman, 2018; Otheguy & Zentella, 2008; Rosa, 2019; Zentella, 2016), soon after, CLAp included speakers of Spanish in both English as an L2 and mainstream classes as well as Spanish as a heritage language (HL) (Lacorte & Magro, 2022). CLAp proposals in the field of Spanish as an HL started with Martínez (2003) and Leeman (2005) and were followed by a second wave of studies by scholars such as Beaudrie et al. (2021), Holguín Mendoza (2018) and Leeman (2018). However, at the time of my research, there was no record of any study investigating the link between the integration of SPC in the classroom to raise CLA and motivation. Of course, motivation is not by any means the final justification for adopting an antiracist pedagogical approach, but rather a side point that deserves this discussion.

Motivation has been studied in depth from a psycholinguistic perspective, especially from those more progressive approaches within the field. Nevertheless, some language educators, especially those L2 researchers and instructors who are still more concerned with linguistic proficiency issues from a traditional cognitive perspective – or in what Flores (2017) calls 'language-as-resource' from a neoliberal understanding of language learning, and not so much about the developing of the student as a whole from a social perspective (and/or in what Flores calls 'language-as-struggle') – may ask themselves, 'So what if linguistic awareness increases motivation?'

This is a valid question in an increasingly threatening environment for the humanities, one where there is an intensification of the demand to instruct specific technical skills from a neoliberal perspective aligned with an empiricist epistemological framework according to maxims of competitiveness, efficiency and profitability. This neoliberal attempt to adapt education to the changing demands of capitalism has also become a factor in the conceptualization of language and multilingual education imagined as a way to raise the value of individuals in the various neoliberal workplaces (Flubacher & Percio, 2017). Under these circumstances, it is also understandable that some instructors, especially those trained or instructed by their supervisors to focus exclusively on learners' linguistic development, and despite their will to commit to an antiracist change, may fear that the integration of SPC may interfere with the maximization of language acquisition and with meeting the expectations their employers impose on them. This is particularly common for those instructed under those linguistic-cognitive paradigms that share, in Ortega's (2019: 23) terms, 'post-positivist logics, quantitative rigor, and generalizability as values in their research'. To calm these fears, the answer to this question of *so what if CLA increases motivation* can be found in the theories of motivation, both from the fields of social psychology and SLA. This answer leaves no excuse for not implementing antiracist pedagogies if you are compromised to fight racism: an increase in motivation is related to the development of linguistic proficiency (e.g. Dörnyei & Ushioda, 2013; Masgoret & Gardner, 2003; Lorenzo, 2006). Consequently, SPC interfering with the linguistic development of the language learner is not a valid excuse to not implement the antiracist pedagogical approach to language instruction proposed in these pages.

In summary, from a social-psychological perspective focused on the student – aiming to meet their needs, not only cognitive and linguistic, but also affective, cultural and political – the main question of my dissertation research was whether the integration of SPC influences:

(1) The development of CLA (assessed by content analysis of argumentative essays, semi-structured interviews and observation).
(2) Motivation, measured (through questionnaires, semi-structured interviews and observation) as the desire to continue learning Spanish by continuing in Spanish courses, enrollment in study abroad programs, involvement in Spanish community service, etc.

(3) Linguistic proficiency, assessed through different tests integrated into the syllabus designed to quantify it (both in oral and written format, both in comprehension and production).

I embraced a mixed methodology to answer this question. Thus, I collected both quantitative data – through questionnaires and assessments – and qualitative data – observations, speech analysis and interviews – that were analyzed from a CLA perspective and the aforementioned interdisciplinary approach.

This conceptual framework led to the formulation of the following hypothesis: *the use of a pedagogy that integrates SPC will influence the development of CLA, student motivation and, consequently, linguistic proficiency.* I will not elaborate on this research since it is available in my doctoral dissertation (Magro, 2016a), in which the reader may dwell on these three relationships, my research questions and the mixed methods utilized to answer them, including how I granted agency to my participants and interpreted all this data, taking into consideration the individual characteristics of the participants. In sum, the analysis of the data obtained through the initial and final interviews, and the discourse analysis of the final exam, indicate that the integration of SPC in the curriculum influences the awakening of CLA of the students of an L2. The analysis of the data collected through the three quantitative questionnaires, the qualitative questionnaire, the final interview and the case study showed that the awakening of linguistic awareness influences the increase in the motivation of students and that this influence is attributed to the awakening of CLA. The data analysis obtained to assess language proficiency through a series of quantitative instruments (oral and written final exam, tests, essays, partial oral exam) corroborate motivation theories: there is a relationship between an increase in motivation and an increase in linguistic proficiency. Thus, the evidence points to the confirmation of the hypothesis: the use of a pedagogy that integrates SPC influences the development of linguistic awareness, motivation and, consequently, the linguistic proficiency of the student. My dissertation also discusses the obstacles I encountered when conducting quasi-experimental research in a natural context and how the limitations that could be considered weaknesses (and could question the rigor and reliability of my investigation from a positivist point of view of so-called neutrality and objectivity) became strengths from my critical and qualitative approach.

Note

(1) The names of the school and the participants in this study are pseudonyms, to protect their anonymity.

2 'Trabajo más que un negro': An Ethnography of Racism Within a Spanish Department

Coming from a fundamentally antiracist department at a public university with one of the strongest programs in sociolinguistics in the US East Coast, I was shocked by the racist uses and practices I was exposed to when I joined the Spanish department at X University (XU), first as an adjunct and later as a visiting assistant professor. In previous job positions, and after I left XU for a better opportunity at another university, I had the chance to teach, lecture and observe at other local, national and international universities. Based on this experience, I can affirm that the racist practices I encountered at XU's Spanish department, as well as its demographics, are not an isolated case. This chapter aims to promote reflection in faculty working at (Spanish) language departments through an example based on ethnographic research. This research exposes some of the ways in which racism manifests in these departments in the hope that it will provide educators working in other (Spanish) language departments with some analytical tools to identify and take action against the manifestation of racism. The purpose of the snippets and examples provided in this chapter is to highlight the need for metain-struction, that is, the instruction of language instructors. These snippets also provide a look into institutional power dynamics in US universities through concrete experiences, while warning about the professional risks for educators implementing antiracist pedagogies.

In 2017, the National Center for Education Statistics reported that less than 6% of full-time faculty in degree-granting postsecondary institutions were Hispanics, not reaching 3% for full-time assistant professors and 2% for professors. Blacks had similar statistics. However, although the National Center for Education Statistics does not offer race-related data within the Hispanic faculty (notice how in this statistic, Hispanic is constructed as a racial instead of an ethnic category), every Spanish department in which I learned or taught shares a common absence: Afro-descendant faculty. I would state that these departments are pre-dominantly White, but this affirmation would imply that the majority of these Hispanics/Latinxs are White. Even though many self-identify as White, White America does not recognize them as such, which is a point that I would like to discuss in depth when I talk about identity in Chapter 3. The point I want to make with these facts is that XU is a rather good example of an expensive private university in which the lack of ethnoracial diversity is a recognized issue by the same institution that (re)produces it.

Racism in (Spanish) language departments in the United States (from elementary school to higher education) is a topic that needs to be further investigated. Finding statistical data to back up the claims I make based on my personal experience and ethnographic research has been extremely difficult, mainly because Hispanic ethnicity is understood as race (e.g. National Center for Education Statistics, 2020). The lack of diversity and the racist practices in Spanish departments are unexplored areas at this time and would require investigations of their own. However, this is outside the scope of this book, which focuses on combating that and other forms of racism through pedagogical approaches. There is a need for studies aimed at developing and using demographic data collection tools and information systems to map the demographic infrastructure of Spanish departments in the United States, analyzing their racial (and class, place of origin, migrant generation, linguistic background, gender, etc.) composition as a function of race. This would allow researchers to empirically expose the lack of representation and potential proportional control over Spanish departments in educational institutions as a function of race.

It is important to consider the type of institutions we, as antiracist educators, are facing in our daily practice. Michael Apple (2004) makes a clear point when he states that as institutions of control of cultural and economic capital, schools – in this case, university Spanish departments – dictate what is legitimate 'real' knowledge by positing a false consensus on what are appropriate contents, skills and outcomes, and the way these should be assessed. I would go further and state that these institutions are also gatekeepers of who should instruct this knowledge. These ideas, presented to us as 'the only rational universally valid ones', as Marx and Engels (1972) articulated in *The German Ideology*, dialectically link the economic to the cultural apparatus, which in turn links a culture of racism to economic profit and vice versa.

A fundamental principle of antiracist pedagogies is finding out and fighting the connections between these normalized dominant ideas and the interests of particular groups in a society through questions such as: Whose knowledge is it? Why is it taught to particular groups in particular ways? What are the overt or covert functions of teaching this knowledge within the larger complex industrial society? Why is it accepted as a universal truth? As Michael Apple argues, only after responding to these questions can we promote the acquisition of particular forms of cultural capital and inquire about our success in doing so. The lack of this type of critical thinking in (Spanish) language departments is what makes it impossible for them to disengage from racist approaches and practices in language teaching and embrace antiracist pedagogies.

This chapter aims to provide context about the dynamics of racism within higher education and, particularly, within Spanish departments in universities in the United States. Within the scope of this chapter, I aim to describe a Spanish language department, the context in which I conducted the research that informs this book, to shed light on racist language and practices within that context. I hope this information helps to reflect, identify, denounce, amend and act against these practices, which may also appear in other language departments. I will start by describing the university where I conducted my research, followed by a description of the Spanish department. Next, I will examine racist language practices in this institution, overview the students participating in my research and finally discuss positionality in curriculum and ideology. As an example of a Spanish language department in a private higher education institution in the United States, I will also provide an overview of the participants in the research that informed this book, since their sociocultural and economic characteristics had a meaningful impact on the approach taken to develop and integrate sociopolitical contents (SPCs) in this context, as we will see in Chapter 4.

2.1 XU: A Pricey Private University

First, let us provide an overview of the larger context in which the Spanish language department where I conducted my research was located: X University. Before describing this traditional institution, I would like to unconventionally start this section with two examples that illustrate how one of the main power groups in this institution exercises its privileges, to illustrate the scope, presence and power that power groups have within US university campuses. Depending on the institution, these groups may vary. One such group at XU is the pro-Israel Jewish community.

During the semester in which my investigation was conducted while I worked as a Visiting Assistant Professor at XU, a scandal broke out on campus when a Palestinian-American medical student was forced to remove a Palestinian flag from his dorm window. Palestine Legal reported in 2016 that campus police appeared at the door of this medical student's dormitory. The officer at the student's dorm door explained that the campus police department had received numerous complaints about the flag and that he would leave only after the flag was removed. Although a legal non-profit organization wrote to XU asking the university to withdraw the warning letter issued to the Palestinian-American student and apologize in public, the damage was already done.

Let us provide another example exposing how this community does not hesitate to exercise its power. The same semester, a colleague informed me off the record that a student had reported me to the chair of the Spanish department the previous semester. I still remember the incident that triggered this complaint. A female Jewish student defending a Zionist position had a heated discussion with an international female student from Turkey during one of my advanced Spanish classes. The incident occurred when I asked the class to provide examples of Irvine and Gal's (2000: 34) concept of fractal recursivity after I had explained it – that is, 'the projection of an opposition, salient at some level of relationship, onto some other level'. The Turkish student used the example of Israel and how this state acts toward the Palestinian population in a similar way to how Nazi Germany acted with the Jewish people. A debate broke out. Since debates were one of the main output tasks utilized in advanced Spanish classes, I utilized this teaching opportunity to help students practice their Spanish language skills as a final output activity for that class. During the debate, the Jewish student had difficulties defending her position. She showed symptoms of cognitive dissonance, the unpleasant emotion that results from believing two contradictory things at the same time. Some of the manifested symptoms I could observe included ignoring the facts presented by the Turkish student (and other students who joined the debate) and showing physical signs of discomfort, such as increased movement, removing her jacket and an anxious rictus on her mouth. Although I only intervened in this debate to provide linguistic feedback, made sure they respected their turns, kept the conversation in a respectful tone and even provided linguistic support to the Jewish student, a short time later the Jewish student reported me to the chair of the department, claiming that the personal Facebook account I use as an artist contained a post that read 'Israhell'. This was a repost of something a friend and member of my rap group – who is of Moroccan descent – posted on his page after one of the multiple bombings of the Palestinian civilian population during that time (as I write this, Israel is air-striking Gaza). Because during that semester, the department chair was a Jewish Latin American professor, I guess the student saw an ally to make her complaint to, hoping I would be fired. However, either because the chair was not sympathetic to Zionism (not all Jewish people are), or because it would have been ethically and legally inappropriate, the complaint never reached my ears until my colleague told me a semester later during an informal conversation. Although the incident did not escalate, the outcome could have been very different. Let this be an example of the risks we face when implementing antiracist pedagogies, particularly in universities with student populations such as XU. Nonetheless, regardless of the risks, these anecdotes motivated the integration of critical reflection on the complexity of student religious, racial and linguistic identities intersecting in the classroom in future class activities in this program (and later on, in my current program). As a preview of the activities proposed in the second part of this book, in the program at XU, the discussion of fractal recursivity in subsequent semesters compared and contrasted the example of the Palestine–Israel conflict, the Jewish Holocaust in Nazi Germany and how Jewish people 'became White' in the United States. The activity also promoted the comparison of the hierarchical relationship between English and Yiddish with that of Hebrew and Arabic. This was done with the intention of raising critical linguistic awareness (CLA) about the intertwining of language, identity and power with its manifestation through fractal recursivity.

However, to further understand the student population that XU attracts, it is necessary to overview its socioeconomic characteristics. Although I have extensive information that documents the characteristics of this institution, to protect its anonymity, I will hide the sources and summarize them to give the reader an idea of the type of university where my research was conducted and where I designed/integrated an articulated critical linguistic awareness pedagogies (CLAp) program with a focus on racism based on the implementation of SPCs for the first time. I include this extensive information to provide the reader with context to better understand the students' voices in Chapter 7, section 7.1.

XU is a private university with an urban feel in the heart of a big city on the East Coast. A well-known newspaper published an article in 2015 in which a senior XU student who was in deep debt and had invested considerable time getting and working internships described it as the world's most expensive trade school. Another student mentioned the abundance of rich students whose parents were essentially buying them a degree, giving them a fancy-sounding diploma the way they might gift them a new car. As the same article mentions, until the late 1980s, XU was an inexpensive commuter school transformed by its last dean two decades later into a nationally recognized research university with expanded facilities and several specialized new schools. The money for this conversion came from the students and their families, and it became, for a time, the most expensive university in America. Like many other similar universities, the highly criticized lack of ethnoracial diversity and the scarcity of financial aid make their student population quite homogeneous in terms of race and social class: the vast majority were upper-middle-class Whites. At the time of my research, almost 65% of XU's student body was declared White, approximately 12% Asian, less than 7% Black, 9% Hispanic, and the rest declared unknown or other.

The statistical data is self-illustrative, but the couple of incidents I used to document the culture of this university are, perhaps, clearer evidence of how asymmetric power relationships are reproduced on US university campuses through what may look like minor incidents. Of course, more spectacular incidents happen across US campuses every day. I could name a few that recently happened at the campus where I am currently lecturing. These incidents include unjust arrests based on racial profiling; nooses placed in Hispanic fraternities and mainly

Hispanic-run campus kitchens; linguistic discrimination such as banning cleaning staff from using Spanish during working hours; and even murder, such as the stabbing to death of Army 2nd Lt Richard Collins III by a member of a racist Facebook group. Nonetheless, all these incidents, major or minor, align with demographics on campuses and the maintenance and control of particular forms of (hegemonic) ideologies that, when challenged, the group(s) that benefit from them exercise their power to maintain. But let us see how this plays out in the microcosmos of the Spanish department at XU.

2.2 A Very Typical Spanish Department

Before proceeding with this section, it is important to highlight that every Spanish language department in the United States is different. It is not the goal of this section to generalize my observations to all Spanish departments in the United States. Nonetheless, the department that I am about to describe may share common areas with many other language departments. I will try to document in-depth the peculiarities of this department and its faculty to better understand where racist language and practices occur. This is not to say that XU's Spanish department was particularly racist, but rather an example of what is going on in US Spanish departments, which seem to reflect the general elitist hegemonic trends present in the foundation of US higher education.

As Geiger (2005) pointed out, the term 'higher education' was primarily meant to educate society's elite while reflecting and reinforcing social inequality. Higher education was not meant to be a populist form of education but rather an exclusionary institution that actively (explicitly and implicitly) recruited White males and excluded non-White, non-male and non-wealthy students. For example, many Ivy League institutions put quotas on the number of Jewish students, and Princeton, as absurd as it may seem, went as far as to give preference to taller students under the belief that these were young men who would be seen as potential future leaders (Karabel, 2005). Several authors (Gusa, 2010; Karabel, 2005; Thelin, 2004) argue that similar logics of exclusion also applied to faculty hiring, thereby establishing an institutional cultural norm around Whiteness in the foundation of US higher education. What follows is important for understanding not only the type of faculty enrolled in the Spanish department at XU and their work environment and conditions but also my degree of knowledge and awareness about the type of program where I conducted my investigation and the challenges I was facing when I designed it.

This Spanish department was part of a department that conglomerated a few other 'modern languages'. It was subdivided into Literature Studies and Language Studies. At the time of my research, the department chair was a (non-Hispanic) linguist who took over the position previously held by a Spanish literature professor.[1] The Spanish language studies sub-division, directed at that time by a traditional cognitive-oriented linguist, had more students and faculty than the sum of all other departmental divisions. Despite the high number of instructors in the Spanish language department (15), they were not enough to meet each semester's demand, and numerous students remained on the waiting list to take Spanish classes, which were often a requirement for their academic programs.

Additionally, the teaching staff mobility within the Spanish Language Department was remarkably high, especially in contrast to that of His-panic Literature, which had only two tenured associate professors, a ten-ure-track professor and a visiting professor. The language program had only one associate professor (non-tenure track and the only one holding a PhD). The rest of the faculty included an instructor with a three-year renewable contract (with a master's degree in a field unrelated to second language acquisition [SLA]), two full-time professors in a visiting posi-tion (as an ABD, I was one of these two), four part-time instructors and seven adjuncts (of whom six were new entries that semester). Three fac-tors could have contributed to the high mobility that made this depart-ment look like a revolving door: a low salary and lack of job security/ benefits, a high workload and the problems associated with highly stan-dardized programs (such as excessive supervision or lack of curricular freedom and inflexibility). It is important to discuss these factors, since they outline the socioeconomic and individual characteristics of the fac-ulty that stay and teach in this department as well as of the faculty who leave every semester.

Nowadays, it is a well-known inside joke for most educators that higher education professions in the humanities are only for those who are wealthy or willing to live precariously. It is also well known that university Spanish instructors' salaries in the United States are below the mean compared to their corresponding positions in other departments in the same universities.[2] It does not help either that universities responded to the so-called crisis of the humanities with corporation-like economic policies and practices aligned with a neoliberal ideology. Tenure-track positions seem like something from a better past, while universities, globally, create more and more part-time and short-term contracts without any long-term guarantee (Blommaert, 2020b). This results in an overall picture of workload intensification, standardization, account-ability requirements and micromanagement practices in higher educa-tion globally. To put this in perspective, in some school districts, a high school teacher without a PhD – in many cases, without a master's degree – makes as much as double the salary of a short-term or part-time profes-sor working as a Spanish instructor in a university (double the salary of a full-time lecturer if the teacher holds a master's degree and has more than five years in his/her position).[3] Of course, it is arguable that some (many?) of these instructors teach at universities because they can afford it and, more than economic compensation, the main motivations may be, among others, a passion for teaching (rarely, since teaching positions at K–12 schools offer teaching opportunities and pay more), or the prestige that teaching in higher education may grant. Research, another plausible motivation that could justify an unworthy salary, is off-limits in most of these positions since time restrictions imposed by teaching duties make it almost impossible to conduct.

Nonetheless, a yearly salary of $40,000–$50,000 is, in most cases, more than three times the average wage in the country of origin of many of these instructors. However, considering that, in the state where XU is located, the poverty level for a household of four is around $25,000, the salary for a short-term full-time Spanish professor is not high. Thus, it is not surprising to find, among these instructors, the otherwise unoccupied spouse of a diplomatic government official or the partner of a momentarily exiled corrupt politician working for an international financial institution. Although these representations of faculty may sound exacerbated, they are two real examples. In the first case, the instructor verbally admitted to me that, although convenient, she did not need the money but, otherwise, she would stay at home without much to do. In the second case, the instructor was the sentimental partner in a well-known corruption scandal in a Spanish-speaking country (the country is not mentioned to protect anonymity). These job posts offer an opportunity to enrich their CVs or perhaps just grant 'bragging rights' when they go back on vacation to their country of origin because of the social prestige that university professors have in other countries. But for those who need to work to make a living, the workload/salary ratio is something to be weighed with more profitable or better quality-of-life opportunities.

Moreover, the workload, demand and expectations were exceedingly high in this department. This made it difficult for instructors to teach a greater number of classes, in this or other universities, to compensate for their low remuneration. This problem was intertwined with the high standardization of the program – across and within levels – which required level coordinators and class instructors to constantly manage an enormous technological and assessment apparatus. Additionally, the program required instructors to create and integrate new didactic materials frequently, along with an exhaustive evaluative component that required the development of new tests, plus grading and providing feedback for both tests and daily homework (imagine all this when you teach four classes of 20 students per semester). Teaching 80 students four days a week, four hours each day, adding a commute of one hour each way, had me grading homework and exams on a playground bench while my – then little – kids begged me to play with them, only to continue working during the rest of the evening and on weekends.

Beyond all this, part-time and full-time instructors had multiple department service duties such as the overview of standardizing requirements for study abroad programs; evaluating students' placement in courses; various extracurricular activities such as writing workshops and film presentations; the administration and maintenance of online materials; the creation of new didactic materials; instruction and coordination of adjuncts; professional development workshops for faculty; coordinator meetings; beginning- and end-of-semester faculty meetings; finding out room locations for exams; and administration and coordination of exams, among others.

Also – and perhaps this paragraph may serve as advice about what not to do when directing a language program to avoid the reproduction of asymmetric power relationships – instructors were under the impression that they were under constant surveillance. In this department, the program director, often threatened and mistreated by her tenured partners from the literature department, projected this pressure on her faculty through her overcontrolling practices. The program director commented more than once on the pressure to which she was subjected by the two male tenured literature professors. She was aware that the language department she directed had much higher student enrollment rates than the literature program, which granted her some sort of power when negotiating money allocations and budgets with the Office of the Dean. However, the program director told me that the two tenured professors belittled her by denying the intellectuality of her work and thinking of her as a sort of technician, not as a 'real professor'. These pressures could be part of the reason behind the obsessive control over the program and the exacerbated focus on quantitative data by the program director as a way to have evidence ready to prove her effectiveness as a leader of this program.

The struggle for intradepartmental power was evident. Instead of bridges, both sub-departments were engaged in building walls to separate language and literary studies. The Spanish language program director had organized her department in such a hierarchical order that each level of Spanish had a coordinator responsible for ensuring that all instructors followed the syllabus daily and taught and evaluated the students using the same criteria, adhering strictly to the general rubrics created by the department. The program director oversaw the level coordinators, who were required to intervene when, for example, there was a statistical disparity in test grades when compared across sections (or rather, I should say, when the director thought that there was a statistical disparity, since the fact was that the samples were too small to establish any significant difference). As a level coordinator, I was frequently asked to talk to an instructor because the director thought they were grading too high. She suspected that instructors, to obtain better student evaluations at the end of the semester, did this intentionally. Furthermore, the director had access to all the instructors' electronic grade books, which she would regularly access without notification to ensure that every coordinator complied with her rules. Many of these instructors felt uncomfortable with the situation, something they commented off the record during my investigation. References to Orwell's novel *1984* were a common joke among the instructors. One of them even promised to dress as a rubric for Halloween right before he told me that he could no longer stand what he thought to be an oppressive situation and quit. This organizational system is habitual in university departments. How are we going to contest power structures in our classrooms if we, as scholars and educators, reproduce and work under the very same practices that we critique?

This high mobility of instructors affected the program so much that there was always a high demand for instructors with pedagogical training in content-based instruction (CBI) and task-based methodologies. However, the market's low supply of this type of instructor caused several classes to be canceled a few days before the beginning of the semester, with the consequent economic loss for the college. In addition, it was mandatory for full-time staff to function as coordinators, use numerous resources to coordinate each level and train and ensure that all instructors worked under the program standards. In a sense, this program functioned as a task-based and CBI teaching methods academy. Most adjuncts and professors entered this program without any preparation on SLA or teaching methods foundation, but they left trained, or at least with an idea of how a standardized program of these characteristics works.

I am not trying to make a case here for unstructured disarticulated Spanish programs in which every instructor teaches the way they please. My argument here is that this Spanish department (like many others) is a microrepresentation of the university culture, which, in turn, is a microrepresentation of society. Hierarchically organized and with a strict surveillance system, this department's director implemented a language program based on the 'objective' and 'neutral' premises provided by 'science', in this case by the field of traditional cognitive linguistics to which the director adhered like a religion. Of course, hypothesis-testing and inquiry procedures are of paramount importance in the scientific process; even, as Ortega (2019) proposes, rigorous quantitative research within post-positivist epistemologies should not be incompatible with a social justice agenda. However, scientific argumentation and counter-argumentation are a major part of it as well. Theories and the way to proceed within disciplines become norms that lead to conflict between groups of scientists. This conflict is central to progress in science, but it is hidden from both students and faculty through the imposition of a particular paradigm.

In this case, the imposition was implemented through a forced consensus of SLA methods informed exclusively by traditional psycholinguistic approaches simultaneously informed by a 'language-as-resource' (Flores, 2017) perspective. Thus, the program director rejected conflict by erasing and silencing voices that proposed the inclusion of other valid research-based methodological paradigms, such as those based on a sociocultural approach, or simply requested a more realistic workload for both instructors and students. Moreover, many instructors, especially those who really needed the job, feared crossing the director and having their contracts canceled the following semester; many of them were visibly stressed and living under constant pressure.

Another aspect that needs to be highlighted in order to understand this Spanish department is the nationality or national origin of the teaching staff. As happens in many Spanish departments in the United States, this aspect was somewhat shocking considering the Latina demographics in the United States. The program director publicly acknowledged making explicit efforts to diversify the department as much as possible regarding national origin. Anecdotally, she almost did not hire me, she jokingly confessed, after finding out my national origin. During my first job interview, she did not identify me as Spanish (she had the decorum to avoid that question during our first interview, which could have been interpreted as racist). However, she never mentioned seeing an issue in the lack of diversity regarding gender – we were only two male instructors – or – more noticeable due to the penetration of its construction and its major role in all social structures in US society – race. There were no Black instructors in this department, and the majority of the instructors self-identified as White (as they told me when I asked them about their racial identity directly, or when referring to themselves in comments such as 'ahí estaba yo, la única blanca', 'there I was, the only White female'), even if this was questionable considering how Whiteness constructs race in the United States (the construction of Hispanic ethnicity as a race in the United States, regardless of the adverse consequences for Hispanics of African descent, has been extensively documented; see for instance Arlene Dávila, 2012).

For this department director, diversity was more a question of national origin than other aspects of identity, such as race, which plays a major role within the US context. This could be interpreted as thinking within a colorblind ideology (see Chapter 1). Despite the director's efforts to diversify her department, out of 15 faculty members, eight were born in Spain (including her). The rest were Ecuadorian (one), Mexican (one), Argentine (one), Venezuelan (one), Salvadoran (one) and American (two, White American). This fact is important because, among other cultural aspects, it influenced the (geo)varieties of Spanish predominant in the program, with a bias toward the use of, mainly, certain phonetic, syntactic, lexical and pragmatic features as opposed to others (in this case, Peninsular Spanish from the center-north region of Spain).

In a sense, this language program reproduced the neocolonial ideological order fostered by institutions of linguistic disciplining such as the Royal Spanish Language Academy (RAE) or Association of Academies of the Spanish Language (ASALE): 'an institutional apparatus through which Spain intends to maintain a degree of cultural preeminence over the Spanish-speaking nations of America' (Del Valle, 2019). Of course, all regional Spanish language varieties were accepted and respected in the language program, but under the umbrella and tolerance granted by these legitimized Spanish institutions and represented, in this case, by the program director and the majority of its faculty, including both Spanish and Latin American faculty, therefore exemplifying how coloniality survives colonialism.

Intradepartmental relationships were cordial, or at least I never detected excessive tensions, despite the extremely fast-paced work, which was a common topic of complaint during casual conversations. However, interdepartmental relationships were a different matter. The constant disputes between the Spanish language and the Spanish literature departments led to an external review that concluded with a poor evaluation report and, two semesters later, the removal of the language program director. I will not go into detail about this report. However, I will address something that I consider especially important and, as usually happens, was left out of this report: the manifestation of racist ideologies through the use of language by faculty at XU's Spanish language department. In the following section, I will document from an ethnographic standpoint those racist ideologies that I was able to observe from my privileged position as an insider. In some instances, I will push aside the academic tone in which this monograph is written to highlight the emotional effect that these racist occurrences caused me.

2.3 Racist Language Practices at XU

During my time at this university, I heard the recurrent use by faculty of expressions such as 'trabajar como un negro' (working like a Black); the diminutive form of *negro* (black), 'negrito/a' (blackie, darkie), to refer to an adult Black male/female as well as Black kids; or 'le ha escrito el libro un negro' (a Black wrote the book for him – an expression to refer to a ghostwriter). I will use two examples to illustrate these unacceptable racist language practices and how they intertwine with ideologies and attitudes. This will be followed by a brief examination of, first, Spanish faculty identities from my conceptual perspective on identity and, second, the neoliberal educational policy framework in which these racist practices appeared. The main purpose of this section is not to label certain linguistic practices as racist or point a finger at certain curricula and educators as 'incorrect' and needing to be fired, but rather to point out how certain practices by educators are acceptable while others are not under a neoliberal educational context focused on 'language-as-resource' (Flores, 2017). Thus, the goal is to facilitate identification, reflection, analysis, understanding, resistance and action regarding these practices.

On one occasion, to my disbelief – and interrupting my burst of anger – the program director reprobated an elder instructor from Spain after she used, right in front of us and casually, the expression 'trabajo como un negro'. The director's immediate reply to this instructor was 'Decir eso está feo' (saying something like that is wrong) and, looking puzzled, asked her if she used that expression in front of her students. With serenity and peace of mind, the instructor from Northern Spain answered with a shameless yes, justifying that this is a quite common expression, everyone in Spain uses it and she did not mean anything by it. Now, let us visualize for an instant how this instructor's few Black students – and all her students in general, racist and antiracist, for that matter – in a country with a history of more than 400 years of systemic racism and an economy based on a plantation system that still intersects all aspects of this society may feel when they hear her use this expression. Notice, however, how the director showed her nonconformity with this racist use of the language, but no measures were taken at all. Moreover, somehow, I still have the feeling that my presence triggered the director's response. To this day, I still doubt this dialogue would have happened in my absence. The expression would have been used and not given the slightest importance. And you may wonder why this is. My interpretation is that, within this Spanish department culture, an incident like this is not as important as, for example, inflating grades, not following a rubric or printing a test with a typo (actions that could lead to a warning). Meanwhile, any type of misconduct that could interfere with any of the stipulations stated at each level of this program within its traditional psycholinguistic approach to language teaching had important consequences, such as being fired. However, the manifestation of racism – by a faculty member in class! – was relegated to the background and disregarded as anecdotal, similar to how antiracist curricular content was seen. Last time I heard, this instructor still worked full-time at this department and probably kept using this type of expression, completely normalized in racially homogeneous or reactionary contexts in Spain, although nobody would say it in front of Black people unless explicitly trying to show racist attitudes (yes, even in Spain).

On another occasion, a Catalan female instructor called my kids 'negritos' after she inquired about the 'beautiful' Black woman (my wife) in my family picture on my laptop's screensaver. Of course, as an antiracist linguist scholar, I had to reply! You may think that it could have been better to take my time after the meeting to explain to her how what she said was a racist otherizing and inferiorizing expression. But racist behaviors demand immediate responses. Besides, as many of you readers can probably relate to, after many previous similar encounters in which the user of a racist expression will justify themselves as non-racist by saying things such as 'I have a Black friend' or something similar – making things worse – I knew better than that. So instead, I used another strategy to help her self-reflect about her use of race and a diminutive as a marker to refer to my children. I decided that it would be better to manage to diminish her sympathetic smile by – following Lee *et al.* (see Chapter 1) – making her Whiteness strange and uncomfortable. So I just asked her, with another sympathetic smile, if she had any 'blanquitos' (Whitey children). I am certain she, and everyone sitting around us, perceived my answer as confrontational, especially because her statement was apparently inoffensive (and most probably she meant no harm, and her intention was just to praise my family). But racism – overt or covert, intentional or unintentional – must always be confronted everywhere, particularly in educational settings. Doing otherwise would be racist.

Our ideologies inform our attitudes and behaviors. I have no doubt that a racist ideology is at the core of these racist language uses that, as the Northern Spanish instructor in my example confessed, emerge in the language classroom, naturalizing them, offering them as valid tools of expression that index a particular (often exoticized) foreign culture. Moreover, through these practices, Spanish is presented as a foreign language in the United States when it is not (after Mexico, the United States is the country with the most Spanish speakers: 41 million, over 13% of its population according to the 2019 US Census).

In the daily use of Spanish (and any other language), we find frequent examples of the reproduction and perpetuation of certain stereotypes and attitudes that, not having a malign explicit intention in some cases, end up forming a discriminatory representation of social groups that are inferiorized and represented as otherness in – as in this example – Spanish society, and, through translocalization – the process of adopting and adapting global practices to the local context (Pennycook, 2007) – in US society and even within the smaller context of the classroom itself. The language uses I just exemplified respond to a series of normalized hegemonic ideologies. 'Working like a Black man' or the use of 'Black' to designate a ghostwriter (one who writes an artistic work without receiving credit for its authorship) constitute a reflection of the cultural and moral values of a great part of Spain's society that aims to construct and inferiorize these others.

Bañón Hernández (1996) listed the examples I provided along with other common uses such as 'hacer el indio' (acting like an Indian), meaning to act like a fool; 'merienda de negros' (late afternoon tea of Blacks), to indicate chaos and disorder; 'ir hecho un gitano' (have the appearance of a Gypsy), implying being dirty and wearing ragged clothes (notice the long history of discrimination in Spain against Spanish Roma people); 'hacer una judiada' (doing a Jewish thing), in the sense of betraying someone; or 'engañar a alguien como a un chino' (cheating/tricking someone like a Chinese, meaning easily), among many others. The values represented through these very common and completely normalized language uses are reinforced, perpetuated and, in the case of some Spanish language programs, transmitted to students without taking into account the ethical and moral implications; the establishment of asymmetric power relationships; and who is included, who is excluded and who identifies with which group within the classroom.

This body of knowledge can be articulated in the classroom with the following example that anticipates what I call later in Chapter 6 guerrilla tactics – that is, using those moments that appear during instruction that offer an opportunity to integrate critical content. This activity is an example of how, through raising awareness about racist linguistic practices of this type – those that are apparently said without malicious intent – we can provide tools for our students to fight these practices, which are sometimes perpetuated by their own instructors without them being aware. In a recent basic Spanish class, the word *moreno* appeared in an activity to describe brunets. However, a very participative male student of Indian descent who lives in a primarily Hispanic neighborhood pointed out that *moreno* is also the word to refer to Black people. This comment opened up an opportunity to discuss the underlying racist ideologies of this word and its use in different semantic and sociolinguistic fields. I asked the students to write sentences in groups using the word *moreno* with as many meanings as they could think of. Most of those sentences referred to hair, such as 'El pelo de Sarah es moreno' (Sarah's hair is brown), one group came out with 'Tariq es moreno' ('Tariq is brown' to refer to a Black student) and I added 'Me pongo moreno muy rápido en la playa' (I tan very quickly at the beach). This was followed by linguistic feedback and an explanation of the problems involved in the use of *moreno* as Black. The use of this word is widespread among some Spanish speakers, especially from Central America, but also used by some Latinx immigrants, including Dominicans and Puerto Ricans in New York City (some of them of obvious African descent), to refer to African Americans and, sometimes, Afrolatinxs to avoid the word *negro* (Black). Avoiding *negro* grants a negative connotation to being Black, as if being Black and using its equivalent word in Spanish to refer to Black people is some sort of taboo, a way of sugarcoating a negative attribute, something that could inflict shame on the person you call *negro*. This use of *moreno* is also commonly used among Spaniards with racist and xenophobic views in casual conversations when they attempt to hide their racist attitudes toward Black people. However, in Spain, the use of *moreno* instead of *negro* is generally taken as an insult by people proud of being of African descent, as seen in different social media outlets such as Afroféminas on Instagram or comments by some of my Black Spanish friends (some of their interactions with people using *moreno* to refer to them resulted in physical confrontations). Spanish Afrodescendants argue that there is nothing bad about being Black and they are proud of being Black; therefore, they claim the word *negro*. This awareness against the use of *moreno* to avoid using *negro* is widespread in the Spanish-speaking world, including countries such as the Dominican Republic, which have more complex racial nomenclature, as Torres-Saillant (1998) explains. To exemplify this point, I referred to one of the music video clips we had already watched in that class, 'Demasiado negro' (Too Black) by Dominican MC, Patógeno Musa (2020). In this music video, several Dominican MCs of unambiguous African descent rap precisely about this issue, claiming the word *negro* instead of *moreno* or others to refer to Black people.[4] The example of this video triggered an extension of our discussion. The same student told the class that he loved this song; however, he was hesitant to play it and sing its lyrics ('demasiado negro') while cruising through Black neighborhoods because he was afraid that Black people would think that he was using the word 'negro' in English. This opened another opportunity for the group to briefly discuss their thoughts about this matter and how different contexts (and the dynamism and fluidity of contexts within the United States), cultures, language uses and what is commonly understood by languages have an impact on the semantics of the same word.

Paradoxically, XU's Spanish language department insisted on and constantly promoted the use of reflection through workshops and emails. This was part of the director's attempt to promote faculty development based on new pedagogical trends that she learned of in conferences or read about in publications. But this professional practice aiming to facilitate change was not understood the way social scientists, such as Kondrat (1999, as cited in Sisneros *et al.*, 2008: 20), do: 'examining one's own biases and prejudicial attitudes, particularly when one is learning about and working with different identity groups, facilitates a process of change'. A critical approach within a multicultural perspective, such as Kondrat proposes – in my case, rather than multicultural, an antiracist perspective – allows us to evaluate how behavior, speech, attitudes and the way individuals interact can contribute to biases or discrimination toward those social groups constructed as others, further inferiorizing and marginalizing them instead of empowering them.

Instead, this Spanish department director's idea of reflection was far from this. Once again, within the director's epistemological framework, 'reflection' was focused on language acquisition techniques (which strategies/activities work, which do not) while omitting completely critical reflection. As seen in Magro (2016a), critical reflection works not only to achieve the goal proposed by Kondrat: of identifying and correcting behaviors/attitudes and breaking the cycle of bias and oppressive behaviors, which will help us to develop a more tolerant, critical and moral citizenship as a result of higher education. It also considers linguistic outcome goals; critical reflection oriented to raise CLA helps influence language acquisition in students through an increase in motivation.

On the one hand, it is our duty as educators to fight these widespread racist language uses reproduced by Spanish instructors, especially by newcomers to the United States or those who, for one reason or another, have resided in the United States for a while but have not been able to become aware of these uses or simply refuse to get rid of them because they see no harm in them. They may think of themselves as non-racialized subjects in US society – i.e. they identify as White, as I exemplified earlier – or exoticize their racialization or deny it by adhering to a position of *us* in their country of origin. Although I will delve more deeply into the concept of identity in Chapter 3, it is convenient to advance here that race, as part of our identities, is a dynamic social construct that depends on multiple factors, including perception, time and place. As Carmen Lee (2017) argues, identities are always open to reappropriation, recontextualization and transformation. Furthermore, as Nortier and Svendsen (2015) argue, although not every language choice is an act of identity, there is much identity work in the intersection between linguistic form, language use and language ideologies associable with society at large. In addition, we must consider how the symbolic value of linguistic markets (Bourdieu, 1991) restricts or influences identity and the indexical order of signs linking the micro-interactional instantiations to the macro-societal level. But how are educators going to address race in their daily practice if they are unaware of its intricacies as a social construct? This is, in part, the goal and the reason for including the first part of this book.

On the other hand, we must also resist the neoliberal educational policy framework in which racist language practices are performed, a framework within which Spanish departments and universities in general operate. This policy pushes toward a marketplace-oriented education centered around the economy and performance objectives based strictly on a connection between education and paid labor, a policy that, as Michael Apple (2004) explains in *Ideology and Curriculum*, produces more inequalities, not fewer. An antiracist pedagogy must combine, in its curriculum, social criticism with rigorous, disciplined academic content and teaching practices, always aiming for a more critical approach that truly places into practice a counter-hegemonic narrative not only by integrating and empowering *others* but by centering the curriculum around *others* while making Whiteness strange. For example, in another 'guerrilla tactic' activity implemented in a basic Spanish course that I want to advance here, the four 'White' Colombian characters used in the communicative activity presented in the textbook were problematized. The students were asked, '¿Has notado algo en la selección de los "cuatro colombianos"?' (Did you notice anything about the selection of these 'four Colombians'?). The students discussed it in groups (in Spanish). Some of the answers included: 'Los cuatro tienen piel clara' (all four are light-skinned); 'son blancos' (they are White); 'son "famous"' (they are famous); 'son ricos' (they are rich). After listening to their answers, we review what was discussed in previous classes about identity and how in the United States these Colombians would not be generally considered

White by the mainstream, but in Colombia they are – how the *us* vs. *them* dichotomy changes depending on the context. The following question was how the authors of the textbook may consider the introduction of these Colombians as an act of diversity when, in the Spanish-speaking world, they are mainstream. This conversation led to (1) a discussion about the authors of the textbook, who are White Americans, and how they look into these issues from a different perspective, through a different lens; (2) a discussion about Whitewashing and antiblackness in Colombia (and in Spanish-speaking countries and in the world in general). This part was in English for reasons of time, but with extra programming could be conducted in Spanish. This conversation was followed by a two-minute video from a Colombian news program (in Spanish with subtitles in English) about the exclusion from the gallery of presidents and the alteration of the features and skin color of the first Afrodescendant Colombian president's portrait, which exemplifies the rooted history of Whitewashing, antiblack ideologies and the erasure of Blackness from hegemonic contexts. The students were asked if they would be able to improve this textbook activity and they offered, in Spanish, solutions such as substituting the characters with Afro-Colombians who have the same professions as the textbook's characters, which they did (each of the four groups in class searched for two singers, a famous athlete and an actress). Then, they were asked if they thought that the professions chosen by the textbook were representative of Colombians and how this was linked to the circulating stereotypes in the United States about Latinxs, either positive or negative. We will see more examples of this type of guerrilla tactics and working within the cracks of the curriculum in Chapter 6.

The narrative of making Whiteness strange needs to admit and be informed by the fact that the story of the United States and many other nations, including all Spanish-speaking nations, is one of racial oppression that has benefited some groups over others. This history of racial oppression influences and informs the ideologies, attitudes and representations of all the social groups involved. An antiracist language curriculum must be detached from (exotic/romantic) ideas of (legitimate/authentic) *us* vs. (illegitimate/inauthentic) *them*. It must include *otherness* in our programs in a significant, significative and effective manner, not in the margins but as an integral part of our curricula, as the core of our curricula, empowering discriminated social groups and raising antiracist awareness among those privileging from power. Unfortunately, based on my experience, Spanish departments' cohorts tend to assimilate and reproduce the neoliberal educational policy framework in one way or another, naturalizing ideologies that relegate to the background critical sociopolitical content that could counteract neoliberal ideological impositions and their effects on equity and social justice.

This depiction of a Spanish language department is circumscribed to a very specific example: XU's Spanish language department. Nevertheless,

I am afraid this example is not an exception; on the contrary, I believe it is a good representation of Spanish departments in the United States. It is up to the educator to use this chapter to reflect on their own institutional context and identify similar practices to analyze, denounce and take action against them.

2.4 White Students in L2 Classes: The Case of Students Enrolled in XU's Spanish Program

Who were the recipients of these racist practices and ideologies? In Chapter 1, I offered a general overview of the sociocultural characteristics of the students enrolled at XU. In this section, I will describe the general features of a representative sample of these students. These are the participants in the research that informed the activities in Chapter 5 and the testimonies in the first section of Chapter 7: 35 students from two different sections of the Advanced Spanish II course. Of these 35 participants (20 females and 15 males between 18 and 22 years old), 30 completed the research. The purpose of this exhaustive description is (1) to highlight the importance of the individual characteristics of our students when developing antiracist materials and (2) to provide a broader picture of the Spanish department in which I developed the activities in Chapter 5 so the readers may have a referent to compare and contrast with their own instructional contexts in order to adapt the materials I propose or create their own materials.

In terms of the participants' linguistic background, all of them, except for three in the experimental group and four in the control group, declared English as their first language (L1). At the beginning of the semester, the linguistic proficiency level for all participants was between intermediate mid and advanced low. The department controlled this via a placement questionnaire that all students completed at the beginning of each semester. Jonatan and Sara in the experimental group and Abelardo, Ginés, Emma and Maribel in the control group were students of Hispanic heritage who grew up listening to Spanish at home. Kyra, in the experimental group, grew up with both Gujarati and English at home. These seven bilingual students were an unexpected exception. During the two previous semesters teaching this class (over 60 students), I only encountered one Hispanic heritage student who identified herself as White and Latina – her father was Puerto Rican and her mother, White American. I discussed the enrollment of these seven bilingual students with the director of the program. She confirmed the unusualness of this situation, admitting that during the more than 10 years in her position, she had never heard of a similar situation in her department.

The participants' socioeconomic status (SES), with two exceptions, was medium/high, reporting a total annual income per household of more than $100,000. Although there were no data on SES in the previous semesters, with the exception of an excellent African American student from the Bronx who came on a scholarship, I do not believe that there were lower-middle SES students in my classes. However, during my research, I had two students from a working-class background (both of them of Hispanic descent).

In the initial questionnaire (see Appendix A), all my students declared identifying racially as White or Caucasian except for these seven bilingual students. Twenty-six students checked the 'White or Caucasian' box; one student marked 'Asian' (and specified 'Indian' next to it); seven checked 'Hispanic or Latino/Latina'; and one student checked two categories, 'White or Caucasian' and 'Hispanic or Latino/Latina'. There were no African Americans enrolled, which seems usual in Advanced Spanish classes in this language program; I had only two African American students in the four sections I taught the previous two semesters. I did not discard students for my research, but these individual differences were considered an important factor when analyzing and interpreting the data. See Figure 2.1 for the breakdown of participants by race, a construct that, in Chapter 3, I will explain and problematize (for a more exhaustive and complete view of each participant in this research, see Magro, 2016a).

This overview of the students enrolled in the two classes I used for my research is a representative sample of the linguistic, socioeconomic and racial profile of Spanish students in a predominantly White private university in the United States. In line with other scholars (e.g. Alim & Baugh, 2007; Del Valle, 2014; Leeman et al., 2011; Leeman & Serafini, 2016; Martínez, 2003; Pennycook, 2007), I believe that empowering students belonging to racialized groups through a critical curriculum is an effective pedagogy. However, raising antiracist awareness among those students belonging to the power groups exercising and benefiting from racism is not only an effective pedagogy but also a priority. After all, it is *they* who consciously or unconsciously support, perpetuate and benefit

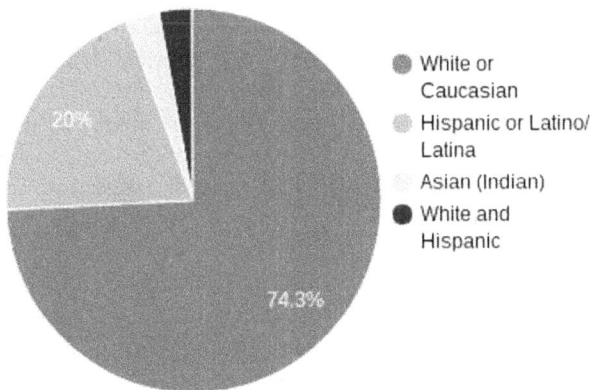

Figure 2.1 Participants by race

from racism. That question continually asked W.E.B. Du Bois as a Black man whenever racial issues arose – 'How does it feel to be a problem?' – should be directed to Whites and not to racialized persons. Over a century after DuBois's insightful comment, higher education scholarship and praxis still apply this method of (indirect) racial framing. As Chun and Feagin (2020) argue, when 'diversity' initiatives are created, or a racist issue occurs on college campuses, the focus tends to be on racially minoritized campus populations, which implicitly ignores the cause of the racial issue; the educator often ends up 'preaching to the choir'. Only acknowledging the grievances of students of color is not enough. We need to acknowledge the role played by Whiteness in racism if we are aiming to make substantive progress in fostering a racially inclusive curriculum and campuses.

By promoting CLA, antiracist pedagogies help to acknowledge the role of Whiteness in racism. They also help to develop allies that can effectively fight racism from within and transform the world into a more just place. But before I continue, I consider it necessary to attend to issues of positionality: how my positionality drives my research and practice, who am I trying to reach and for what purpose, some of the ideologies involved in this process and how they affect me personally and professionally, and how all this affects my field(s) of study.

2.5 You, the Reader, and I, the Writer: Positionality in Curriculum and Ideology Matters

As a critical researcher, I consider it crucial to position myself regarding my ideological values, overtly embracing them and admitting that they lead my research and praxis. Like Edward Said (1994), I consider it important to explicitly establish the locus from where I investigate, write and teach. With my life-long journey fighting racism within different (academic, artistic, militant) fields, it is not surprising that the transformative mission of my research would continue within this tradition. I already offered a reflection about my identity when I tried to answer that infamous question of 'what are you?' in the introduction to this book. All those experiences that preceded me as a scholar and forged my (stigmatized) identities are necessarily going to permeate my production, plus guide and influence my scholarly practice, which, framed within a critical paradigm, necessarily denies notions of value-free research.

I drafted this book to address educators, whether they are scholars, in- or pre-service teachers or graduate or undergraduate students, across a wide array of fields of study with different disciplinary-specific outcome goals but with the general common goal of eradicating racism through pedagogical strategies. Therefore, this work is not addressed solely to linguists. I am aware – and I want you to be aware – of the dialogue that, as Garrett (2001) explains, is established when trying to transmit the scientific knowledge of linguistics to a broader public, and how to change public attitudes where there is resistance. When asked about the scientific facts that the non-linguist is willing to deal with, this dialogue opens up other discussions that have to do more with ideology: who is the public, who are we trying to reach and who are these non-linguists? This book is not only trying to reach you as a (future) educator and/or scholar. With a focus on helping educators to implement antiracist pedagogies, it is ultimately targeting a very diverse audience, a diverse array of mainly non-linguists (or rather latent linguists): our students, who, all of them, are potential educators either in future classrooms or informal discussions outside classrooms.

But who do I mean by 'our students' in this book? As I briefly mentioned in this chapter, there is a considerable body of studies in the field of critical applied linguistics (CALx) that aim to empower heritage students by raising their linguistic awareness. However, research focused on raising linguistic awareness among US mainstream students is scarce, even though Whites are the ones who implement racism and benefit from it. Why do we not go then to the direct source of the problem instead of trying to mend its symptoms? Would it not be more effective to raise mainstream students' linguistic awareness instead of reproducing an ideology that grants heritage students all the responsibility for fighting these racist ideologies but, in the process, makes them indirectly responsible for them? This idea is not a novelty, as I previously exemplified with W.E.B. Du Bois's insightful explanation over a century ago (Chun & Feagin, 2020). After all, the construction of these ideas, although also internalized and perpetuated by those suffering from them, has its origin in the main racial and socioeconomic group with which these mainstream students identify: middle-class Whites. According to Chun and Feagin (2020), this problem has to do with the invisibility of Whiteness and this method of racial framing in higher education, both in scholarship and practice. By this, I do not mean that the pedagogical strategies suggested in this book are exclusively oriented to White mainstream students. As you will see, the practices that I propose are also effective with other racially minoritized populations within mainstream students – e.g. African Americans or Asian Americans – as well as with heritage students.

But what about those ideologies that influence public attitudes? My position in society would make it difficult for me to ignore the current political and social moment. Thus, I consider it necessary to address the present coexistence of contradictory linguistic ideologies that I perceive as very salient. On the one hand, within a monolingual ideology perspective, bilingual students are forced – as a sort of punishment – to attend English as second language (L2) programs. Within a subtractive paradigm, these programs aim to linguistically assimilate these students while erasing their other language(s). In the process, these programs ostracize and taint these students with stigma for the rest of their academic careers as 'incomplete' or 'defective' speakers of both English and their native language(s) (Rosa, 2019).

On the other hand, the media echoes those studies conducted in linguistics that repeatedly argue about the benefits of bilingualism. These programs tend to privilege mainly middle-class White students who flood language immersion programs wherever they are offered. Meanwhile, these same programs are avoided by native speakers of languages other than English who want to assimilate linguistically because they – or most commonly their guardians – believe this subtractive assimilative linguistic process will grant them greater social mobility and reduce discrimination. At the same time, they lose a remunerated skill in the job market, a trait of their identity and all the cultural and cognitive benefits associated with bilingualism (García & Otheguy, 2015).

But these contradictory ideologies are rooted in the beliefs of most members of our society – including many linguists, as DeBose (2007) argues – who are deeply (unconsciously) invested in the hegemony of the 'standard language'. Either with diverse student populations or with mainly mainstream ones, and both within the dominant language versus dominated languages dichotomy and with variation within each language (and this happens from early childhood education), educators are in charge of the socializing process of educating culturally and linguistically. However, educators are permeated by the same entrenched linguistic hegemonic ideologies that penetrate most citizens. Nevertheless, they are in a position of great power because they oversee the enforcement of those top-down imposed 'rules' that maintain the sociolinguistic order (Paris & Alim, 2017). My position toward standard language ideologies, as you can imagine, is overtly critical.

Before I continue, I should point out that I am conscious that my following explanation of the sociolinguistic order runs the risk of reproducing another linguistic ideology detrimental to hybrid speakers: the view of languages as discrete units. Thus, I want to clarify that what I understand here by *a language* is a sociopolitical construction. Intralinguistically – that is to say, within what has been constructed as *a language* – this order has to do with the imposition of a 'chosen' language variety and, in the process, the inferiorization of language varieties that do not adhere to the prescribed rules of this 'chosen' standardized language variety. Interlinguistically – that is to say, between what has been constructed as two or more different languages – within the US context, this order is closely linked to the ongoing heated debate about English Only, a debate recently revived after the 2016 US presidential campaign and its results. In this debate, racist discourse takes the form of linguistic debate as a reaction to fear of what Harvard political scientist Samuel J. Huntington (2004) called the Hispanic threat. What is known as the 'Latino threat narrative' (Chavez, 2008) is a constant in both pre- and post-9/11 public discourse that perceives Latino groups as a dangerous invading force. This discourse predicts, against all linguistic knowledge, a Spanish invasion that will break the illusion of US political unity and cultural homogeneity in, probably, the most diverse country in the world, and whose elites want to impose on their image and similarity.

Another ideological issue is the lack of attention to the relationship between academic knowledge and extra-academic phenomena. It is in this area that curricular content plays a central role. To better illustrate this issue, let us examine the following example. Recently, in an intermediate Spanish language program, I witnessed the switch from using materials that utilize historical and sociopolitical contents to teach Spanish to more 'aseptic' cultural content, such as topics related to food, travel or the job market. This selection process was put through a committee of instructors – including professors of a diverse range and graduate students teaching these classes – who voted after more than six months of reviewing different proposed materials. Of course, a decision such as this one takes into consideration many factors, which, as you can imagine, had a different priority status for each member of the committee – for example, the type of digital platform, ease of use of materials for untrained graduate students instructing these classes, printed versus digital-only materials, integrated versus non-integrated assessments, approach to grammar teaching, organization, content, cultural and sociolinguistic aspects, price and support.

There is no perfect standardized teaching material, and its selection mostly depends on the program's priorities and needs at a given moment. However, although I perceived improvements in the methodology (e.g. the new materials focused more on communication than on grammatical structure acquisition and the students were able to communicate better within more aseptic, although simpler, sociolinguistic fields by the end of the semester), this switch, which deprioritized content over method, brought up complaints by numerous students who claimed the materials to be unexciting, boring and even insulting due to their puerile nature. Who cares, right? The students are learning Spanish, which is the main outcome goal. However, the question remains, how many of these students will be willing to enroll in the next class? How many will continue using Spanish? Should our main goal as language educators be to teach Spanish from a neoliberal framework in which language acquisition is a commodity?

Against what many critics of curricula may think in a case like my example – i.e. educators did so because they did not know better – this curriculum switch, as I detailed, was not a mindless decision. Instead, I believe the decision taken in this example had to do with what Michael Apple argues in *Ideology and Curriculum*: schools were in part designed to teach precisely what they do. That is, hidden or tacit content related to the teaching of socioeconomic expectations, economic functionalism, values and moral norms is contextualized within a larger and much more powerful nexus of economic and political institutions. This relationship, which gives schools their meaning, is often overlooked by educators and administrators that are more focused on certifying a technical competence under certain internalized standards – linguistic proficiency measured as X, cultural aspects understood as Y – rather than taking into consideration broader educational goals and a critical transformative mission. In other words, speaking a language is the goal because it is a useful skill in the labor market. What you speak with that language, which materials the students use to learn that language or what the students will do with that language should never interfere, under this neoliberal ideological framework, with the maximization of providing this technical skill.

In this particular language program (despite its diverse nucleus of resistance), and in most of the programs where I taught, schools do what they are supposed to do, what they are designed for: to maximize the production of technical knowledge while deprioritizing ideological considerations other than those naturalized by hegemonic economic and political institutions. As Michael Apple (2004) argues, at least up to a point, the problem here is not analytic (what should be constructed as knowledge?), technical (how to organize, store and teach knowledge to facilitate learning?) or psychological (how do we get students to learn?) but ideological. This ideological problem has to do with what is accepted as legitimate knowledge, which responds to pre-chosen educational ends. It has to do with what should be included as content and what should not because, for instance, it may make some students feel uncomfortable when it challenges their ideologies or, in the best cases, press them to enter the realm of cognitive dissonance. Negligence to overlook these issues – in my opinion, covert negligence, at least in my example – maintains the purpose of the educational system as it was designed. In other words, just as there is an unequal distribution of economic capital, there should be a similar distribution of cultural capital, not only by restricting access to 'legitimate' knowledge but also by delegitimizing, silencing and erasing certain knowledge that challenges the status quo.

The erasure of content related to inequality, asymmetric power relationships and racism from language curricula hurts CLA development and motivation toward language learning and interferes with linguistic proficiency. In this sense, I agree with Apple that the educational system works, but it works for *them*, those in groups of power who benefit from it. *They* justify the existence of massive parts of the population struggling to survive in order to serve the conservative social interests of stability and social stratification. Moreover, they do it while maintaining a well-lubricated social system of oppressors and oppressed through one of the main tools of social control ever created: education. Thus, from my ideological standpoint, it is both a professional and moral duty for educators to act on these ideological considerations.

Of course, as Larson and Ovando (2001) argue, embarking on the change needed to achieve racial equity in education – or any transformative change for that matter – is rather difficult because it calls into question how the norms, practices and routinization of institutional members have long grown comfortable with what may in fact be the cause of racial inequities injuring racially minoritized students, faculty and staff, and even the surrounding community. This is the reason why, more often than not, educational institutions' public commitment to racial justice ends up in 'just talk', because any impactful action would cause the institution to break away from the ease of norms it has long benefited from (Welton *et al.*, 2018). Authors such as Castagno (2014) and Lewis and Diamond (2015) pointed out that this 'we had good intentions' approach is not only not enough but why true institutional change for racial equity often never comes to materialize.

I would like to stop here, fully understanding that much more could be and needs to be said about the topics I have raised in this section. My positionality and views on free-value research drive me to consider certain ideological topics as central to developing and implementing content aiming to aid the critical transformation of language students, both explicitly and implicitly. Explicitly, by developing and implementing content related to the sociopolitical nature of language in order to raise CLA in both L2 programs and in heritage language (HL) programs, which should be more like English courses for English speakers (Leeman, 2015). Implicitly, by working within a pedagogical framework that integrates practices that consider these ideological aspects in language teaching. Departing from this ideological standpoint and answering the need identified by Garrett (2001) to adequately integrate the study of language ideologies as an essential component of CALx, in the following chapters, I propose a pedagogical framework and concrete research-based tools to increase CLA and change attitudes toward the *other*, with the goal of initiating educators and students into an antiracist path. This framework and tools will do so by promoting reflection focusing on both the *us* and the *I*.

Notes

(1) I will avoid being too specific to protect the anonymity of this institution.
(2) See *The Chronicle of Higher Education* for data (https://data.chronicle.com/category/ccbasic/30/faculty-salaries/).
(3) For example, for a 10-month appointment, in 2019, a K–12 teacher in Washington, DC, with a PhD had a salary ranging from $65,697 to $116,408 ($76,728 to $130,346 for a 12-month appointment). Source: https://dcps.dc.gov/page/compensation-and-benefits-teachers.
(4) Another transversal activity that I use, which includes alternative voices and materials in basic level Spanish classes, is a playlist of videos from different non-hegemonic artists representing different Spanish-speaking countries, as well as traditionally excluded from academia, social and racial groups. These videos are played a couple of minutes before the class starts while I am setting up the room and they are followed by simple questions (e.g. in basic Spanish, '¿De dónde son?' [where are they from?]).

3 Let Us Talk About Race ... and Language ... and Power

3.1 Introduction

With a few exceptions, the reality we face as educators in higher education institutions is that, on the one hand, Whites are overrepresented in most of our classrooms, and, on the other hand, racially minoritized students 'have learned through their presence in "White" spaces (such as universities) what they can and cannot say' (Rebollo-Gil & Moras, 2006). Consequently, those counternarratives that 'tell on' racism, as Bell (2003, as cited in Rebollo-Gil & Moras, 2006) puts it, are often excluded from any discussion in our programs. Moreover, resistance – or silence, which according to Willis (2004) is a form of resistance – to explicitly thinking about race and racism in discussions of language programs in hallways, classrooms, faculty meetings, conferences and even over email is the norm rather than the exception (Inoue, 2015). These discussions must happen. However, after the merciless public execution of George Floyd on 25 May 2020, a new urge to include antiracist pedagogies at all educational (and publishing) levels is perceived by some of us, antiracist educators working in this field for years, as an opportunistic drift or, in the best cases, a movement that, despite being long-awaited and welcome, runs the risk of turning into a passing trend.

With the goal of establishing antiracist pedagogies as a long-term educational effort to eradicate racism, this chapter will first focus on the rationale behind the inclusion of counternarratives as a central component of antiracist pedagogies. Second, focusing on how to integrate these counternarratives in the language classroom, we will analyze the articulation of counternarratives through content related to the sociopolitical dimension of language (sociopolitical contents or SPCs). To do so, I will start by reviewing key intersecting concepts and tenets from the field of critical race theory (CRT) which inform this book, whose understanding is necessary in order to underpin our curriculum on counternarratives: identity(s), race and racism. This will be followed by a discussion of the question: why is the focus on race? Lastly, I will address the rationale behind the inclusion of content related to the sociopolitical nature of language.

3.2 Counternarratives: Justification and Strategies

I agree with Rebollo-Gil and Moras (2006) that counternarratives that 'tell on' racism are pivotal to promoting antiracism among our White students. Moreover, I also believe that these counternarratives must be the core of our curriculum, not marginal/peripheral or anecdotal knowledge, and they must be carefully planned, integrated and articulated into our language programs. The manifestations of these counternarratives within the curriculum, however, will be markedly different for each educator. These manifestations will reflect how their race, racial identity, antiracist education and their (race) life experiences and subjectivity necessarily intersect their experience in classrooms. These individual differences will inform what we think we can and cannot say in our counternarratives. Regardless of these differences, however, they should be honest reflections on privilege and/or the experience of subordination. This is pivotal and will necessarily have different repercussions for White and racialized educators.

As Rebollo-Gil and Moras (2006) argue, White educators' 'confessionals' can be a starting point to introduce counternarratives. If you are a White educator, by doing it yourself, you can open the space for White students to, one, create spaces that privilege racialized voices through recognizing and legitimizing experiences of racism and their continued power and incursion in the classroom; and two, publicly tell on yourselves and your families, by bringing up the topic of your own personal racism and your struggles in combating it within yourselves and the people closest to you. If you are a White educator with experience in antiracist activism, you may also include those experiences to legitimate antiracism not only as a valid stance but as a necessary one.

As a racially minoritized educator, the strategies will be different, but the goal will be the same: White students must be oriented toward breaching racist beliefs consciously and actively. Until very recent times, these beliefs used to be generally communicated among White Americans through coded language, in trying not to sound racist at any cost, as Bonilla-Silva (2003) argues in *Racism without Racists*. However, after the electoral campaign in 2016 and Trump's takeover, there was a turning point. Now, we face a different scenario. More and more White Americans have returned to overt, shameless, explicit racism, especially remapping it onto language (Zentella, 2016). Although many Whites still spend enormous amounts of energy to avoid being seen as racists, almost half of the US voting population supported an overt racist in the White House. An overview of the demographic composition of this electorate shows that 88% of Trump voters in 2016 were White, 88% were from rural and suburban areas, 63% were noncollege Whites (26% college Whites) and 54% were Christian affiliated (34% Evangelical, 20% Catholic), something that did not change in the US presidential elections of

2020 despite Trump's defeat (Pew Research Center, 2018, 2020). Many of these far-right populist policy supporters have taken off their hoods and reproduced and amplified Trump's racist discourse in both private and public spaces. Thus, our experiences in dealing with racist encounters and how we may link them to different, yet racist, experiences faced by other racially minoritized students (all our experiences differ and intersect different subordinated identities such as gender and religion), how we feel about these encounters and how we resist them can be a starting point to bringing these counternarratives to our language classrooms.

Therefore, if we want to develop and implement valuable antiracist work, we should not only be able to actively break the coded speech protocols that camouflage racism and expose the speaker publicly, as Rebollo-Gil and Moras (2006) propose; we must also report, deconstruct and strategize against those not-so-coded speech protocols of overt racism and how they are interwoven with specific economic and political interests. Our curriculum must address students' stories in the classroom, both racist and antiracist stories, both active and passive ones, as perpetuators or victims of it. Our programs must be effective in dissecting, pinpointing and highlighting the racist underpinnings of certain modes of thought, speech and behavior in order to be effective in openly discussing strategies to contradict them, challenge them by any means necessary through conversation and promote either intellectual or physical action, as well as to reflect on and imagine the possible repercussions and outcomes of antiracist actions. By exposing these normally invisible systems of privilege, subordination and inferiorization, both White students and White educators will be able to dissect their own Whiteness and make racism a localized and personalized issue. Simultaneously, racially minoritized students and educators will be empowered in this process, validating our experiences and helping us develop strategies to deconstruct racism and articulate resistance against it.

In this respect, the antiracist pedagogical approach I propose is also rooted in critical Hip-Hop language pedagogies (Alim, 2007), which work within a Freirian critical pedagogy of language framework (Freire, 1970) that aims to educate linguistically profiled and marginalized students about how language is used and how can be used against them. That is to say, how language can be used to perpetuate asymmetric power relationships and how can be used to, as (Alim, 2007) support, resist, redefine or reverse these relationships – or rather, as I support, not to reverse but to eradicate these relationships. Moreover, based on critical Hip-Hop language pedagogies – which draw heavily from the perspectives of critical linguistic awareness (CLA) (Fairclough, 1995; Wodak, 2012) – I view educational institutions as perpetuators of the sociolinguistic order, teaching but not challenging it.

Thus, antiracist educators must challenge this linguistic order. However, in doing so, we must also address issues related to fractal recursivity

(Irvine & Gal, 2000: 39), which 'involves the projection of an opposition, salient at some level of relationship, onto some other level', and avoid the reproduction of this order at other levels, always looking for a more just society, free of racism and any other form of discrimination of inferiorized groups. We must report, challenge and promote action against those practices conducted by individuals from some racially or otherwise discriminated groups who project that discrimination toward groups perceived as inferior (e.g. discrimination wielded by some African Americans or Chicanos who see themselves in a privileged position of power over recently arrived migrants, even within heritage language [HL] courses, as Lacorte and Magro [2022] argue). Moreover, we must be careful in doing so, verifying that the relationship between racism and power, as well as the difference between racism and racial prejudice, is understood by the students and by us to avoid falling into the widespread ideology of racism as intrinsic to human nature, such as the absurd belief that humans are inherently racist. Complex behaviors and attitudes are learned, not genetically transmitted (Montagu, 1976).

Therefore, our curriculum should aim to create cognitive dissonance in our classrooms, purposely and frequently, in which a rigorous research-based curriculum disarticulates coded and overt racist discourse. Our content may depart from the anecdotal life experiences of our students – and/or our own experiences as educators – but should halt the casual conversation and redirect the class toward deeper antiracist analysis, understanding and action. As Rebollo-Gil and Moras (2006: 393) explain, 'the goal is for racism to stop informing the conversation between Whites and instead become the topic of their talk'. Whereas these authors refer exclusively to Whites, I want to emphasize, once again, the need to deal with possible instances of fractal recursivity of discrimination conducted by discriminated groups over groups perceived as inferior, thus stopping the reproduction of the mechanics of racism.

In order to achieve this goal, we will use different pedagogical strategies depending on our teaching environment and the course goal objectives. Regardless of these, I concur with Zapata and Lacorte (2018) that our starting point is to develop a curriculum that takes into consideration our students' life experiences, needs, interests, communities and affiliations and personal worlds (i.e. their diverse social and cultural backgrounds). This is Kalantzis et al.'s (2005) notion of belonging, the need for students to feel they belong to their instructional environment while connecting at a deep, personal level. Furthermore, according to Lacorte (2007), we must attend to our students' communicative needs and grant sociocultural meaning to our pedagogical strategies, such as paying attention to specific linguistic forms that allow students access to comprehensible input and opportunities to negotiate meaning in a social context while participating in natural communication. The pedagogical approach I suggest follows Lacorte's (2007) and Zapata and Lacorte's

(2018) recommendations about incorporating a social psychologist's focus on second language (L2) acquisition – incorporating social, cultural, psychological and political behaviors – and understanding the attitudes and motivation within the classroom. In line with Lacorte's perspective, I understand motivation as a dynamic space, an idea that intertwines with motivation theories (Dörnyei, 2003; Masgoret & Gardner, 2003). All this is necessarily going to be linked not only to the content but also to the type of format we use to present the information to our students, which must address these needs. Now, I am not saying, and I believe that neither did these authors, that if we encounter in our classroom a student belonging to, for example, a far-right group, we should promote such views by including them in our curriculum. Nonetheless, we should consider how such a student's affiliations and views can be utilized to cause the student dissonance and promote change toward an antiracist stance.

Another component of importance promoted by learning by design (Zapata & Lacorte, 2018) and closely related to the notion of agency is to involve and engage the student in the learning process. This is crucial because of agency's relationship with the transformation process (Kalantzis *et al.*, 2005) that we are seeking by implementing antiracist pedagogies. And for this transformation to succeed, we must 'take the learner into new and unfamiliar terrains. However, for learning to occur, the journey into the unfamiliar needs to stay with a zone of intelligibility and safety. At each step, it needs to travel just the right distance from the learner's lifeworld starting point' (Kalantzis *et al.*, 2005: 51). This idea has to do with Vygotsky's zone of proximal development, and for this to happen, we must consider and promote agency within our students. For example, granting agency was necessary not only during the data collection process for my investigation (Magro, 2016a), as Willis (2004) proposes, but also central as a pedagogical strategy, as Duff (2012) and Leeman (2005) advocate. The student must feel like a part of his/her learning process, not a mere recipient of it. In this regard, we need to be careful with the labels we impose on our students because, as Duff (2012) argues, these will position people and their abilities and aspirations in particular ways. For instance, think of the following labels and the different social and psychological effects they may have on students: *interlanguage speaker, fossilized second language users, immigrants, limited (English) proficient speakers, refugees, non-native speakers, heritage-language learners, generation 1.5 learners.* As we will see next, a critical perspective on the construct of identity(s) plays a pivotal role in an antiracist approach to pedagogy.

3.3 Counternarratives in the Language Classroom

Before we start developing our curriculum around the idea of counternarratives as a central axle, we, as educators, must understand the constructs that will inform them. In this case, identity(s), racism and CRT inform the pedagogical approach I propose. After introducing them, I will explore the rationale behind the use of SPCs to fight racism in the language classroom.

3.3.1 Identity(s)

Norton (2012) already explained the growing interest in the study of identity within the field of second language acquisition (SLA). She attributes this to the current change in the conceptions of the individual, language and learning in this field, which is related to the ongoing switch from traditional psycholinguistic perspectives toward approaches with a major focus on the social and anthropological dimensions of language learning, particularly with reference to sociocultural, poststructural and critical theory (Norton, 2012; Ortega, 2019). Accordingly, researchers interested in individual differences that have to do more with social than cognitive aspects of language consider it necessary to study not only input–output issues in SLA but also the relationships between the language learner and the larger social world. Additionally, Norton (2012) states that a view of the learner as a binary being (e.g. motivated–unmotivated, introverted–extroverted) is not sustainable from this perspective, since these affective factors are generally socially constructed, changing over time and space and, quite possibly, coexisting in a contradictory way within the same individual depending on the context. All this theoretically justifies a need to analyze the various social, historical and cultural contexts – including issues related to race, resistance, inequality, ethnicity, class and iconization of different linguistic varieties – in which language learning will take place. Thus, students will have the opportunity to negotiate and even resist the various positions that these contexts offer. When developing and implementing SPCs, we must always bear in mind that this analysis – and the opportunities to negotiate and resist that it offers – is jointly intertwined with the development of our students' agency. With this in mind, let us look at what is understood by identity(s) in this book.

To begin with, my views on identity are aligned with Goffman's (1956) analogy of identity as a theatrical performance. I understand identities as socially constructed through discourse, making our language choices of paramount importance. Identities constantly change due to various factors, such as the context of interaction or the ways speakers interpret the identities being projected. In social interaction, people are constantly making decisions about whether they wish to express or reveal certain aspects of their identities, constantly trying to highlight some features of themselves and hiding others. Despite the speaker's attempts to influence how others perceive them, it is the hearer who ultimately creates the speaker's identity (Goffman, 1956).

I use the plural form *identities* instead of the singular *identity* in view of the multiplicity and multifaceted nature of identity understood from a constructivist approach (Vygotsky, 1980). As Lee (2017) states, certain aspects of identity are considered more static than others (e.g. age, gender and nationality), while aspects such as hobbies, interests and social networks are more subject to change with time. Moreover, social domains (e.g. work, family and education) and/or relationships (e.g. friends, colleagues and family) shape aspects of identities. Likewise, historical and socioeconomic domains shape race and ethnicity.

Some examples I often use with my students may help to illustrate this point. In Chimamanda Ngozi Adichie's novel *Americanah* (2013), the main character, Ifemelu, insightfully reflects on becoming Black soon after leaving Nigeria to reside in the United States. After being raised in a (middle-class) social context in a country in which people of African descent are obviously not subjects of Black racial profiling, she is shocked by these racist practices when she experiences them in the United States. Another example, based on personal experience, is how I became racially identified as 'ragatón' in Kenya when the local lifeguard in the hotel I was staying at for a wedding had issues finding a racial category to identify me. During an informal conversation, he pointed out that he could not place me within the other guests' identities – Black American, White American or Indian (a common racial group in Kenya). However, for him, I looked like those (Puerto Rican) artists featured in reggaetón videos playing at that time in Kenya. He was not familiar with the US term Latino/Hispanic to categorize me, but since he thought I looked like those artists, against my will (I am not a big fan of reggaetón), I became 'ragatón' (his phonetic rendering of 'reggaetón').

A third example is informed by various stories in social media and other information outlets that show astonished Spaniards when they are racialized in the United States by Whites. That is, they see themselves as White in Spain, but when they arrive in the United States, they are 'turned' into Hispanics and/or Latinxs. This Spaniards' identity conflict responds to the rhetoric resulting from the economic and sociopolitical agenda of 'whitewashing' Spain by 'Spanish powers, especially by the government and the media as being sustained over a false myth of pure Europeanity' (Toasijé, 2009), which aligns with the interests of neoliberal neocolonial projects launched and supported by corporations (e.g. PRISA) as José del Valle (2005) argues when discussing Spanish as a neoliberal/neocolonial project. As Carmen Lee (2017) explains, identities are always open to reappropriation, recontextualization and transformation. Therefore, this conceptualization of identities rejects an essentialist conception of identity as given categories of who individuals or groups are or belong to (Lee, 2017: 55). Thus, identities are dynamic, not fixed, always changing in time and (social, cultural, geographical) space.

Furthermore, although not every language choice is an act of identity, there is much identity work going on in the intersection between linguistic form, language use and the ideologies of language associable with a society at large (Nortier & Svendsen, 2015: 14). Thus, the symbolic value of linguistic markets (Bourdieu, 1991) restricts or influences identity as well as the indexical order of signs linking the micro-interactional instantiations to the macro-societal level. Depending on the linguistic market (e.g. academic context vs. Hip-Hop), features associated with contemporary urban speech styles may have a different 'price' (Magro, 2016b).

Let us expand on this idea. What is considered the prestige language variety in the linguistic market of a college – i.e. normative top-down standardized linguistic features – loses its value when used in a different linguistic market such as Hip-Hop. In the linguistic market of Hip-Hop, the vernacular language is the prestige variety. Conversely, as Androutsopoulos (2010) argues, while in one context (e.g. Hip-Hop) these features may be considered prestigious and index in-group solidarity and positive associations to a certain locality, in another context (e.g. academics), they may be considered as having low prestige and evoke negative stereotypes of, for example, prototypical migrant descents.

Hence, as educators, we need to enhance our understanding of the fine-grained ways of performing identity within a specific space, whether racial, political, historical or economic; whether urban, suburban or rural; whether socially homogeneous or heterogeneous and diverse spaces. Moreover, in this new age of technology, we need to pay attention to how these ways of performing identities intertwine with how these specific spaces are displayed globally through social networking sites such as Instagram or Snapchat. Also, we must be ready to understand how identities are performed from a translingual perspective, in which multilingual speakers utilize their linguistic repertoires as an integrated communication system (Canagarajah, 2011), and from a heteroglossic perspective, which embraces the coexistence of different varieties within a single language (Bakhtin, 1981). In sum, we must consider the dynamic and dialectic nature of social positioning and identity management, forged by the total linguistic fact, and the great importance of hegemonic ideologies, shaped by the socioeconomic and cultural positions of groups in societies.

3.3.2 Racism

I explained in Chapter 1 what is understood by racism in this book. In Chapter 2, I unveiled some of its manifestations in a Spanish language department and the rationale behind them. Let us argue why it is so important for educators to understand racism and its linguistic component as well as its recent history. Before we start with racism, let us first see the main tenets of CRT, to which this work adheres. Afterward, let us follow Bonilla-Silva (2003), who does a brilliant job explaining race, in examining the different perspectives adopted by social scientists regarding this social construct (and to avoid theoretical assumptions, I will state my position overtly for the benefit of both readers and potential critics), the concept of racial structure and racial ideology.

Counternarratives are a central tenet of CRT (Dixson *et al.*, 2018; Solórzano & Yosso, 2002). They provide a way for communities of color to share their stories without Whiteness being centralized, and, additionally, they challenge the master/dominant narrative. They are asset-based and provide a fuller story where antenarratives, or partial stories, once existed (Wolgemuth, 2014, as cited in Welton *et al.*, 2018). But what is CRT?

According to Martínez-Avila *et al.* (2015: 28), CRT emerged in the United States during the mid-1970s. It started with lawyers, activists and researchers in the field of law. This group of scholars and professionals proposed new theories and strategies to fight racism, which had gained ground since the stoppage in civil rights advances during the 1960s (Delgado & Stefancic, 2001: 3–4, as cited in Martínez-Avila *et al.* 2015: 28). Currently, based on Martínez-Avila *et al.*, the CRT movement comprises a collection of activists and researchers interested in studying and transforming the relationship between race, racism and power. This field has a close relationship and intersections with other movements such as legal studies and radical feminism; with philosophers and theorists such as Antonio Gramsci and Jacques Derrida; with the radical US tradition of Sojourner Truth, Frederick Douglass, W.E.B. Du Bois, Malcolm X, Cesar Chavez and Martin Luther King, Jr; and with the Black Power and Chicano movements of the 1960s and early 1970s.[1]

CRT understands that there is little disagreement among scientists that race is not a fixed biological or natural reality but a socially constructed category (Gallagher, 2011; Wagner *et al.*, 2016). As Martínez-Avila *et al.* (2015) argue, the concept of race and all notions of difference based on race are human creations. Race is not proven as something natural, essential or absolute, neither fixed nor an eternal category. From a biological standpoint, race is, instead, a grouping of artificial elements in the function of biological similarity criteria (and very often confused with ethnic or cultural attributes such as language, religion or geography). This grouping of attributes is commonly used to discriminate or for identity purposes. However, from a social constructivist perspective, the non-natural characteristic of a concept does not make it unreal. A position that denies or ignores the existence of race because it is not natural does not seem to be an effective solution against racism, while third parties construct identities – actively and passively – with discriminatory endings. The impossibility of scientifically proving the existence of races, dividing natural lines that differentiate elements of one race from another, has not prevented individuals from adopting artificial criteria to identify with a group and differentiate from *others* (which, following Derrida, will be defined by their differences) (Martínez-Avila *et al.*, 2015: 29).

Another important tenet of CRT, which I utilized both during the research that informs this book (Magro, 2016a) and in my pedagogical approach, is that it recognizes the right of every individual to self-identify with a race, especially – and this is important not to confuse with cases such as the one of the former president of the Spokane chapter of the NAACP, Rachel Dolezal, a White female who self-identified as Black for personal profit – when it is utilized to explain the discriminatory acts motivated by the definitory aspects of the group to which the individual was assigned (Pérez-Peña, 2015). Therefore, based on Martínez-Avila *et al.* (2015), CRT cannot be racist nor equivalent to racism, which is performed over the subordinated groups, which in the US context is non-Whites. Thus, as David Ingram (2004: 55, as cited in Martínez-Avila *et al.*, 2015: 29) states, affirming Black Power is not equivalent to affirming White Power because the former is a defensive strategy whose goal is to rectify a negative stereotype.

However, as Bonilla-Silva (2003) explains, even within a constructionist perspective on race, social scientists have three distinct approaches to it. The first one, which is gaining popularity among White social scientists – and among students – is that race is socially constructed; therefore, it is not a fundamental category of analysis and praxis. Some supporters of this perspective go even as far as to suggest that social scientists who use this category are responsible for its existence, making it real.

The second approach focuses on 'racial' differences in different areas, such as academic achievement, crime and standardized tests, such as SAT or writing assessment scores, as if these differences were truly racial. In doing so, it fails to highlight the social dynamics that produce these racial differences, such as the pervasive unequal distribution of resources and opportunities in our students' lives. Because they omit the discussion on these social dynamics, these analysts – typically most White sociologists writing on race – propagate racist interpretations of racial inequality and help to reinforce the racial order.

The third approach insists on the social reality of race, which is to say that it is true that race is a social construct and biologically does not exist; but once it is constructed, it has real effects on actors racially constructed as White or non-White. Within educational contexts, this has to do with racial habitus (Inoue, 2015). Whether we promote it, critique it, fight it or actively promote something else, '[a] White racial habitus exists beyond or outside of bodies, in discourse, in methods of judging, in dispositions toward texts, etc.' (Inoue, 2015: 47). Racial habitus spotlights the macro-level phenomena and the structures and social structuring, spotlighting 'the patterns among many people who associate or find themselves geographically and historically in the same places and circumstances, without forgetting that these patterns exist in individuals who augment them' (Inoue, 2015: 47).

Now, this third approach is my position regarding these three theoretical approaches to race as socially constructed. The first approach to race aligns with the widespread, naive and romantic idea that there is only one race, the human race (most probably in a world cohabited by other races such as the unicorn race). This apparently non-racist idea – which from a biological standpoint is true – denies the existence of racism because of the nonexistence of race. But the reality is that police officers arrest and murder certain humans belonging to racially minoritized groups at a higher rate than others. Answering racism by ignoring race and believing that doing so will make it go away is an absurd idea. I believe this perspective to be useless and detrimental to fighting racism. Race does not exist, racism does, and American society revolves around it. As Inoue (2015) puts it:

> Doing so [ignoring race] tells me that my experiences of racism in school and out are just figments of my imagination, that they must have been something else, that we just cannot know if there is racism anymore, that we just have to ignore it and all will be well, that we just wait a little while longer. As a middle-aged man, I know better. Waiting is complicity in disguise. I've seen and experienced too much. It ain't my imagination. Any denial of racism in our writing assessments is a white illusion. It upholds a white hegemonic set of power relations that is the status quo. It is in the imagination of those too invested in a white racial habitus, regardless of their racial affiliation. Hell, I denied it when I was younger. I had to. (Inoue, 2015: 24)

The second approach promotes racism by not discussing and challenging the social dynamics at the core of any 'racial' difference in any field, from sports to academia. However, the third perspective on race, to which I adhere and position this book, takes into consideration the two other perspectives. However, it is helpful for fighting racism because, aside from viewing race as a nonscience-based ridiculous construct, it sees it as founded on economic and political interests to perpetuate asymmetrical power relationships. It studies, questions, discusses and challenges these relationships and, importantly, aims to understand how society works under this construct and challenges it. This approach fights the real race effects, the systematicity and institutionalization of racism, its practices and practitioners, as well as those that do not take a proactive stand against it. This conception of race also aligns with my views on identity as a dynamic, unstable construct such as gender or class. Nevertheless, according to Bonilla-Silva (2003: 7), race 'has a "changing same" quality as its core'.

However, to understand how this socially constructed category produces real race effects, let us continue with Bonilla-Silva (2003) and the notion of racial structure. Racialized social systems, known as White supremacy in those parts of the world in which White Europeans extended their reach and became a global phenomenon, award systemic privileges to a particular group based on race. You might wonder why humans do not try to get rid of racial thinking after admitting its absurdity. And you can probably already guess why: members of the dominant groups receive material benefits from the racial order, whether they struggle to maintain these benefits or passively accept them. In order to defend its collective interests, the dominant group will rationalize the status of the different races. Bonilla-Silva (2003: 7) termed this notion *racial ideology*: 'racially based frameworks used by actors to explain and justify (dominant race) or challenge (subordinate race or races) the racial status quo'.

All the races in a racialized system have the power of developing these frameworks. However, the dominant race usually imposes the master framework upon which all racial actors base their ideological positions, either in favor (dominant group) or against it (subordinated group). Moreover, 'the ideology of the dominant group provides a moral framework that touches every aspect of life' (Jackman, 1994: 69), but with astonishing strength in educational contexts. From a Marxist perspective, the reason for this lies in the idea of the ruling material force being the same as its ruling intellectual force (Marx & Engels, 1972). To exemplify this notion, think about how the economic and cultural interests of the body of intellectuals composing a hegemonic prescriptive institution such as the Royal Spanish Academy (RAE) align with those of big corporations such as Grupo PRISA (a communications and publishing corporation conglomerate mogul, whose main stockholders are Spanish banks) (Del Valle, 2013). The power of hegemonic rule, even during harsh overt racist periods such as this one, is not almighty. Subordinated groups – and allies! – will always resist and develop oppositional views. However, these oppositional views are subjected to the power of those who rule a society to influence – or 'color', as Bonilla-Silva puts it – the views of the ruled.

Among the components of racial ideologies, I want to highlight what Bonilla-Silva (2003) defines as *common frames*. These are the symbolic representations of a racial group to explain how the world is or ought to be, what is or should be 'normal'. These frames bond together a particular racial ideology and are rooted in group-based conditions and experiences. On the one hand, because hierarchy and domination lie beneath the group life of the various racially defined groups, what is 'common sense' – what should be considered 'normal' – is the ideology imposed by the ruling group, which represents its interests. On the other hand, oppositional ideologies 'challenge that common sense by providing alternative frames, ideas, and stories based on the experience of subordinated races' (Bonilla-Silva, 2003: 8). It is within communicative situations that actors utilize these elements for manufacturing alternative versions of actions, self and social structures. These elements are loose-jointed, of flexible application, allowing social actors to use them to maneuver within different contexts, such as discussing racial issues in a language classroom, responding to a race-related survey or joking with friends on a street corner. This looseness also allows for different representations of self – e.g. portraying intolerance, radicality or ambivalence – and reinforces 'the legitimating role of racial ideology because it allows for accommodation of contradictions, exceptions, and new information' (Bonilla-Silva, 2003: 8). As Jackman (1994: 69) points out, 'an ideology is a political instrument, not an exercise in personal logic', and its strength resides in that looseness.

These ideologies are widespread in our society and can be manifested in different ways. Of course, there is a manifestation of overt racism in our society, but narratives that are the product of racist ideologies are more difficult to confront when they are more subtle. For instance, Bonilla-Silva (2003) identified four frames of colorblind racism, an ideology that most readers are probably familiar with. The first frame, abstract liberalism, is an individualistic discourse that downplays the environment and structural limitations. This colorblind racist ideology attributes success or lack thereof to individual motivations, talents and (free) choices. Common expressions such as 'I don't see color', 'we are all humans', and 'people are people' are usually inherent to this narrative. The second frame, naturalization, understands social facts such as segregation as the result of 'human nature'. That is to say, there is nothing wrong, it is completely natural; it is just a benign desire to be with people most like oneself. Cultural racism is the third frame. This interprets social facts such as racial differences in income, housing or education as 'nothing to do with race', but a result of cultural factors (i.e. lack of 'family values', work ethic or education). The fourth frame, minimization, rejects claims of racially minoritized people facing discrimination. Colorblind racists do this through rhetorical devices like distancing ('I am not Black, so I don't know') or projection such as reverse racism ('Blacks are the ones discriminating').

Now that I have overviewed race and racist ideologies, let us examine racism and its relationship with language. It is going to be within this relationship that our counternarratives need to aim to unveil the particular social, political, economic and ideological mechanisms of social control responsible for the reproduction of racial privilege in a society and their manifestation into, and reproduction through, language.

As John Baugh (1992: 1) argued, racism has a linguistic component. Racists believe that their language – along with most aspects of their culture – is superior to those of the 'inferior' races. Such an attitude, if sustained by political domination (remember how I argued in Chapter 1 that power is necessary for racism to exist), be it overt or covert, is used to justify attempts to impose various doctrines on subordinate racial groups. Ironically, this policy is often proposed in the name of 'improving' the situation of less fortunate groups of people. We have discussed in Chapters 1 and 2 how racism has been remapped onto language (Zentella, 2016) and the diverse ways in which linguistic policy works under institutionalized racism.

It is not the goal of this book to make a genealogy of racism (see Inoue, 2015: 167–172, for a history and etymology of racism); however, it is important to mention that despite the relative novelty of the concept of racism, the phenomenon it designates is ancient. Nonetheless, the concept of racism had its apogee in the period between the First and Second World Wars, with Nazism being one of its main diffusers (not the only one), associating itself with different expressions of contempt, rejection and discrimination. As early as the first half of the 19th century, social thought was concerned with its study, contributing to its doctrinaire and scholarly formulation, even reaching popularity among the medical and scientific community in the form of pseudoscientific currents such as eugenics. These pseudoscientists adorned themselves with a halo of scientificity to legitimize themselves.

Thus, particularly within the social sciences, but also within other fields of knowledge, a privileged place was given to the concept of race as a category capable of explaining social and historical change. In this way, the knowledge of racial belonging – that is, the possession of inherited and genetically transmissible provisions – provided the key to moral, cultural and social differences (Asturiano, 2005). After the Second World War and the crimes of the Holocaust, the concept of racism suffered a huge setback. Currently, as I explained, the idea of race is rejected by most Western authorities. At the same time, those groups that this idea of race had excluded and had historically oppressed – and still excludes and oppresses – welcome it and use it as an act of empowerment (Asturiano, 2005: 3).

I have discussed how racism became overtly manifested after Trump's takeover in 2016. Nevertheless, many still do not want to be perceived as racist and manifest racism more subtly. Let us see Asturiano (2005: 3) to better understand how racism is manifested more subtly in society. This scholar argues that racism is not based on the knowledge of the other but rather on ignorance about them. This ignorance is a restriction that manifests through stereotypes and the construction of distorted knowledge, aimed at legitimizing a biological categorization of the biased group. It relies on mythical elaborations, consisting of integrating, in a single image, various constituent elements of a national culture and organizing a representation of the origin. For some years, Asturiano keeps arguing, we have witnessed a new manifestation of racism that is moving away from overt prejudices to give way to more subtle forms articulated under the heading of symbolic racism. This can be characterized by its distance from the grossest stereotypes and apparent discrimination and by keeping a certain contact with reality, which, although distorted, is not replaced by mythical or imaginary prejudices but rather has the capacity to elaborate rational explanations that refer to the idea of very real social problems. We would be faced with symbolic racism, for example, when affirming that a school with a high rate of foreigners who do not speak the national language is detrimental to the rest of the students.

Numerous definitions of racism can be found in the current literature. Michel Wieviorka (1992, as cited in Asturiano, 2005), for example, explains that in these definitions, there needs to be a link between the attributes – physical, genetic or biological heritage – of an individual or a group and their intellectual and moral characteristics. But this type of generic definition runs the risk of not doing justice to the social context where racism occurs because historical power relationships can be lost. In these generic definitions, those instances when the oppressed group represents the oppressor by linking their physical, genetic or biological attributes to certain intellectual and moral characteristics could be understood as racism. From a CRT perspective, these definitions are useless. This is illustrated by Spanish scholar Asturiano (2005: 5–6) when he argues that in a cultural lecture in his city of Murcia, during the 1998 academic year, Cervantes award winner Cabrera Infante, a great cinema enthusiast, assured the brutal racism currently practiced when dubbing actors of color, such as Eddie Murphy. Also, Asturinano keeps arguing, viewers have been able to confirm, with some indignation, the racism of some American series in recent years, such as *Family Matters*, where the presence of White characters was practically nil, and their occasional appearances always embodied the role of the stupid, the perfidious or the clown.

Even though Asturiano's study attacks racist uses of the Spanish language (in this case, racist practices when dubbing actors), he uses racist language by choosing the term 'of color' to avoid the term 'Black' when referring to African American Black actors (or 'racialized' if he was referring to racially minoritized actors in general, which is not the case). He also equates and puts at the same level of racism the cultural representations of Whites in *Family Matters* with the strategies of racism currently practiced in dubbing actors (Asturiano, 2005: 5). By doing so, Asturiano reproduces – I want to think, unintentionally – the ideology of reverse racism. As we will see in the next section, from a CRT standpoint, the idea of reverse racism is not valid but unacceptable, because whereas for most Whites, racism means racial prejudice, racism and racial prejudice are not the same. Racism is systemic, institutionalized and therefore needs power to exist. Therefore, as explained in Chapter 1, my working definition of racism is the one set forth by Pat Bidol: 'Racism is racial prejudice (the belief that one's own race is superior to another race) combined with the power to enforce this bias throughout the institutions and culture of a society' (1972: 1). Moreover, for this work, it is even more important to understand who is racist within the United States social context. In this sense, following the argument provided by the National Education Association (NEA) in 1973, and in alignment with the more current concept of White privilege, this work understands that:

> All white individuals in our society are racists. Even if a white is totally free from all conscious racial prejudices, he remains a racist, for he receives benefits distributed by a white racist society through its institutions. Our institutional and cultural processes are so arranged as to automatically benefit whites, just because they are white. It is essential for whites to recognize that they receive most of these racist benefits automatically, unconsciously, unintentionally. (NEA, 1973: 13)

This is why, building on the views of scholars such as Apple (2004), Irizarry (2009) and Martínez and Welton (2015), the radical position of this work focuses on explicit antiracist pedagogical approaches rather than on diversity and multiculturalism. I am aware that some readers may have difficulty with this all-encompassing view. However, if we want to address inequity and social injustice, we must start by addressing its most aberrant manifestation, racism. From racist mass shootings to police brutality and murder, from lack of access (to housing, voting, health, education, wealth, justice, etc.) to the propagation of racist ideologies; these are some of the many reasons that from my geo-sociopolitical locus justify such an approach. Yes, I am aware that the foregoing NEA statement from 1973 (by the way, written by White educators) is unlikely to foster potential allies among some White educators due to its explicitness and unapologetic tone, which may seem out of context in contemporary academic texts. However, I believe that acknowledging statements such as this is a first step toward reflecting on racism and becoming antiracist. It should be acknowledged that, perhaps, not everyone reading this text is ready to become an ally. Nonetheless, sugarcoating or avoiding statements such as this to make readers feel more comfortable or self-censoring myself for fear of losing potential allies seems to me a strategy destined to fail. My views on inherited privilege have nothing to do with McWhorter's (2021) comparison of White privilege to original sin. Its purpose is not to blame and make Whites feel bad about being White; it is, rather, to help them acknowledge how society is set to provide a head-start for some while providing handicaps to others based on their race. This is perhaps a good first step in deciding to be part of the solution or keep being the problem. I will delve into the rationale behind this unapologetic 'in your face' position toward racism and its critics, but first, let us discuss why the focus is on race.

3.3.3 Why race?

In a world where discrimination is acted upon by individuals based on multiple identity factors other than race – ethnicity, religion, disability, gender identity, sexuality, immigration status – you may wonder why to focus mainly on race. In fact, the focus of the pedagogical approach I propose is not solely on race, although race is its central axis. In this section, I address intersectionality, followed by a discussion of the dangers of generic inclusivity and what antiracist pedagogical approach toward discrimination there is apart from race. Last, I answer those concerns about the unapologetic antiracist language of this pedagogical approach and why racism must be addressed directly, without softening it.

I agree with authors who call for educational leaders to consider how race and racism intersect with cultural identities and inequities (e.g. Mayo, 2018, for gender identity and sexuality; Wiemelt & Maldonado, 2018, for native language and immigration status; Patton & Haynes, 2018, for Black womanhood) because focusing on a single identity only narrowly depicts how marginalized groups both experience and use their cultural assets to navigate the racial injustices they confront in educational institutions (Yosso, 2005, as cited in Welton *et al.*, 2018: 3). This phenomenon is what Kimberlé Williams Crenshaw (1991) defines as 'intersectionality', a dynamic of oppression in which multiple structures intersect, such as class, economics, gender, culture and race. Thus, race is central to this book, but when I speak of it, I consider all these other patterns as much as I do racial structures because they intertwine with racial structures. As Inoue (2015) explains, intersectionality creates diversity within locally diverse communities, but we can still find patterns as well as exceptions. Like this author, I am not interested in the exceptions but in the patterns. The latter comes from the structures, and racial constructs are affected by particular structures. Additionally, I believe that the overfocus of US society on the exceptions is an ideological strategy to make us believe that 'because there are exceptions, the rule no longer exists or that it's easily broken by anyone with enough willpower or hutzpah' (Inoue, 2015: 6).

Likewise, in line with authors such as Apple (2004), Irizarry (2009) and Martínez and Welton (2015), we should be overly cautious of frameworks that focus on generic inclusivity of multiple inequities. The overusing of concepts like diversity and multiculturalism – and even equity and social justice – 'might lead educational leaders to "depoliticize," "soften," and in essence water down the critical work needed to promote long-lasting change for racial equity' (Irizarry, 2009: 194; Martínez & Welton, 2015, as cited in Welton *et al.*, 2018: 3). We must acknowledge and name racism explicitly, loud and clear. This is an integral step when attempting to dismantle something so omnipresent in education – and pervasive and devastating to society.

I do not deny that such factors as economics or gender are involved. For instance, African Americans and Latinxs in New York City are often some of the poorest in their area, with poverty rates that are much higher than those of Whites. This is not a coincidence, so it should not be addressed as such. As Inoue (2015: 57) points out, these factors intersect and make up racialized experiences as political and as asymmetrical relations of power which, in the United States, 'usually are organized around three nodes of difference: gender, race, and economics. These structures become racialized when they pool or gather into patterns in groups in society, creating distinctions from the white hegemonic group'. These structures are then used as markers of difference that justify the denial of privilege, power and access to opportunities, such as education. For example, as Inoue (2015) explains, using a standardized language variety as a way to determine the success of a student in an assessment or her/his fitness or value for higher education are clear examples of societal structures that become racialized when they are used to maintain White privilege. Not talking, discussing or critiquing the penetration of a racist dominant discourse in our programs does not stop it from being racist.

Yes, this loud, unapologetic and explicit inclusion of the direct language of antiracism sparks some concerns about the fear and withdrawal it may provoke in White students, and feasibly even White educators (see Stengel, 2008). But what these fears suggest is that educators tend to sugarcoat the narrative of race and racism to overprotect students – and other educators – when it comes to addressing racist thoughts, beliefs, values, ideologies and actions. As Welton et al. (2018: 3) explain, 'History in and of itself should prove that pacifying white people does not work'; meanwhile, racism exists freely, without protection for those who suffer it, while privileging those identified with the group exercising it. The outcomes of racism are far worse than those of being exposed – from the comfort of a desk in a classroom – to the narratives of the raw reality that it produces. An antiracist pedagogical approach must keep in mind that this softening of the narrative of race and racism does not directly address the issue; it only further endorses White supremacy.

As painful and unjust discrimination based on identities other than race may be, despite the fact that their dynamics are similar and an antiracist approach must understand and address the many ways they often intersect race, the histories of oppression – as well as their outcomes – are different. An antiracist approach must address race directly and prior to the specifics of particular diverse local communities. Addressing these specifics is a must, but in doing so, we must avoid at any cost relegating race to simply one more specificity and getting stuck in 'the platitudes and unsubstantiated generalities of generic pedagogical perspectives' (Ladson-Billings, 2000: 210). Moreover, Stewart (2018) warns about the concept of diversity because it simply focuses on the inclusivity and numerical representation of social groups but does not critically question whose perspective still weighs power as majoritarian, and whose does not. As a result, a dominant view of diversity is imposed.

Although racism translates easily to other social phenomena that come from other kinds of diversity in our classrooms (e.g. ethnic differences, linguistic differences, religious affiliation, gender, sexual orientation and disability), their histories of oppression and outcomes are different. An antiracist pedagogical approach understands race as the axis intersected by these other differences, never as one more difference. Thus, aligned with the CRT goals proposed by Furner (2007: 146), an antiracist language pedagogy seeks to rectify – and, I would add, eradicate – situations of unjust White privilege by describing and explaining these instances of racism and acting from a triple commitment: an epistemological commitment to the social construction of concepts such as race (and, I emphasize, racism as a central axis), an ethical commitment to social justice and a methodological commitment to both physical and intellectual radical actions.

3.3.4 Why SPCs?

My incursion into antiracist pedagogies started as an intuition after noticing a motivational change in my students when content related to the sociopolitical nature of language was introduced into the classroom. This intuition sparked my doctoral dissertation research (Magro, 2016a) and, by extension, this work. But a personal intuition does not suffice to justify the pedagogical approach I propose in these pages; there is a solid theoretical framework based on CLA that supports and informs the use of SPCs to, on the one hand, raise students' CLA, motivation and linguistic proficiency, and, on the other hand, raise educators' CLA and promote a reflexive analysis of their own language behaviors and ideologies that, eventually, will help them develop and implement an antiracist curriculum. In this section, I first aim to justify the inclusion of SPCs in language programs based on the relationship between race and language. I will then explain the way SPCs address three matters: (1) the transforming mission demanded of radical pedagogies; (2) the benefits of CLA for educators; and (3), keeping in mind language program directors and curriculum coordinators in the United States, how the integration of SPCs could help to amend the crisis in the humanities, particularly within Spanish language programs. I will conclude this section with a brief discussion of two sociolinguistics-based approaches to language learning with quite different agendas: the expansionist model and the CLA model, to which my pedagogical framework adheres.

As part of critical pedagogies, and similarly to what critical discourse analysis and new literacy studies do, antiracist pedagogies 'draw from cultural and social theory and emphasize the ways in which language and language practices are tied up with issues of power and social control'

(Leeman, 2018: 348). As I explained in Chapter 1, race has been remapped from biology onto language (Zentella, 2016), and racism is inseparable from its linguistic component; it is based on it. The linguistic dimension of racism is one of its fundamental tools for expressing it; therefore, it is an excellent input for analyzing, understanding and combating it. Jonathan Rosa (2019) investigated the construction of US Latinxs as an emergent ethnoracial category and its linguistic indexes. Rosa shows how contingent processes, rather than naturally occurring cultural essences, structure these contexts by emphasizing the production of racial categories and linguistic varieties through interrelations among institutions, actors and ideologies. For example, Jennifer Leeman (2018: 347) explains how 'for Spanish-speaking and Latinx children, English-only education and the concomitant failure to recognize and value children's home languages and experiences constitute symbolic violence as well as educational malpractice, given the well-documented educational benefits of bilingual and mother tongue schooling' (e.g. Carreira, 2007; Darder, 1991; Gándara, 2012; Macedo, 1997; Nieto, 2009; Valenzuela, 1999). Moreover, it has been argued that prioritizing English language acquisition at the expense of subject matter content and segregating emergent bilinguals in programs – such as Structured English Immersion – limit students' opportunities and academic development (Gándara, 2012, as cited in Leeman, 2018). English hegemony in the United States – plus English-only ideology and its resulting educational policies – has directed the attention of critical researchers toward the subordination of Spanish and Spanish speakers. But within the Spanish-speaking world, similar hegemonic ideologies of inferiorization of linguistic groups are also reproduced. It is important to point out those sociopolitical issues related to linguistic variation within Spanish (and other languages) and linguistic behaviors and practices associated with subordinated groups within the Spanish-speaking community, such as hybridity or translanguaging. By exposing these interrelations (contained in the SPCs proposed in this work), the explanatory power of how language intertwines power and identity – and the institutions, actors and ideologies involved in this relationship – influences students' and educators' CLA.

Moreover, the integration of SPCs answers the transforming mission of radical pedagogy (Giroux, 1983). The SPC-based didactical units that I propose in the second part of this book aim to spark a transformation in the students by promoting reflection on the eradication of inequalities, wealth and privilege. These units serve as a mediating vehicle in the exploration of the role that, as Talmy (2010: 129) explains, language has in producing, maintaining, challenging and transforming asymmetries of power, discrimination, inequality, social injustice and hegemony in relation to race (as well as ethnicity, class, gender and other intersecting constructs). Thus, SPC units assist students in gaining what Leeman *et al.* (2011) call a critical understanding of how language is interwoven with social and political structures. To this extent, the implementation of these contents helps students see the relationships between language, power and identity in a new light. For example, in the context of Spanish in the United States, this pedagogical approach pushes students to question and understand the educational practices that materialize hierarchies and power structures over students through the current monolingual ideology in US public schools. In doing so, this approach facilitates insights into how language is linked to power, identity and the results of the asymmetric power relations that it conveys, among other issues.

Also – and this is one of the main arguments on which this book is based – training in critical language issues can help educators to transition from a 'well-meaning' stance to an educated one capable of addressing students' questions about the imposition of dominant language norms (Alim & Baugh, 2007; Alim *et al.*, 2016). The integration of these SPC units not only addresses what Alim and Baugh point out but also educates instructors on the relationship of these ideologies of normativity with the imposition of dominant groups and how this interplays with linguistic ideologies. Furthermore, educators can benefit greatly from reflexive analysis of their own language behaviors and ideologies, which – as we have seen in Chapter 2 – are reproduced daily even in the more well-intended language departments. In fact, as Alim and Baugh (2007: 173) argue, 'it is only once teachers develop a metaideological awareness that they can begin to work to change [their own language behaviors and ideologies] – and be more fully prepared to teach all students more effectively'. Suggestions for preparing pre- and in-service educators to effectively teach courses under a CLA framework with an antiracist approach can be found in Lacorte and Magro (2022).

The last reason that I want to discuss to justify the inclusion of SPCs has to do with how it addresses the crisis – already exposed as early as 2006 by John Lipski – that a large number of Spanish departments are going through in US universities. The inability or, in many cases, resistance on the part of these departments to articulate courses in language, literature, cultural and ethnic studies, linguistics, sociology, etc., as well as negligence to promote an interdisciplinary approach, result in the loss of students' registration in Spanish courses and the disappearance of majors and minors in numerous language and literature departments (Lipski, 2006; Colburn, 2017; Looney & Lusin, 2019). This long-lasting issue – interwoven with recent socioeconomic, cultural and technological changes (see Lacorte, 2017) – has been affecting the institutional and administrative demands and expectations within a framework that pushes toward a service provider–client relationship (Ciller & Ortín, 2019) and the neoliberalization of academic goals looking for an economic-oriented short-term reward such as the L2 teaching for the professions movement (e.g. Spanish for business, Spanish for health professions, Spanish and the law, etc.). Let us see some initiatives that attend to this crisis, how SPCs help to overcome the much-criticized traditional separation of language and content courses and an example of how this issue manifests in a US Spanish language program.

There is an urgent need for our language programs to be assessed and redesigned if we want to address this crisis and, especially, if we want to break away from racist pedagogies and start designing antiracist curricula. However, authors such as Gironzetti *et al.* (2020) acknowledge the limited body of research on the process of curricular evaluation and redesign of L2 Spanish undergraduate programs in United States universities in contrast to other languages. Unfortunately, the few curricular evaluation initiatives conducted tend to focus mainly on addressing bureaucratic-administrative needs and demands within the program instead of aiming to improve its quality and the educational experience beyond external demands related to administrative or accreditation criteria (Davis, 2015, as cited in Gironzetti *et al.*, 2020).

There are exceptions to this over-focusing on market demands without attending to cultural and social students' needs. However, we should be careful with the tendency to cover the needs of the majority and neglect the needs of racially minoritized groups. Needs can be differentiated into two types: objective and subjective (Brindley, 1989; Richterich, 1983, as cited in Gironzetti *et al.*, 2020). Objective needs are related to observable aspects linked to sociocultural and educational factors (e.g. level of language proficiency), while subjective needs are related to cognitive and affective aspects (e.g. motivations for taking a course). It seems logical that a neoliberal education framework will push toward objective needs, while a radical critical pedagogy, such as the one I propose, will push toward subjective ones. It is understandable that under the current pressure toward maximum performance and profitability, language departments may perceive curricular redesigning as a futile task. Nonetheless, this scenario is not as doomed as it seems. Some successful current redesigning attempts include Gironzetti *et al.*'s (2020) effort, which resulted in implementing programmatic evaluation guidelines and instruments based on students' needs in a US public university. Leeman and Serafini (2016) did likewise, but from the perspective of critical pedagogy, within a Spanish heritage speakers' program in a private university. From an antiracist perspective, I believe we should concentrate our efforts on critical approaches to redesigning programs if we want to fully address our students' needs.

Furthermore, it has become increasingly important, at an academic and curricular level, to leave behind the separation between language courses and content courses (e.g. Allen & Maxim, 2013; Kalantzis *et al.*, 2005; Levine & Phipps, 2012; Modern Language Association, 2007, 2009; Paesani & Allen, 2012, as cited in Giorinzetti *et al.*, 2020). This traditional division between language courses – offered at the initial levels of the program and focused on communicative approaches that frequently privilege oral skills over reading and writing skills – and content courses – offered at the most advanced levels of the program (levels 300 and 400) and focused on literary and cultural analysis that prioritize literacy skills – impedes the promotion of an integrated approach to language, culture and literature throughout the entire program. In this regard, I believe the focus on an integrated approach to language, culture and literature exclusively must open to an approach in which linguistics – particularly sociolinguistics and language ideologies – as well as race and ethnic studies, anthropology, sociology and many other interdisciplinary connections, are acknowledged as an important component in L2 programs at all levels, including initial levels. Yes, I want to emphasize this in initial levels too. Let us illustrate how all of this interplays in a real scenario with an example from my experience at X University.

After an external evaluation of XU's Spanish language program (in which I did not participate), the recommendations highlighted the department's need to conduct an extensive curricular review of all its course offerings: language, literature and other options. The committee observed that there had not been such a review for some time and heard from more than one faculty member about a serious disconnect within language programs between the lower and upper levels. Thus, the committee recommended that such a review include an examination of the courses and hours required for the major, the minor and any language certificate, the number of tracks in the major and the possibility of offering larger lecture courses in English on various aspects of the foreign culture (e.g. culture, cinema, media).

The reviewers believed that such courses could increase enrollment, build bridges to other college programs and entice students to take further courses, including language/linguistics study. Additionally, they urged considering the addition of more tracks to the major. The review committee also observed residual tensions and unspoken anxieties about the renewal of the curriculum, which had the potential to attract large numbers of enthusiastic majors, certainly double or triple their current levels, if the department would engage in how the profession is evolving (i.e. to embrace literary studies smartly integrated with linguistics, film and media studies, digital communications, gender studies, material culture, environmental studies and much more). One of the demands was for senior faculty to create many of these new courses and not leave all the work for a few non-tenure-eligible and even contingent instructors rewarded for crafting fresh designs on the edges of the canon. The report stated that the committee was told repeatedly that there had been no discussion in recent memory of how faculty colleagues are approaching literature, defining culture or even thinking about how their respective fields have evolved over the past 25 years. Some colleagues mentioned cultural studies to the committee; others eschewed the concept, arguing that the appropriate focus is and remains a study of language-based cultural ideas. Still others dismissed the concept of language and student interest in language learning per se, noting that it is the ideas that count; the language of the expression of the ideas does not. Any regard for applied linguistics and its research base was characterized as not intellectual by senior members of this department. These were issues that impeded any substantial discussion of moving forward as a collective; it seemed to the committee that each individual was at odds with the group and, thus, there could not be a larger vision.[2]

As noted, this program's evaluation addressed many of the issues, if not all, linked to the crisis in our language departments. It may be argued that the integration of SPCs in language programs aligns with the current needs of US language and literature departments and the development of courses that articulate SLA with sociolinguistics, literature, cultural studies, cinema, etc. This is not only because it is the direction recommended by hegemonic institutions such as the MLA or the American Council on the Teaching of Foreign Languages (ACTFL), external program evaluators or distinguished scholars (e.g. Lipsky, 2006) for addressing the new needs of students, but also because it affects the students' motivation and attitudes about the study of other languages and, consequently, their linguistic competence (Lado & Quijano, 2020; Magro, 2016a).

Before concluding this argument, I would like to contrast two popular approaches to language learning, both informed by sociolinguistics but quite different: the CLA model and the expansionist model. As Jennifer Leeman (2018) explains, those of us who are advocates of CLA approaches clearly support the discussion of social and contextual variation within the curriculum through calls to include discussion of sociopolitical aspects of language within language education. From this perspective, the incorporation of sociolinguistics is designed to help students develop an understanding of how language and linguistic variation work, not just at the formal – i.e. linguistic – level but also with regard to sociopolitical and aesthetic concerns. Moreover, the focus of awareness is not only on geographic variation but also on social variation and variation associated with language contact. This approach does not adhere to an expansionist perspective (e.g. Valdés, 1995) in which the incorporation of sociolinguistics serves primarily as a means to acquire prestige norms and assimilate students to the status quo. Although both the critical language awareness and expansionist model approaches are informed by sociolinguistics, they are quite different in their philosophies and goals.

On the one hand, expansionist models – popular in programs teaching Spanish as a heritage language (Martínez, 2003; Valdés, 1995) – tend to rely on 'appropriateness'-based accounts of sociolinguistic variation in which non-standard varieties and practices are described as linguistically valid but 'appropriate' only in specific settings, such as with family or friends. In contrast, only the standard variety would be appropriate in professional or academic settings (Leeman, 2018; Magro, 2016b). Their goal is to expand heritage speakers' linguistic repertoire to help them perform in academic and professional settings, without questioning why this repertoire is the prestigious one. Often, this process resembles a kind of linguistic 'evangelization' of the native.

On the other hand, a critical language awareness framework endorses the integration of content related to the sociopolitical nature of language as a way to spark discussions of sociolinguistics that will promote student CLA and agency and question given assumptions and normalized ideologies (including those that expansionist approaches don't question, such as the elevation of some varieties versus the denigration and stigmatization of others and the people who speak them). Therefore, a critical language awareness approach like the one proposed in this book facilitates an understanding not only of students' (and instructors') own circumstances and society but also of imagining and strategizing how one might transform the sociolinguistic order and society.

Let us examine the pedagogical foundations of SPCs before seeing how to put all this into practice with concrete pedagogical proposals.

Notes

(1)   Derrick Bell, a New York University law professor, is considered the intellectual father of the movement, while other figures of importance include Alan Freeman, Kimberlé Crenshaw, Angela Harris, Charles Lawrence, Patricia Williams, Neil Gotanda; Asian authors such as Eric Yamamoto and Mari Matsuda; Robert Williams as the principal Indian author; and Richard Delgado, Kevin Johnson, Margaret Montoya, Juan Perea and Francisco Valdés as principal Latinx authors.
(2)   To protect the identity of this institution, I paraphrased this report and omitted the name of its authors.

4 Pedagogical Foundations of SPC Units

Before moving to the second part of this book and providing concrete examples of when, where and how to integrate critical linguistic awareness pedagogies (CLAp) with a focus on antiracism in (Spanish) language classes, this chapter will review the principles on which this pedagogical approach is based. First, I will discuss the antiracist framework of the sociopolitical content (SPC)-based units I propose. This will be followed by an examination of the foundations and goals of SPC units in the language classroom. Finally, I will address issues of first language (L1)/second language (L2) usage while teaching language under a CLAp approach.

4.1 Antiracist Framework of SPC Units

A key tenet of Paulo Freire's pedagogical approach is the urge to regard education as a path to freedom, a liberatory experience achieved through a mutual process of 'conscientization' between educators and students (Freire, 1970). A central component of this engaged pedagogy is that 'teachers must be actively committed to a process of self-actualization that promotes their own well-being if they are to teach in a manner that empowers students' (hooks, 1994: 15). Students and educators alike are transformed into active participants, creating, changing and recreating their narratives as they progress by using a reflexive dialogical approach. In this Freirian approach, there is a focus on the individual. In antiracist pedagogies, this focus on the individual translates into the idea that it is the individual who ultimately complies with or challenges the existing system of racism, regardless of the ultimate goal of antiracism being to target societal and institutional racism (Young & Laible, 2000, as cited in Welton et al., 2018). Thus, as part of their learning about how language works, based on CLAp, SPCs are designed to encourage individuals to 'question taken-for-granted assumptions about language and to analyze how such assumptions are tied to inequality and injustice, with the ultimate goal of promoting positive social change' (Leeman, 2018: 345).

The SPC units and other materials that I present in this chapter are antiracist pedagogical tools because they teach and practice antiracism. These units recognize majoritarian historical narratives and challenge these assumptions to allow for counternarratives and counterstories to these narratives. Furthermore, in an effort to decolonize the curriculum and prevent the substitution of one dominant group with another, these materials are built to 'eliminate the element of power relations and address the potential needs of all potentially marginalised sub-groups of learners rather than focus on just one sub-group' (Ade-ojo, 2021: 2). In alignment with authors such as Ade-ojo (2021), this is done by integrating a multiplicity of voices (also referred to as multiliteracies) from a sociocultural perspective of literacy that draws on Bourdieu's concept of capitals (social, cultural, economic) and linguistic markets (Bourdieu, 1991). Based on Bourdieu's idea of linguistic markets, depending on the context (time, space), the appreciation of capital will be different; therefore, it cannot be a singular construction of capital. Grenfel (2012b, as cited in Ade-ojo, 2021) suggests that Bourdieu's theoretical framework not only provides a standpoint for studying language but also its political impetus. This political dimension of language is central in the articulation of antiracist materials designed to raise CLA as well as the articulation of CLAp designed to promote antiracism.

Such an antiracist approach is framed by the idea of multiplicity. Multiplicity recognizes that different elements, different narratives, different ways of curriculum delivery and, more importantly, different curricular goals exist and must be included in the development and delivery of curriculum by all the stakeholders, from policymakers through educators to students (Ade-ojo, 2021). However, this requires recognizing non-dominant voices, narratives and even delivery methods as legitimate and valid. This is difficult for the educator who clings to their position of power after spending multiple years going through multiple educational filters imposed by hegemonic frameworks focused on maintaining asymmetric power relationships.

Thus, before putting the materials I propose into practice, educators should take three pivotal steps that I attempted to help with in previous chapters. First, educators should dig deep into the history of racism and race relations and their influence on culture and society today. Second, before attempting to facilitate critical thinking and change through these units, educators must first examine their beliefs, views and assumptions regarding racialized others and check themselves for never-resolved underlying attitudes regarding race and racism (Davila, 2011). Unresolved underlying attitudes will thwart the implementation of these units and will hinder true action and change (Dlamini, 2002, as cited in Davila, 2011). Third, while implementing antiracist content such as this, educators should be aware of resistance and objections toward it and be able to argue for the urgent need for antiracist pedagogies and their rationale. Let us examine this last point further.

As I write this chapter, protests worldwide against police brutality following the murder of George Floyd by racist White police officer Derek Chauvin are turning the long fight against racism and the Black Lives Matter movement into a trend. Antiracist organizations are emerging everywhere, including my children's progressive and diverse public school, which is notorious for several racist incidents (one of them reached TV news nationwide when, right after Trump's takeover, a graffiti in a 4th-grade bathroom that read 'Kill Kill Kill N*****s' was found). Nevertheless, there is still resistance against the use of the term antiracism because of alleged negative connotations. Antiracist pedagogies, regardless of this recent awakening about racism worldwide, and although many educators and scholars have integrated or are in the process of integrating antiracist pedagogies, still have a long way to go to become the core of the academic curriculum, as I propose. Some of these objecting voices, e.g. Stengel (2008), claim that the term antiracist is 'in your face' and triggers fear for some (White) students (and educators). This resistance occurs in both PK–12 and college/university classrooms and department meetings where participants use tools of Whiteness to avoid engaging in discussions about race (Picower, 2009; Swanson & Welton, in press, as cited in Welton, 2018). These voices object – as I recently heard from a schoolteacher and an administrator (both Black females) in a meeting with the newly created antiracist organization at my children's school – that the term antiracist 'sounds negative and aggressive', that they feel uncomfortable talking about antiracism to their students because it may cause them to shut down and disengage from discussion and that 'it doesn't sound nice'. Stengel (2008) further argues:

> Fear and racism go together in our individual, social, and institutional experience. And the fears of the students I observed have individual, social, and institutional objects. They don't want to think of themselves as personally guilty of the moral evil that is racism. They don't want to be held accountable for an acknowledged social evil. They don't want to be forced to consider that their own understanding of the institution of schooling may be fatally flawed. (Stengel, 2008: 70)

Stengel, and the staff at my children's school, suggest changing the terminology, which plays into economies of niceness. However, in line with Galman *et al.* (2010), I believe that this sugarcoating of racism distracts us from the urgent need for more critical examinations of racism. Fear, anger, avoidance or silence in discussions about race only reinforce the racial status quo (DiAngelo, 2011; McMahon, 2007, as cited in Galman *et al.*, 2010). The behavior shown by the Black staff at my children's school can be explained by DiAngelo's description of how people of color in mixed-race settings are placed in the vulnerable position of softening their own emotions about racism in order to appease White people's feelings and avoid conflict. As a result, some racialized people are burdened with explaining racism to Whites in the 'right' way that 'is generally politely and rationally, without any emotional upset' (DiAngelo, 2011: 61). But racism is neither polite nor rational; it is brutal and 'in your face', it is uncomfortable, it murders innocent people and turns lives into a hell on Earth. Resistance to coming out of the comfort zone and facing authentic racial engagement in a culture and economic system based on racial disparity prevents any change in mindsets and viewpoints on how racism manifests in society and how it can be fought. Consequently, resistance to antiracism 'limits the ability to form authentic connections across racial lines, and results in a perpetual cycle that works to hold racism in place' (Diangelo, 2011: 66). In this sense, I agree with Malcolm X when, defending the idea that '[e]xtremism in the defense of liberty is no vice; moderation in the pursuit of justice is no virtue' in the 1964 Oxford Union Debate, he urged us to move us away from Aristotelian ideas of virtue as a mean and toward an awareness of virtue as justice. 'Anytime anyone is enslaved or in any way deprived of his liberty, that person, as a human being, as far as I'm concerned, he is justified to resort to whatever methods necessary to bring about his liberty again' (X, 1964).[1]

Moreover, self-reflection on why one has negative attitudes to antiracist pedagogies can trigger admitting that racism is a problem, a necessary first step to start the journey toward antiracism. Squire *et al.* (2018: 15) argue how 'David Bohm (1996), a renowned physicist and theorist, noted that to break out of a normative mindset, we must engage in not just creativity, but confusion'. Immersion in this confusion provides space for new thinking. Bohm also believes that creation is not the competence of a few selected people such as scholars, artists, musicians or politicians; anybody can be a creator. Therefore, antiracist pedagogies embrace the confusion that antiracism may create, since antiracism calls on all individuals to confuse themselves into creative liberation.

In addition, educators do not receive adequate instruction in their preparation programs to successfully facilitate critical discussions targeting race relations (Davila, 2011; Ladson-Billings, 2000). This is something that I have observed both in PK–12 and university programs. Even educators who received some instruction on diversity and multiculturality (e.g. graduate classes, workshops) have difficulty implementing theory into practice and offer resistance to antiracism, viewed as something difficult to integrate into the curriculum and manage in daily instruction (Davila, 2011). At a macro level, there is an urgent need to restructure teacher and leadership preparation programs and learning to begin implementing antiracism education in both the classroom and at the institutional level. Nonetheless, as educators, we have the responsibility to do so regardless of the curricular and administrative restrictions and impediments imposed on us, which, after centuries of racist-oriented curricula, have become normalized and believed as something unavoidable. No, they are not.

4.2 Foundations and Goals of SPC Units in the Language Classroom

Grounded in CLA-oriented pedagogies (Leeman, 2018), the units I will present have as a central component the examination of the four types of language variation (social, geographic, contextual/stylistic, temporal) and the ideologies, attitudes and mechanisms by which those linguistic varieties, associated with racialized or low socioeconomic status speakers, are stigmatized. They examine how, simultaneously, those varieties associated with power groups are chosen, legitimized and become prestigious – a process that has nothing to do with the linguistic fact (Tusón, 1996: 90) – as well as the sociopolitical implications of these processes of stigmatization and legitimization. However, within a decolonizing agenda of the curriculum (i.e. decentering Eurocentrism and empowering and bringing from the margin to the center of the curriculum those voices historically stigmatized, excluded and silenced), these units also examine how the symbolic capital of these varieties depends on the linguistic market (Bourdieu, 1991), switching value depending on the cultural context in which they happen (e.g. academic environment versus Hip-Hop). Much like in any other market, in linguistic markets, nothing is free, and power relations predetermine the standards according to which linguistic capital is allocated, thus preserving the rule of the elite (which speaks the most prestigious language) (Bourdieu, 1991, as cited in Lacorte & Magro, 2022).

In addition, these units emphasize the socially situated nature not only of language but also of literacy practices. They build around the notion of multiplicity of voices in the design and implementation of the curriculum to decolonize it. By including research that examines the rich and varied kinds of literacy practices such as rapping, social media, comedy or storytelling, SPCs aim to engage and bring to the core of the curriculum those voices and practices that have been historically excluded from academia and educational contexts, visibilizing and empowering them. From this approach, in line with authors such as Alim (2005), these practices are considered different, not deficient, stressing that different kinds of both literacy and linguistic varieties are valued in different cultural contexts. While doing so, these SPC units not only aim to validate a wide range of linguistic and literacy practices but, simultaneously, as scholarship in new literacy studies also encourages, attempt to build bridges to academic-based literacy (Leeman, 2018). They do so by expanding linguistic repertoires through the incorporation of peer-reviewed readings and by analyzing the utility of academic-based literacy while simultaneously pointing out its historical and sociopolitical discursive construction as prestigious varieties and literacy practices. Moreover, using the notion of multiplicity of voices to decolonize the curriculum may trigger critiques and resistance from college students to these materials (e.g. 'I do not pay college to listen to rap songs'). These critiques/resistance (and possible formal complaints against the instructor) may come from White and racialized students alike because hegemony permeates deeply, even in those who suffer from it. Although it is not common, this effect is also part of this pedagogical approach. On the one hand, students need to critically understand why some materials/voices are appropriate in an academic context and not others, who legitimized them and why, whom they benefit/harm, what their purpose is, why they bother them and how some materials legitimate nowadays were once silenced/excluded/stigmatized. On the other hand, colonized curriculum, like Whiteness, must be exposed and felt as something strange.

SPCs' pedagogical approach takes into consideration the US context in which the CLA framework was first put forward as an educational model for speakers of stigmatized varieties of English. CLA focused primarily on African American Vernacular English (AAVE) (see Lanehart, 1998) and, soon after, speakers of Spanish and Latinxs in both English as a second language and mainstream classes. Building on these studies, explicit antiracist proposals emerged aiming to eradicate from the curriculum racist approaches that empower prestige language varieties and inferiorize others (e.g. Inoue, 2015; Paris & Alim, 2017). Due to the widespread circulation of negative discourses surrounding Spanish and the stigmatization of varieties of English that show signs of Spanish contact and vice versa in the United States (Del Valle, 2014; Leeman, 2018; Othegy, 2012; Rosa, 2019; Zentella, 2018), the pedagogical units I propose, while taking into consideration that these processes occur globally, focus mainly on Spanish. Thus, they build on the first theoretical proposals of CLAp as a framework for the design of Spanish heritage language (HL) courses (Leeman, 2005; Martínez, 2003) and the more recent efforts continued by authors such as Beaudrie et al. (2021), Holguín Mendoza (2018) and Leeman (2018). However, the units proposed in this book do not focus solely on HL education but rather are designed to work with both HL and mainstream L2 programs. They can also be adapted to English language programs, sociology, anthropology and, of course, linguistics courses, among others, due to their interdisciplinary approach.

Moreover, in line with authors such as Rebollo-Gil and Moras (2006), SPC units push for counternarratives, confessions and breaching strategies that require educators to remain engaged and invested in their classrooms and students. These units aim to become the lesson plan for our classes by intertwining research with disconcerting and troubling facets of educators' and students' lives. As educators, we are – and must be

– inextricably linked to our students' self-formation. But we also must be cautious. When planning and organizing the topics of our instruction and study, we should do it not only around the topics of our own lives, from which it is almost impossible for us or our students to remain detached, but around rigorous sociolinguistics and critical race theory (CRT). This strategy will allow us not only to legitimize discussions that, otherwise, some (White) students must consider personalized issues, but will also help to channel and direct our classes to achieve our goal of capacitating our students to be able to create counter-hegemonic narratives and moments of dissonance purposely and frequently. Because it is in these moments of dissonance during casual or formal conversation that coded racist speech encounters antiracist talk strategies.

A philosophical goal of the pedagogical approach I propose in these pages aligns with Squire *et al.*'s (2018) priority:

> to urge scholars of race and racism in higher education to reclaim their ability to think divergently and creatively about the future of higher education – that is, to allow oneself to engage in creative storytelling that imagines a world that is free of the oppression that currently exists. The ability to think in this way is often lost as one ages and becomes indoctrinated into the hegemonic notions of reality. However, scholars such as Walter Mosley (2016) argue that we should be able to shirk the systems that constrain us and to at least engage in creating utopias, or new worlds that 'praise and raise humanity to its full promise' while also recognizing the variety of thought and practice that exists in our world today. (Squire *et al.*, 2018: 15)

To help achieve this goal, SPC units scaffold from a micro-level analysis of the linguistic elements within discourse toward a macro-level analysis of language: how these linguistic elements connect to the broader sociohistorical, political, economic and ideological contexts in which they are situated. Based on critical discourse analysis and new literacy studies, which, like critical pedagogy, draw from cultural and social theory, these units highlight how language and language practices are tied up with issues of power and social control (Chilton, 2012, as cited in Leeman, 2018). According to Pennycook (2001), these units include the two primary domains for critical discourse analysis with a greater focus on the second one: (1) how power is exercised in interactions (e.g. through the analysis of turn-taking or control of the topics discussed) and (2) the examination of the construction and reproduction of social categories, power relations and ideologies through language.

The field of sociolinguistics is broad; it is not the goal of these units to exhaustively cover the entire field. The goal of the pedagogical approaches I introduce in the following sections is praxis-oriented. It integrates sociolinguistics-based theory, aiming to increase CLA. Thus, these pedagogical units, strategies and content are intended to be a guide, a sort of template that should be adapted to the needs of each particular program/course/section. I will provide examples of how and when to integrate antiracist pedagogies in advanced and lower-level standardized programs (in Spanish). Moreover, for those unfamiliar with sociolinguistics theory, I will explain in each unit those concepts that we will introduce to our students. Also, I will discuss a syllabus for an introductory class in language and antiracism. As I was developing the first draft of this book, I had the privilege of designing such a class – in English – for incoming university students interested in literacy and language education. I had complete freedom to focus the curriculum exclusively on the sociopolitical nature of language, and we will see the results through students' testimonials at the end of this course.

The first program I will present is based on the first time I articulated SPC units into an advanced Spanish language course. I did it by adding 20 extra minutes of instruction each week for 12 weeks. The language program where I was teaching did not allow me to make any changes to accommodate these contents within the regular classroom time. So, after my language program director granted permission, I asked my students if, once a week, they would start 10 minutes early and leave 10 minutes later than scheduled. They all agreed. I mention this because curricular restrictions/impositions are among the greatest obstacles to implementing antiracist pedagogies in the language classroom. We must think outside the box, be flexible and find our way through. Regardless of the vehicular language, or if you are teaching a language learning class or a content class, regardless of the field in which your class is situated (linguistics, second language acquisition [SLA], pedagogy, sociology, anthropology, etc.), the following pedagogical proposals are built on the same principles and content.

Before I move on to these proposals, I would like to highlight the importance of understanding what Rebollo-Gil and Moras (2006) point out when discussing their antiracist pedagogical experiences. When talking about race in academic settings, regardless of your course level, you can never assume a set starting point for the conversation. Through my research on CLA, motivation and language proficiency, I developed instruments that somehow inform us about our students' level of CLA. However, the disparity in starting CLA levels between students makes it difficult to establish a departure point. As Rebollo-Gil and Moras explain, 'there is no checklist of books, no keen mathematical formula that can help gauge or determine the degree of "progressive" racial thinking an individual might or might not have' (2006: 387). In the experience of these authors, and in my own, conversations, for the most part, seem to go back and forth endlessly between different areas, such as personal stories, political ideology, news accounts or even celebrity gossip. These stories are important to integrate into classroom conversations, but they must be structured so that the conversations do not deviate toward, and remain on, the anecdotal aspects. To do so, the units I developed for the different courses exemplified in this book do not make any assumptions and start at a considerably basic level of critical awareness. They are scaffolded and structured around research-based and theoretical sociolinguistic aspects that aim to progressively provoke critical thought and antiracist linguistic awareness by integrating counternarratives and students' assets.

Following Lacorte and Magro (2022), some of the critical issues and topics proposed for discussion in CLAp classrooms informed by the field of language ideologies are:

- The language standardization process, which aims to reduce language variation within a language variety selected by powerful social groups and established as the prestigious one.
- Language, identity and power and how they intertwine to (re)produce asymmetrical power relationships.
- Linguistic indexicality and iconization, the semiotic process in which 'linguistic features that index social groups or activities appear to be iconic representations of them, as if a linguistic feature somehow depicted or displayed a social group's inherent nature or essence' (Irvine & Gal, 2000: 38).
- Bilingualism, bidialectalism and the expansion of linguistic repertoires.
- Attitudes toward linguistic hybridity, that is, the mixing of linguistic practices associated with different languages and/or language varieties.
- Hispanophobia, the fear, distrust, hatred of, aversion to or discrimination against the Spanish language, Hispanics and/or Hispanic culture, an ideology on which the English Only movement is based (Zentella, 1997).
- Language variation and 'appropriateness', that is, the idea that all varieties are valid, but some are more appropriate than others in certain contexts and, therefore, students need to learn an appropriate language variety for each context (e.g. Gutiérrez, 1997; Potowski, 2005). CLAp contests this approach because 'appropriateness' legitimizes/promotes the dominant position of standard varieties and simplifies the complex nature of language variation and power relations in society (Leeman, 2005).

Although many of these topics are informed by the field of Spanish as HL education, the pedagogical approach proposed in these pages considers the integration of these topics fundamental to raising antiracist critical awareness in second language programs, especially, although not exclusively, in content-based and general education courses (regardless of the vehicular language). As I argued in previous chapters, it is the responsibility of those profiting from racism to understand its dynamics and ideological intertwining with language. Thus, the curriculum that I propose articulates these topics, expands them to include others and organizes them, scaffolding from a very basic point of departure and always building on sociolinguistics theory and research-based investigations that seek to link with the students' life experiences in a meaningful manner. This is done from a position of equal partnership with our students that attempts to break with instructor-centered instruction approaches and the asymmetric relationships between students and instructors that emerge from this approach. Our students' identities, experiences, motivations and purposes for attending school are articulated in the classes by integrating and, sometimes, even deconstructing them. Although the following proposed activities present templates and examples that facilitate a student-centered approach, they are open-ended. It is in this aspect of instruction that being knowledgeable in CRT and education methods and having experience, skills, inspiration, creativity and even improvisational capacity play a fundamental role.

I would like to finish this section with an example that further illustrates a way to do this in more advanced classes. This example is based on a History of the Spanish Language class that I was recently asked to teach as an adjunct professor for a small group of PhD students (five) at a prestigious university on the East Coast of the United States. The syllabus that was provided to me had a strong focus on a traditional structuralist approach based on the historical evolution of the Spanish language from Latin to 'modern Spanish' that included numerous narratives (some of them historically inaccurate, others utilized to push concrete sociopolitical agendas) with the goal of granting prestige to a particular hegemonic construction of the Spanish language. A critical sociopolitical perspective was mostly absent from the syllabus of this seminar. What I could infer from the syllabus that I received was that this PhD program had a special interest in its students learning about the evolution of Spanish grammar in order to (1) decipher ancient texts (for students specializing in literature) and (2) learn in depth about grammatical aspects of the Spanish language through its evolution (for students specializing in SLA). In our first meeting, we sat in a circle and I explained and tried to make clear that we were equals in this learning journey (I myself had to dust off my notes on the History of Spanish before preparing for this seminar). I emphasized, as I do in all my classes, that I was there to facilitate their learning and that I expected that we would discuss and produce knowledge together. One of the first questions after reading the proposed syllabus was, 'Why are you here?' This open-ended question was guided toward finding their fields of specialization, interests and what they expected they could use this class for in their professional and non-professional lives. As a result, I found out that the students were fed up with classes on Spanish morphology and phonology (a strong component of what they were facing in this history class); all except two of the students were teaching Spanish, and all of them wanted to teach Spanish in the near future (accordingly, my inference 1 was discarded); the field of specialization was, for all of them, SLA with a strong interest in sociolinguistics. I explained to the students that it seemed that their department had a strong interest in achieving a minimum set of outcome goals regarding form and, therefore, I had the responsibility to make sure that our seminar would cover these contents. However, I proposed the idea of seeing these contents through a parallel critical lens through the inclusion of critical sociolinguistics and antiracist contents that would offer counternarratives and a critical sociopolitical history of the Spanish language based on language ideologies and gloto-politics. I warned them that this would include more work, but that we, as a class, could decide to reduce some of the content focused on Span-ish structure in the current syllabus (we eliminated the support readings and decided to read only the main reading and do the practical exercises before class). We also discussed the load of new materials to add, consid-ering that they were in a doctoral seminar (we decided to add one more article per week and, instead of exercises about this article, to answer a question focused on their interests with a focus on its practical implica-tions). I proposed a trial during the first week and then made adjustments accordingly. Thus, the syllabus worked as a script that changed several times as the seminar progressed. These adjustments were based on stu-dents' feedback as well as on decisions I made based on how the students progressed. I also proposed reflecting on how these materials could be utilized in our daily practice and whether they were effective and worth the extra work, thus granting the students agency in their own learning. Also, part of each seminar was conducted by a student each week, and I tried to balance my amount of output with that of the students. In the first classes, I tried to stimulate their imagination on how to integrate into presentations one's interests regarding counternarratives and different voices from a critical perspective.

As a result, on the one hand, this was one of my greatest experiences as an educator, not only in developing and stimulating a rich relationship with my students, but also in learning from the process. I left each class with a fulfilling feeling of accomplishment. On the other hand, these are all of the anonymous testimonies of the students as posted in their course evaluations (I would have liked to include dissenting voices, but there were none): 'This was an exceptional course. The instructor always came prepared to class and the Prezi presentations were great. The restructur-ing of this course to make it more relevant and updated compared to how it has been traditionally taught was greatly appreciated. The instructor created a wonderful atmosphere for discussion and made participation very enjoyable. I would love to take another class with Dr. Magro'.

'The semester with Dr. Magro was outstanding. His expectations were clear and he effectively led group discussions that aided us in thinking outside the box and reading between the lines. His charisma and reasonable teaching style made this a great semester'.

'Hands down best course I have taken at [this] University and he isn't even a full professor here! *Qué lástima*'.

'José is the best professor I have had in my PhD program. He is compassionate about students' lives, enthusiastic about class content, and overall a really fabulous individual. He has a very effective teaching method through which we learn a lot of information in a way that doesn't feel overwhelming or boring. I was excited each week for the carefully-planned lessons and discussions he prepared, and never felt judged or insecure about being a non-native Spanish speaker. José is open-minded, accepting, and truly willing to learn from his students and adapt to their needs. I sincerely hope [this university] tries snagging him in the future because the department could use a good sociolinguist.

'Gracias por un increíble semestre, de verdad que se necesitan más profesores como tú, instructores que no olvidan que además de ser estudiantes … somos personas' (Thank you for an incredible semester, we really need more professors like you, instructors who do not forget that in addition to being students … we are persons).

4.3 L1 or L2 While Teaching SPCs in the L2 Language Classroom?

Neither, or both. Research regarding this topic of vehicular language in the L2 language classroom supports both perspectives. After reviewing the literature, one may conclude that these two confronted approaches that aim to postulate the optimal strategy for L2 teaching are fundamentally based on beliefs. While numerous researchers in the field of language teaching and learning support the use of L1 in L2 classrooms to facilitate learning (e.g. Atkinson, 1993; Cook, 2001; Eldridge, 1996; Ellis, 2008; Mahmoudi & Amirkhiz, 2011; Mohebbi & Alavi, 2014; Turnbull, 2002, all as cited in Almoayidi, 2018), a significant number of researchers contend that the use of L1 in the L2 classroom hinders learning and deprives learners of exposure to the L2. Krashen (1981) was one of the first researchers to promote the latter approach from an empirical perspective with his comprehensible input hypothesis. He argued that the L2 should be the exclusive vehicle in the language classroom (Almoayidi, 2018).

However, the aim of this study is not to argue for one or the other perspective. Instead, while rejecting a rigorous position of outright exclusion of L1 in the language classroom (such as in Krashen, 1981), I argue that this decision is going to depend on different factors, such as taking into consideration our antiracist goals, the level and outcome goals of the specific course and the instructional guidelines of the program in which we will attempt to integrate an antiracist program.

Thus, the goal of the following pedagogical proposals being to raise antiracist CLA through content related to the sociopolitical nature of language, the students need to understand the content. Therefore, in L2 acquisition courses, the amount of input in the L1 will depend on factors such as the pedagogical approach to language acquisition and/or the level. We need to consider, for example, if it is a content-based course and/or if it is based on a communicative approach or a grammar-focused perspective. The level of the course – that is, is it an advanced or a lower-level course? – and, sometimes, the specific level of a specific class/section are also factors to consider. We should ask ourselves: are the students in a particular section in the lower or higher part of the linguistic proficiency range for that level? Is there too much level disparity among students? Do we have enough time to present the content in the L2 in a way that students fully understand it? The answer to these questions will help us decide our approach regarding the amount of use of the L1, if any at all. Also, from a critical standpoint, we should ask ourselves what is considered an L1 and an L2. Do we understand language as discrete units (e.g. Spanish vs. English), or do we have a broader view of language and, from an antiracist perspective, embrace hybrid linguistic practices and translingualism?

In the specific case of integrating SPCs in an advanced CBI language class, the first time I conducted my research, the conclusions supported using the L1 in the L2 classroom. Although a greater development of linguistic proficiency could have been expected in the control group, which spent its extra 20 minutes of weekly instruction fully in the target language, the experimental group – which received this 20 extra minutes from a heteroglossic perspective, alternating the use of English and Spanish and allowing hybrid linguistic behaviors during this class time – had a statistically significant greater development of linguistic proficiency (Magro, 2016a). This phenomenon refutes arguments that affirm that the target language must always be used in L2 instruction, both in interactions in general as well as in instructions for activities or behavior management (Curtain & Dahlberg, 2010; Hall, 2001; Lee & VanPatten, 2003; Lipton, 1994; Omaggio Hadley, 2001; Shrum & Glisan, 2010; as cited in Ceo-DiFrancesco, 2013: 2).

In heritage speakers' courses, the considerations will be different. In most cases, these will have to do with the ideologies of languagelessness (Rosa, 2019). That is, can we be more flexible with the use of hybrid linguistic practices or, better yet, integrate them into the curriculum to 'walk the talk' and help to legitimize these practices in academia? Can we integrate translingualism in our pedagogical approach and utilize it to maximize content learning and, therefore, CLA? Again, this is going to depend greatly on the guidelines and flexibility of your program and how you, as an antiracist educator, are going to address these issues in your daily practice, but as it has been explained in these pages, the integration and validation of translingualism validates and empowers HL students whose linguistic practices have been stigmatized and historically excluded from academia (Beaudrie *et al.*, 2021; Holguín Mendoza, 2018; Leeman, 2005, 2018; Martínez, 2003).

In conclusion, regardless of the theoretical orientation of the program in which we teach (and in many of them there will be a push toward erasing the use of the L1 or, at least, minimizing it as much as possible), we must consider that our goal is for students to understand the SPCs. To facilitate this, first, especially for basic, intermediate and first levels of advanced L2 classes, we must consider that the input must be comprehensible, and the output should allow students to express their ideas. Depending on the program, instructors should make accommodations to facilitate this by integrating the L1 or adjusting the input in the L2. Second, especially for HL courses and CBI approaches, we should consider 'walking the talk', that is, being receptive, open-minded and embracing hybrid linguistic behaviors by not criticizing or penalizing them, but rather utilizing them – for example, to trigger critical discussions about stigmatized language use and hegemonic linguistic practices – and validating them in academic contexts. Without further ado, let us now see different ways to integrate all this theory into praxis.

Note

(1)   Malcolm X, Oxford Union Debate, 3 December 1964. 'Extremism in the defense of liberty is no vice; moderation in the pursuit of justice is no virtue' is a quote attributed to conservative Barry Goldwater in his 16 July speech that same year when he accepted the presidential nomination of the Republican Party.

Part 2

When, Where, How: Raising Antiracist Critical Linguistic Awareness in the Language Classroom Through Sociolinguistics-Informed Pedagogies

5 Integrating SPCs in an Advanced (Spanish) Language Class

The following 14 units are designed to be integrated as supplemental instruction for an advanced (Spanish) language course. However, they may serve as a valid guide, with some adjustments, for instructors of all levels of both second language (L2) courses and heritage language (HL) courses, as well as first language (L1) and literacy courses, who are interested in an antiracist pedagogical approach.

The units used as an example in this chapter result from five years of implementing them, entirely or partially, at different levels and courses. These courses include advanced Spanish courses, advanced grammar and writing courses, courses on the translation of technical or legal texts and an interdisciplinary course titled Language and Racism, which introduces sociolinguistics and antiracist pedagogies to incoming university students (see Chapter 6). In all these courses, except for Language and Racism, I was sometimes provided with a syllabus by my university's department, a common practice in standardized courses with multiple sections. On other occasions, the faculty member in charge of curriculum development and supervision handed over a course description and a set of outcome goals. In the latter cases, I had the liberty to design my own syllabi as long as I targeted the department's outcome goals. In the former, I had to integrate these sociopolitical contents (SPCs) into prescribed syllabi and submit the resulting programs for review. On very few occasions, I was asked to adhere strictly to the syllabus provided and not include any of these materials – probably for fear of interference with the course's outcome goals. Regardless of the situation, I had to make adjustments (and perform creative curricular acrobatics) to integrate the content that I propose in the following chapters.

During these five years, I made small adjustments to these materials. Nevertheless, although they have been 'refreshed', the goals are essentially the same. The materials used in the units I am about to describe are tools to reach a set of general outcome goals related to antiracist critical linguistic awareness (CLA) through scaffolded materials. These outcomes include:

(1) Demonstrating 'cross-cultural' competence through reflecting, relating, comparing and contrasting different languages, language varieties and language practices from a critical perspective.
(2) Identifying language ideologies and the discourse associated with them in different sociolinguistic situations, including films, news, music, daily interactions and textbooks.
(3) Analyzing how language, identity and power intertwine in different types of texts, such as films, news, music and textbooks.
(4) Analyzing how language, identity and power intertwine in different cultural and sociolinguistic contexts such as academia, stigmatized markets of cultural production (e.g. Hip-Hop) or daily interactions.
(5) Interpreting language ideologies and articulating how they benefit and harm different social groups in different sociolinguistic contexts, including films, news, music, daily interactions and textbooks.
(6) Reflecting on hegemonic educational practices, how they manifest in their curriculum and how these practices benefit and harm different social groups.
(7) Reflecting on their own linguistic awareness development and agency throughout the course.
(8) Becoming familiar with diverse research methods in social sciences.
(9) Analyzing racism as a form of historical and systemic discrimination in the United States and internationally that may intersect with other forms of power and oppression (this outcome was created by the Diversity Education Task Force and approved by the university senate as 'meaningful changes in the university's general education diversity requirement').

Moreover, this program should not be taken as static or fixed but rather as a guide, a template in which educators may make their own adjustments. There is always room for changes and adaptation to the (racial, educational, economic, social and historical) context and the individual characteristics of the instructor and students. These materials are thought to be further developed, expanded, renewed and adjusted through time and space.

When I first implemented these units for my doctoral dissertation research (Magro, 2016a), they were designed for a content-based instruction (CBI) advanced Spanish course. These classes met for 50 minutes three times per week, except on Fridays, when the class had 20 additional minutes of SPC instruction. This was a hybrid program; the students had an asynchronous online component in which the students prepared for each face-to-face meeting. Within the CBI pedagogical framework of this course, the students learned a particular content while developing their linguistic proficiency in the target language rather than the language being the immediate object of study. In this case, under a theme-based instruction model (Klee, 2015), the students learned about current Latin

American sociopolitical issues while focusing on grammar structures that cognitive linguistics points out as being difficult for L2 students at this level. I emphasize that this program was rigidly 'imposed' onto all instructors across sections by the Spanish department in which I implemented this program.

Due to restrictions related to the highly standardized language program where I first implemented these units, I was not allowed to 'steal' 20 weekly minutes of instruction to integrate the SPCs. Therefore, in order to implement these units, I made adjustments to add 20 minutes of extra time per week.[1] The integration of the SPCs can be rearranged and adjusted to be implemented in other program schedule arrangements (e.g. classes meeting more than three times per week or those meeting for longer than the usual 50-minute periods but only twice per week).

Ideally, to avoid an instructor-centered approach, these units should be implemented using a flipped-classroom approach; that is, the students would read the proposed theoretical materials before each class while, during class time, the output provided by the instructor through the presentations should be minimized. Under an ideal instruction context, this output should be limited to promoting and guiding discussions, helping to answer questions and clarifying any theoretical points (tasks that can be done by the instructor or other students). However, as was the case in this program, it is necessary to take into consideration the pushback that adding extra materials to study at home could generate in a program that was already overloaded with homework. Thus, these units depart from input provided by the instructor during class time that, however, integrates comments and answers as the students pose them during the presentation of materials. When reading across the following units, the reader must be aware that for informative purposes, I emphasized and detailed the input I provided to my students. However, this does not mean that this disproportion in the extension dedicated in these pages to explaining the input should be translated into an instructor-centered approach in which the students' voices are silenced as they become passive receptors of knowledge. The input should be minimized as much as possible, taking into consideration its effectiveness; that is, the theoretical components must be received by the students. The instruction should allow enough time for the incorporation of the students' voices. These two aspects of the instruction should be balanced time-wise. A good example of how to use a flipped classroom approach will be detailed in the second section of Chapter 6.

Based on ACTFL's parameters, the students that took this class ranged from an intermediate-mid level to an intermediate-high proficiency level. The students, aged between 19 and 23, were middle-class White youth with three exceptions (two Hispanic students and one Hindu student). Except for the two Hispanic heritage speakers, all of them had acquired Spanish as a second or third language in an academic environment. The first language for all of them was English, except for the three heritage speakers, who learned Spanish and Gujarati as their first languages (to contextualize the institutional framework of this language program and more details about these students, see Chapters 2 and 1, respectively). As a program requirement across sections, the classes were conducted strictly in Spanish. However, during the SPCs, flexibility was allowed for the use of any linguistic variety of Spanish or English and for hybridity, seeking to promote heteroglossia in the classroom, thus sheltering translingual practices. Nonetheless, these units can be adapted to any level of Spanish as long as measures are taken to make sure the students can understand the input and express their ideas comfortably and freely (see section 4.3 of Chapter 4 for a discussion on vehicular language).

The format of each unit is similar. It starts with the instructor providing input through a graphic presentation that includes different media, including videos, music, pictures, drawings and cartoons. Although the presentations resemble the lecture format, in a pedagogical effort to stay in a student-centered classroom by using a reflexive dialogical approach, they pose questions – during and at the end of each presentation – to promote constant participation, collaboration and, especially, reflection. Each unit ends with an activity aimed at promoting students' reflection on the general contents of the unit. These questions and activities seek to grant agency for students to become actors instead of spectators in their processes of comprehension/acquisition of notions related to the sociopolitical nature of language and their own CLA growth. These units also allow for the inclusion of the students' own narratives and counternarratives. Based on a social constructionist view of learning, working in pairs or small groups is recommended to help promote positive interdependence, individual accountability, promotive face-to-face interaction, appropriate social skills and group processing, among other benefits, such as self-directed learning (Breed, 2016). In an attempt to avoid reproducing hierarchical structures from outside the classroom, the role of the instructor was presented as a mediator, rather than an authority figure, whose goal was to facilitate the horizontal construction of knowledge in groups in an ungraded academic setting (the students were not graded for their work in these units). Of course, the hierarchical organization of the university permeates the classrooms, making it difficult for students to see their instructors as other than authority figures with power over the students. Emphasizing the ungraded nature of the activities, highlighting their freedom of speech, both in content and structure, sitting with aleatory groups of students during their discussions and participating in their conversations as one more member, switching to stigmatized vernacular linguistic varieties (both in English and Spanish) and thus validating them, integrating stigmatized materials, voices and narratives (otherwise prestigious in symbolic markets other than academia), sharing personal experiences and reflections vis-à-vis while connecting them to theory and adapting syllabi to the students' needs and interests are among the strategies that instructors can utilize to break with the reproduction of asymmetric power relationships during these activities. These practices also provide a glance at what education could look like if reimagined through the lens of critical pedagogy.

As a vehicle for these presentations, instead of PowerPoint, which can be seen as boring and commonplace (Craig & Amernic, 2006, as cited in Strasser, 2014) or any other more traditional presentation methods (such as using printed copies or a blackboard), I use Prezi. This Flash-based and cloud-based presentation editor allows for more flexibility and collaboration than is possible with PowerPoint. It better captures an audience's attention because it is visually richer, not as linear in structure and more dynamic (e.g. Prezi allows the user to create presentations that zoom) (Strasser, 2014). Furthermore, Prezi breaks away from the hegemony of PowerPoint as the standard method for presenting information to an audience in educational settings (going back again to the idea of multiliteracies) and aligns better with the way new technologies represent information because Prezi's templates are constantly being developed and updated by its users, therefore facilitating the engagement of 21st-century students.

The program's content is divided into 14 units, which generally correspond with the 15/16-week-long semesters in most US universities. Each section in this chapter corresponds to a unit, and each unit is written to be used as a guide for instructors' lesson plans. Sometimes, I will include some theoretical considerations seeking to promote a deeper understanding for instructors who are not familiar with sociolinguistics or some aspects of it that I utilized in these units. However, the main focus is to provide educators with a framework, resources, examples and tools to raise students' CLA toward antiracism. Appendix B contains a link to access all the presentations.

5.1 Unit 1: Brief Introduction to Sociolinguistics 1

The first two units are the more theory-oriented units of the program. Their goal is to offer students an overview of sociolinguistics. Current pedagogical models often incorporate sociolinguistics (or the adoption of sociolinguistically informed approaches) to promote CLA, including positive attitudes toward linguistic diversity and multiple varieties (e.g. Beaudrie et al., 2021; Carreira, 2007). I have explained how, on the one hand, expansionist models integrate sociolinguistics to expand the (normative) linguistic repertoire of students. On the other hand, critical approaches, such as the one presented here, frame sociolinguistics to promote student consciousness-raising, questioning of given assumptions and agency (Leeman, 2005; Leeman & Serafini, 2016; Martínez, 2003). This book's approach considers it necessary to discuss sociolinguistics

with students so they can understand what sociolinguistics and its different approaches are in order to facilitate engagement and understanding
when discussing topics related to this field.

The following are the procedures organized by the Prezi slide:

(1) Slide 1: the presentation starts with the following quote by Spolsky
    (1999):

    Language is a central feature of human identity. When we hear
    someone speak, we immediately make guesses about gender, educa-
    tion level, age, profession, and place of origin. Beyond this individual
    matter, a language is a powerful symbol of national and ethnic iden-
    tity. (Spolsky, 1999: 181)

Immediately after, the instructor poses this question: 'What is sociolinguistics?' We give students a minute to collaborate in pairs to put
together their answers. Then, the instructor listens to three or four of
their answers and offers a definition, e.g. sociolinguistics studies the different aspects of society that influence the use of language.

(2) Slide 2: 'Basic concepts 1: *Langue* (French, meaning "language");
    and *parole* (meaning "speech")'. The instructor uses Ferdinand de
    Saussure's famous chess analogy to explain how, in the 19th cen-
    tury, Saussure used these two terms to differentiate between *langue*
    (language) – those systemic abstract laws, like the rules in chess,
    which preexist and are independent of the individual users of a lan-
    guage – and *parole* (speaking), the individual phenomenon dependent
    of each speaker that occurs when they use language (the individual
    moves when playing chess). The instructor may ask their students
    questions such as 'if I am thinking where I can move my horse, am I
    using *langue* or *parole*? If I decide to attack a tower with my horse,
    am I using *langue* or *parole*?'.
(3) Slide 3: 'Basic concepts 2' aims to explain descriptivism versus
    prescriptivism. To do so, the display of two comic strips aids the
    instructor in explaining how descriptivism refers to the structure of
    a language as it is actually used by speakers and writers, while pre-
    scriptivism refers to the structure of a language as certain groups of
    people think it should be used (see Appendix B). Then, the students
    are required to collaborate in pairs for two minutes to find examples
    of each position. Here, we expect to hear examples based on stu-
    dents' unfortunate past experiences with prescriptivist teachers and
    professors, which opens an opportunity to advance a brief discussion
    on normativism and standard language ideologies or simply state
    that this topic will be the focus of future units.
(4) Slide 4: 'Basic concepts 3: Grammar and its parts' offers the follow-
    ing content:

Phonetics/phonology: Sounds of language.
Morphology: Structure of words.
Syntax: Structure of sentences.
Semantics: Logical aspects of meaning, sense, reference and interpretation.
Pragmatics: Language in use and how the contexts influence the interpretation of meaning (e.g. taking turns in conversation or text organization).

(5) Slide 5: 'Basic concepts 4: Variety, variable, variant'. These three concepts may be explained by different examples from any language. I generally use the case of /s/ coda in different (regional, social) varieties of Spanish. The slide displays the following text:
Different varieties of Spanish have different linguistic features.
Variable /s/ coda:
Variant 1 > pronunciation /tu.estás.loco/
Variant 2 > aspiration /tu.ehtah.loco/
Variant 3 > elision /tu.eta.loco/

After providing a few examples of situations/regions/social groups in which each variant of this variable may appear, I ask the students to find, in pairs, another example from Spanish or a different language. Notice that this exercise understands languages as discrete systems, which is a concept that will be refuted in further units of this program.

5.2 Unit 2: Brief Introduction to Sociolinguistics 2

The goal of this unit is to point out how language is bound to the concept of speech community across time, region, social group and communicative setting. Following a brief review of the previous unit's content (no more than three minutes), a slide provides a visual aid to explain, through examples, what is known as the architecture of language and the four dimensions of language variation as proposed in Coseriu (1981): diachronic, diatopic, diastratic and diaphasic variation (see Appendix B, Unit 2, Slide 1).

Diachronic varieties are those concerned with the chronological axis. We can exemplify it with variants and historical linguistic stages that follow each other on the diachronic axis, such as extinct, obsolete, old-fashioned, current and fashionable expressions (e.g. Shakespearean English versus current published mainstream authors' English or 1980s rap songs versus later rap songs). Diatopic variation has to do with the different dialects spoken based on regions of the linguistic area (e.g. Colombian Spanish has variants that differ from, for example, Dominican Spanish, *rioplatense* Spanish or Central American Spanish). Diastratic variation attends to the different sociolects used by different social groups (i.e.

according to race, age, sex, profession, etc.). For instance, the English spoken by some African Americans in Los Angeles versus the English spoken by some Chicanos in the same city. Lastly, diaphasic variation attends to the different levels of style/register used in different communicative settings (e.g. two Black female doctors from Los Angeles may use a different linguistic variety when addressing patients versus when they are in private talking about politics or friends over a cup of coffee).

During this explanation, instead of the instructor providing the examples, it is recommended to ask students to provide them. They will introduce their personal experiences, and these examples can be useful for reference in future units (i.e. 'remember when X said that …') while simultaneously recognizing their voices, providing them with agency and providing us with feedback on their understanding.

After this explanation, the students, in pairs, can work on a roleplaying activity:

(1) Randomly assign each pair one dimension of language (e.g. they can pick a card previously written with the word diachronic, diatopic, diastratic or diaphasic).
(2) Give the students a couple of minutes to prepare a conversation that will exemplify their assigned dimension.
(3) After performing it for the class, let the rest of the students guess which dimension they sought to highlight in their performances.

To finish this unit, the instructor will open a discussion after posing the following questions (it is recommended to display the question in a slide; see Appendix B, Unit 2, Slide 3):

• Which Spanish (or English, or French, this depends on the vehicular language of your class) in this class?
• What diachronic, diatopic, diastratic and diaphase variety do you or *y'all* expect me to use? In Spanish classes, I make a pun using the two different uses of plural second-person pronouns, *ustedes* (Latin American and Andalusian regions) and *vosotros* (used in the center-north Spanish regions).
• What do you think this university expects me to use?
• What do you want me to use? (In Spanish classes, in this question, I use *voseo* the way it is used in *rioplatense* Spanish, '¿qué querés vos que use?')
• What do you think I would like to use?
• What do you think we are going to use?

These questions are based on Del Valle (2014), who recommends integrating this discussion into the early stages of language programs because reflecting on the ideological and historical aspects of language architecture helps raise students' CLA. The goal of this activity is to let the students reflect in pairs on the politics of normativity and make connections with their own linguistic experiences. When they present their answers, the instructor may inquire about the reasons for their answers and try to connect them to linguistic ideologies – such as normativity – and attitudes, such as the overt and covert prestige of certain varieties. For example, how some spoken varieties of academic Colombian or Peninsular Spanish are generally perceived as more prestigious than Dominican Spanish, especially varieties of rural or working-class Dominican Spanish, and how this is linked to ideologies such as antiblack racism.

5.3 Unit 3: Language Standardization Process: The Case of Spanish, Part 1

First, although not necessary, if you are teaching a language other than Spanish, and you are interested in integrating the history of that language into your course, it is recommended that you adapt the theoretical content used for this unit to the specific language of your class. This unit aims to highlight the nature of language as a social construct while rejecting the idea of language as a natural entity by explaining the social, political and historical processes of language standardization.

As a warm-up, the instructor may use four minutes to review the past unit with an exercise that compares the language variety of a prestigious legitimized author in academic settings with an equivalent from a non-hegemonic symbolic market such as popular culture. A good example that works well in my classes – because the four dimensions of language architecture are contained within this example, and it tackles issues of racial misrepresentation in the classroom – is to compare Shakespearean English with the iconic rap group Wu-Tang Clan's English. Before asking students to compare both varieties in pairs and state which one they think is 'better', the instructor asks them to consider the four dimensions of language in both varieties. After the students provide a few answers, the instructor may discuss the data provided by big data research available online (Daniels, 2019), which claims that Wu-Tang is lexically superior to Shakespeare. This can be a good opportunity to advance issues concerning big data interpretation (e.g. methodological issues such as 'comparing apples to pears') and, more importantly, how the idea of more elevated or superior varieties is constructed based on ideology rather than facts. In this case, although the underdog (Wu-Tang) comes out as the winner, and even though I am a big fan of this (mainly) Staten Island, New York, supercrew, questioning the methodology utilized to analyze and interpret the data is helpful to inspire your students to be critical. Because big data studies can – and most of the time do – the opposite (i.e. interpret data in favor of legitimized hegemonic attitudes and ideologies by the utilization of a faulty methodology), being aware and self-critical will help students to develop a responsible critical approach toward social sciences that differentiates facts against beliefs and/or emotions. Although I believe Wu-Tang's penmanship is much better than Shakespeare's, I do not think a quantitative tool such as this one is valid to make a quality judgment about something so abstract and dependent on so many variables, such as literary production.

After this warm-up activity, the first slide displays this question: 'What is a language?' The instructor provides a minute for student discussion in pairs or small groups. After listening to several answers (it is to be expected that you will receive answers related to the structural nature of language such as 'a language is a system of signs ...'), zooming into the slide shows the following statement attributed to Weinreich (1945): 'A language is a dialect with an army and a navy' (see Appendix B, Unit 3, Slide 3). To exemplify this statement, the instructor may compare the status of Haitian Creole (the official language of Haiti) versus that of Jamaican Patois (considered a low-prestige dialect by the Jamaican ruling elite). Both languages are analytically very similar: the syntax of both is substrate-based on Western African languages, while the lexical component is based on colonial languages, mainly French for Haitian and English for Jamaican. However, Haiti was the first Black colony to become an independent country after a successful slave revolt (1804), while Jamaica remained a subject of the United Kingdom until 1962. Their different colonial histories and power dynamics are intertwined with the identities and language attitudes and ideologies of these two countries' populations and beyond. The instructor can also expand the conversation to discuss how Jamaican Patois is perceived as a symbol of pride and used as a resistance language by Rastafarian, Reggae and popular culture in Jamaica, defying power and asserting a Black/African-rooted Jamaican identity instead of a colonized one. Notice that the use of this example is not random. A successful Haitian revolution is a symbol of resistance against oppression, despite the economic effects of multiple embargos and debts imposed by the very same colonial powers that Haitians fought to free themselves from. This rarely appears in the history curriculum or is included as anecdotal.

Immediately following this discussion, the instructor plays 'Ebonics' (Big L, 2000), a posthumous music video by an MC from Harlem. In this track, Big L performs a semantics exercise in which he translates standard English to Harlem's late 1990s Hip-Hop 'criminal slang'. Then, the instructor poses a hypothetical case: the independence from the United States of a mainly African American neighborhood in Brooklyn called Bedford-Stuyvesant (a neighborhood popularized by ex-resident rap legend Jay-Z, the late Notorious B.I.G. and film director Spike Lee, and this book's author's hometown for many years). The students are asked to hypothesize about the officiality of its language and the reason(s) why. They must also suggest names for it. When I conducted this exercise, students suggested names such as *Brooklynite* and *Ebonix*. When asked why they chose those names, the students sought to articulate racial demographics and other issues related to identity, power and language. That is the goal.

Next, based on Haugen (1966), the instructor explains to the students that the standardization process is the central object of language policy and planning. This process is conducted by powerful/prestigious members of society who aim to reduce variation in the variety(s) of prestige; that is, it seeks to remove the variants. This process would be inconceivable without writing. However, although, in theory, it does not extend to phonetics/phonology, the linguistic phonetic and phonological traits of these powerful groups can influence a reduced variation by creating an effective phonetic standard. To illustrate this last point, you can use the following example (or an adaptation of it). The instructor explains how Televisión Española (the main public television channel in Spain) and the rest of the major TV stations in Spain transmit their newscasts (their most formal programming) from Madrid, the capital and administrative-governmental center of the Spanish state. The linguistic varieties spoken in these newscasts use central-Peninsular features as the standard. The use of this variety of Spanish during the programming – which is expected to use the more formal-elevated linguistic varieties – is one of the factors that influence, and put pressure for change, on the different varieties of Spanish that ordinary citizens perceive as less prestigious (e.g. Andalusian Spanish).

An example of how this works is based on an instructor's experience. A young Andalusian woman was being interviewed by a New York graduate Spanish student for a sociolinguistics project. When answering, acknowledging that the conversation was being recorded, the interviewee put on an effort to reproduce a formal central-Peninsular variety of Spanish, therefore indexing linguistic formality and exactitude. As soon as the interviewer announced that the interview was over, the interviewee started to relax and talk naturally, and the variants associated with Andalusian Spanish immediately appeared in her speech.

This example can help elicit from students other similar examples in different languages, which is the next activity. The instructor allows two or three minutes for pairs of students to come up with an example. *The Queen's English* is usually one of the examples the students provide, but it would be desirable for students to go deeper and reflect on their own experiences instead.

5.4 Unit 4: The Language Standardization Process: The Case of Spanish, Part 2

This unit is a continuation of the previous one. Thus, the outcome goal remains the same. It starts with input presented by a slide that summarizes the phases of the language standardization process (see Appendix B,

Unit 4, Slide 1). My example is a summary based on the case of Spanish, as theorized by Ralph Penny (2000). The presentation covers the following points:

(1) Status planning.
(2) Selection. As Penny (2000: 197) explains, 'every standard language grows out of some spoken variety or varieties, which are in competition with a much larger number of other varieties, which are not so selected'. After this statement, the instructor explains briefly and in a simplified way the linguistic situation in the Iberian Peninsula during the koineization process (a process by which a new variety of a language emerges from the mixing, leveling and simplifying of different dialects intelligible to each other). Arabic was spoken in most parts of the Peninsula, and different varieties of vernacular Latin (often with features of contact with Arabic) were spoken in the small but expanding northern Christian kingdoms. The instructor then points out the role of politically and economically powerful groups in the selection of their varieties as the standard language. In the case of Spanish, linguistic features used by the economic elite of the politically and culturally prestigious city of Burgos during the 10th and 11th centuries (e.g. /húmo/ vs. /fumo/, from Latin *fumu*, 'smoke') were more favored than those of other varieties (e.g. Castillian spoken in Toledo). Thus, partly due to accommodation and partly to the relocation of populations due to the military expansion of Castile, speakers imitated the speech from Burgos in increasingly broader areas. It is important to highlight that this process requires resources, such as, for example, economic power to publish textbooks and social capital to influence institutions (such as the Church) that play a fundamental role.
(3) Codification. The instructor explains that its objective is to minimize the variation of form (Haugen, 1966), a goal only utterly achievable in written language. The rules are used to convey prestige. As an example, the instructor may use *La gran conquista de ultramar* (*The Great Overseas Conquest*), a 13th-century book in which variation was reduced in subsequent editions, adhering to the elite linguistic norm. The instructor can also comment on how the codification process of spelling is achieved faster than morphology and syntax or than vocabulary, the latter being an ongoing process that cannot be wholly achieved (Penny, 2000: 202).
(4) Elaboration of function. Here, attention is paid to how the chosen varietyering to the elite linguistic norm. The instructor can also comment on how the codification process of spelling is achieved faster than morpholthe language as a code – in the case of romance languages, one different from Latin. The introduction of a spelling system is necessary to raise that awareness (Wright, 1982, as cited in

Penny, 2000). The instructor may use the example of Alfonso X the Learned, a medieval Castilian king who culminated this process of homogeneous consistency when he turned his linguistic variety into a code that became the vehicle for almost all texts inprose narrative, historiography, science (astronomy, astrology, mineralogy, etc.) and jurisprudence (lyric poetry and religion took a bit longer to oust Latin).

(5) Acceptance. Based on Penny (2000), the acceptance of a particular linguistic code establishes and propagates the value of a language, a process that has occurred in more recent centuries. The relationship between the name of a language and political identity is explained; i.e. the speech of a portion of territory whose boundaries are determined by the control exercised by some political entity determines the name of the language (e.g. Castilian is the abbreviation of *romance castellano*, those forms of speech derived from Latin used in the territory of Castile). At least for the first users of this linguistic variety, there is a connection between language and a political entity.

The promotion of a language name is an instrument for building nations. An abbreviation of the example of nationalist exploitation of language provided by Penny (2000) will help students understand this point. Antonio de Nebrija, author of the first Castilian grammar, placed the following quote addressed to Isabella I of Castile and Aragon at the head of his *Gramática de la lengua castellana* (1492): 'siempre la lengua fue compañera del imperio; & de tal manera lo siguió, que junta mente comenzaron, crecieron & florecieron, & después junta fue la caída de entrambos' (Nebrija, 1980, as cited in Penny, 2000: 205). Taking into consideration time constrictions, the instructor may want to translate the whole quote or just refer to the first sentence, 'language was always a companion to empire', and let students discuss its meaning in pairs. After hearing a few of their answers, the instructor should explain how only after 1469, when Castile and Aragon merged their kingdoms, did the term *Spanish* start to be used simultaneously with *Castilian*, one or the other being preferred depending on geopolitics or the historical moment.

(6) Corpus planning. Before concluding this unit, it is recommended that the instructor overview, albeit briefly, Ralph Penny's section on corpus planning (Penny, 2000: 206–217) to further emphasize the relationships between politics and language standardization. First, the instructor would state that, based on Penny (2000), corpus planning has to do with the intralinguistic aspects of the language standardization process. Then, the instructor reminds students that, in Spanish, intolerance toward linguistic variation started in the 13th century with Alfonso X the Learned. The instructor then connects this idea of reducing variation in a top–bottom process to the implementation of orthographic simplification by President Sarmiento

in Chile (1843–1927) and the republican teachers of Madrid. As an example, the instructor may use the new role played by the letters *h*, *b/v* and *j/g* after Sarmiento's policy implementation; these were simplified to provide better access to literacy so, in a democratic effort, the popular classes could have easier access to education. Children (and new learners) did not have to learn difficult 'unnecessary' spelling rules such as those in words that have an h (which in Spanish is mute except when it is preceded by *c*; thus, it was eliminated); when to use *b* or *v*, because in Spanish there is no voiced labiodental fricative sound like, for instance, in English; or reducing the function of *j* for all /x/ sound and its variants /h/ and /X/ (e.g. *general* became *jeneral*), among other changes that aimed to pair spelling and phonics. All printed texts in Chile from 1843 to 1927 followed this simplified spelling system. The instructor may open a brief discussion on the sociopolitical repercussions of this policy and why (and by whom and to what purpose) it was overruled in 1927.

Next, the instructor may explain that in terms of morphology, the process was slower, but that it was already almost completely successful in the nineteenth century, and the syntax still suffered some variation. However, regarding semantics/vocabulary, it still has a high degree of variation despite the restrictions imposed for centuries. The instructor may ask students to reflect on how the vocabulary constantly changes and let them provide some examples based on their own linguistic varieties. Lastly, as an extension (if time allows it), all this can be exemplified, very briefly, by projecting a map of the Iberian Peninsula in medieval times and the evolution of Spanish using Menéndez-Pidal's wedge theory; that is, how Castilian expanded from north to south in constant contact with Arabic, while leaving in its margins Galician-Portuguese in the west and Catalan in the east (see Appendix B, Unit 4, Slide 2).

5.5 Unit 5: Introduction to Language Ideologies

This unit is one of the more difficult to conduct under time restrictions. Because these units are designed to work without readings before each class, we can only aim to provide a general view of the field and highlight the relationships between language ideologies, power and identity. After this unit, the students should be able to understand what ideologies are. They should also be able to understand what linguistics is in order to have an understanding of what language ideologies are and where this field is situated. The ultimate goal of this unit is to understand language as a social construct and to be able to analyze language ideologies and their relationships to concrete forms of power at a basic level.

The unit starts by asking the following question to the group: what is an ideology? (see Appendix B, Unit 5, Slide 1). After listening to a few attempts to define it, the following definition by Ludovico Silva is projected on the second slide, which is incomplete and ends in an ellipsis for the students to complete: 'An ideology is the set of ideas about reality, a general system or existing systems in society's practices concerning economy, society, science and technology, politics, culture, morality, religion, etc. They seek to ...' (1980: 46, my translation) (see Appendix B, Unit 5, Slide 2).[2]

After the students, in pairs or small groups, attempt to identify what ideologies seek, and after sharing a couple of those attempts, the instructor provides the rest of Silva's definition; that is, conserving the system (conservative ideologies), transforming it (sudden or radical, revolutionary, gradualist or reformist ideologies) or restoring a system previously in power (reactionary). The instructor may ask the students to provide examples of each.

Next, a short video explaining Antonio Gramsci's Cultural Hegemony theory is projected.[3] This video should help the students to settle the way ideologies work in praxis.

Then, after defining linguistics (linguistics is the scientific study of language), the following slide offers its different approaches (see Appendix B, Unit 5, Slide 3). First, formalism is explained to students as an approach that deals with the purely formal aspects of the linguistic system. As an example, the instructor can talk briefly about Noam Chomsky's theory of universal grammar and his search for a genetic component of the faculty of language.

Second, for variationist sociolinguistics – the approach to linguistics that studies the linguistic system in relation to social variables – the instructor may use as an example William Labov's (1966) social stratification of language. Labov hypothesized that the higher the social class of a speaker, the more frequent the occurrence of rhotic /r/ in speech. He took his ranging sample in three New York City (NYC) department stores associated with different social classes: S. Klein (lowest social ranking), Macy's (middle social ranking) and Saks Fifth Avenue (the highest social ranking). Labov collected data by asking participants to read a word list and a passage (more carefully considered speech) and to engage in an informal interview (more natural speech). In all social classes, Labov found a higher use of rhoticity when reading the word list as opposed to in the interview, in which rhoticity was less present as the social class lowered. Labov concluded that this linguistic feature was associated with social class.

Third, regarding linguistic ideologies, I recommend using José del Valle's (2007a) definition: '[Linguistic ideologies are] an area of study that interprets language-discursive phenomena in four different fields: political, social, cultural, and economic'. As an example, the instructor may use Lippi-Green's (1997) study on the use of language in Walt Disney films. The study argues how language is used to portray a hierarchical point of view of the world that attempts to maintain certain hegemonic groups in power through the use of stereotypes (whether negative, positive or apparently neutral). After providing examples of animated children's cinema (such as the crows in *Dumbo*, the hyenas in *The Lion King* or the 'Latino' penguins in *Happy Feet*), students are asked for other examples.[4]

Next, a new slide poses the following question to the group: 'What are linguistic ideologies?' Aiming to stimulate critical reflection, this question is written on top of a drawing of 'Uncle Sam' pointing his index finger and saying, 'I want you … to speak English or get out!' (see Appendix B, Unit 5, Slide 4). After listening to a few answers, a definition proposed by José del Valle (2007a: 20, my translation) is displayed: '[linguistic ideologies are] systems of ideas that articulate notions of language, languages, speech and/or communication with specific cultural, political and/or social notions'. This text is followed by an explanation and argumentation about the contextuality of linguistic ideologies – that is, their link to a cultural, social, political and economic order; its naturalizing/normalizing function, which points toward common sense; and its institutionality, i.e. institutionally organized practices for the benefit of concrete forms of power and authority. All this is explained with a comment built on *Lengua, ¿patria común?* (Del Valle, 2007a): the relationship between prescriptive institutions in command of dictating linguistic rules – i.e. the Real Academia de la Lengua Española (RAE) – and the idea of a pan-Hispanic community with neocolonial characteristics that these institutions propagate are linked to concrete forms of power and authority and economic interests (such as publishing, communications, media and even energy and financial holding companies). As an example, the instructor may point out the financial links between Spanish private banks, such as BBVA, or Spanish corporative holdings, such as PRISA, and language/academic institutions such as Fundéu (Fundación del Español Urgente), which was created in collaboration with the RAE.

The penultimate slide aims to explain the objective of the study of linguistic ideas. This objective is to identify the context in which these ideologies make complete sense. From social approaches, this is achieved through the sociology of language; from cultural approaches, through linguistic anthropology; from political approaches, through the field of glotopolitics; and from those approaches that define the context in a hybrid way, through interdisciplinary approaches. Additionally, the instructor approaches the issue of positionality, arguing that every researcher sees and thinks from a specific political, social, intellectual and geo-academic location that frames and contextualizes all their research, whether they are aware of it or not. To illustrate this idea, the instructor may choose any example of their choice related to their own research. I generally use the research for this book as an example: how my own political, social, intellectual and geo-academic location as a researcher influenced me when deciding what and how to investigate; how all this influenced the knowledge obtained; and how the fact that, as a researcher, I decided to deal with all this explicitly is, in turn, representative of its location.

This unit concludes with a collaborative task. The students must discuss in pairs or small groups what a linguistic ideology could be. After a few moments, one of the examples provided by the students is shared with the group, followed by a brief open discussion of the example. The instructor can guide this discussion with questions such as 'How is this linguistic ideology spread within society?', 'Who is profiting from this linguistic ideology?', 'Who is negatively impacted by it?' and 'How could we bring down this ideology?'.

5.6 Unit 6: Introduction to Language and Identity: Their Relationship

This unit is based on the work of Gibson (2004). Its goal is for the students to understand identity as a non-discrete, nonlinear, dynamic construct and to reflect on their own identities and how they are intertwined with language.

The first slide introduces the following statements: 'The term identity literally refers to sameness' (Bucholtz & Hall, 2004: 1) and 'Neither identity nor language use is a fixed notion; both are dynamic, depending upon time and place' (Norton, 1995, cited in Gibson, 2004: 3) (see Appendix B, Unit 6, Slide 1). The instructor asks the students to work in pairs or small groups and discuss examples to illustrate Norton's statement.

Immediately after this, a slide with three bullet points will be shown, which summarizes the following information on ethnic identity and places the focus on race and ethnicity and the central role they play in American society (see Appendix B, Unit 6, Slide 2). The way we perceive ourselves changes with our community of practice, allowing us multiple identities over the years or even within the same day. Thus, in discussions of ethnic identity, it has been argued that a language is not a necessary element to identify with an ethnicity. For example, as Eastman and Reese (1981) and Liebkind (1999) point out, an individual can identify as Irish without speaking Gaelic. Likewise, many Puerto Ricans identify as such without speaking Spanish. Additionally, an ethnic group or individual adhering to that group may have a symbolic attachment to an associated language (and be proficient in it) but may use a more practical one, such as in the case of English versus Spanish in the case of Puerto Ricans in New York or Chicanos in Los Angeles. However, the instructor should highlight that an ethnic group will commonly identify with a language. This is illustrated in the following slide:

For the majority of Hispanics, the Spanish language runs deeply into cultural and personal identities. Anzaldúa's eloquent phrasing of this principle captures the language-identity fusion: 'Ethnic identity is twin skin to linguistic identity – I am my language' (1987, p. 59). To relinquish Spanish either literally or symbolically (which many monolingual citizens of the United States seem to think is appropriate for integration into the country) is to relinquish a significant and powerful dimension of personal and social identity. (Johnson, 2000: 177)

The next slide follows up on the previous one with this statement by Gibson (2004: 4): 'However, all this presumes the speaker is able to self-select their ethnicity, or more broadly, their identity'. This statement is followed by a series of bullet points that organize information about Erving Goffman's (1963) theory of social identity as theatrical performance (see Appendix B, Unit 6, Slide 3, and Appendix C). The instructor uses these bullet points to explain that Goffman's work was influential in showing that the self is constructed entirely through discourse, making our choices regarding the use of language of utmost importance for the construction of our identity. In fact, Goffman (1963) claimed that personal identity is defined by how others identify us, not how we identify ourselves. The speaker may try to influence how others perceive it, but it is ultimately the listener who creates the speaker's identity. If the speaker is not allowed any influence on his own output, then the listener is able to construct an identity for the speaker that may be completely disparate from the identity desired by the speaker. This grants the listener an excessive amount of power and diminishes the self-sufficiency and independence of the speaker. This is a technique frequently used to control populations in settings as diverse as schools, prisons and workplaces. Also, according to Pennycook, this technique 'is used in national language policies to extinguish the power associated with politically subversive and inappropriate languages, such as Catalan in Spain or Hokkien in Singapore' (Pennycook, 1994, cited in Gibson, 2004: 4).

After this explanation, the instructor may feature a short video clip to illustrate identity performed through language. There are multiple videos, but an example that has worked well with my students is a fragment of a television vignette from popular African American comedian Dave Chappelle in which he acts as Clayton Bigsby, a blind Black man who is a fanatical supporter of White supremacy. In this excerpt, Bigsby is transported in an old pick-up truck (a representative vehicle of American rural culture) that stops at a traffic light next to a convertible car in which three young White men dressed in urban clothes are blasting Hip-Hop music. Bigsby immediately starts yelling at them, telling them to turn off that music. Before driving away, he yells at them, 'Boogie, boogie, niggers! Boogie, boogie!' Once Bigsby is gone, the driver of the convertible asks his two friends, 'Did he just call us niggers?! ... Awesome!!' and shakes hands with them. After watching this video, the students are asked, 'Why do you think the kids in the convertible car were so happy after Bigsby yelled at them?' Following this exercise using Chappelle's video, the unit concludes with a game. The students are asked to write on a piece of paper, without their partner being able to see it, the name and identity of their partner and what they think their partner speaks (see Appendix B, Unit 6, Slide 5). For the latter, they are given the instruction 'you can define or describe that language as you like'. Next, each student must print their own name, identity and the language they believe they speak. The pieces of paper are exchanged, and discrepancies are compared and discussed with the class, focusing on which aspects of their peers (i.e. language, phenotype, aesthetics, etc.) they used to construct their identity.

I would like to add a parenthesis here regarding the use of the infamous 'n-word' because it appears in the previous example and, with a different spelling to index a different pronunciation, in the following unit. Even this verbal hygienic (Cameron, 1995) act of using the euphemism 'n-word' is very symbolic. I do not want to delve here into the use of this word, but I would like to point out a few issues and a brief reflection regarding its use based on class and life experiences.

First, on the one hand, we should be aware of the difference between using the word and referring to it, and, on the other hand, we should be aware of who uses it, when, where, with whom and with what intention. Despite not being a big fan of John McWhorter, I agree with his argumentation (2021) about the differentiation between using this word versus referring to it, that is, between statement and quotation. As McWhorter (2010: 3) puts it, 'The pretense that referring to the n-word is equivalent to calling someone the n-word is a kind of incivility in itself – abusive, visceral and dishonest'. I also agree with him in how some situations border on the absurd in the different ways some people react when hearing this word. I think that at this point, no one can doubt that this word (notice how I avoid repeating it) has a sociopolitical charge associated with a history of hateful oppression, profit and injustice. This painful past can surface when this word is used to insult or belittle another person, and in this case, I think that most people agree it is never acceptable to use it. However, I believe it is different when quoting it in a, for instance, linguistics class or legal document. Like many other offensive words, the 'n-word' does not have a kind of magical spell power that, when hearing its sound, unleashes uncontrollable turmoil and despair.

Second, nonetheless, many people, Black, White or non-Black/non-White, feel uncomfortable using it under any circumstance. Personally, I avoid using that word, even considering that in NYC, in the context in which I have lived, it was (and still is) commonly used as a term of endearment among Black people, among some Latinos and between some Black people and Latinos, especially within the linguistic market of Hip-Hop. I am still affectionately called that word by many of my Black friends, which does not mean that I use it back. Of course, there are also multiple dissident voices against its use altogether as an endearment, even by Black people. For example, traditional institutions such as the NAACP condemn its use under any circumstance regardless of its pronunciation, and the Nation of Islam encourages young Black youth to use the term *brother* instead because, as this organization claims, you cannot kill a brother. I also have Black friends whom I have never heard say it (at least not in front of me). Nonetheless, most people agree that it should not be used by non-Blacks and should definitely never be used by Whites. Furthermore, some African Americans think the term should not be used outside of the United States by non-American Black people either because they do not share the sociohistorical context in which this word has developed. But these efforts are, as McWhorter (2010) puts it, as futile as banning the color orange. The symbolic capital of using this word in certain contexts – that is, the coolness, slickness and trendiness associated with it – makes its use appealing for youth worldwide regardless of their race (e.g. the use of *nigga* embedded in Spanish as a term of endearment and appellative is becoming normalized among Black and, although criticized, non-Black people in Spain). Personally, I think the use of this word by non-African Americans is kind of embarrassing, as when I hear teenagers repeatedly inserting maniacally the 'f-word' (that is, fuck; not so much discomfort with this one, right?) in their speech to appear older than they are. But that is a personal opinion, not a fact. As a sociolinguist, I recognize the identity processes inherent to it; as a Hip-Hop head, to use this word while not being African American or, in certain sociocultural contexts, Hispanic, feels non-credible, fake. I believe this is the type of informed conversation that we, as educators immersing in these topics, should have before – loud and clear (and I emphasize *before, loud and clear*) – we approach these topics. Otherwise, you may be involved in situations such as the following one.

In a recent sociolinguistics class focused on language and antiracism, I was reported by an anonymous student to an office of equity and diversity on campus. When the representative of this office called me, it caught me completely by surprise. I was astonished and in disbelief. There I was, the instructor of a language and antiracism course, explaining myself to another Latinx working in this office about this complaint. The conversation was awkward, but I explained more or less what follows. Previously to this conversation, a self-identified middle-class Black female student – born and raised in Maryland – from the same course (probably the one who reported me) told me one day, after class, that I should have not used 'that word' in class because 'you are not Black'. The episode she referred to happened after using for instruction purposes (reference use) the aforementioned video of Dave Chappelle. That day in class, we discussed, very similarly as I did in this reflection but not as in-depth as I should have because of my assumptions based on my experiences, the use of, probably, the word with the most racist load in the English language. And this is why we must be on constant guard about issues of locality, culture, language and attitudes and never assume anything in our class-rooms, or at least constantly revise these assumptions. The conversation with this student happened while walking out of class. Previously in class, this student seemed upset after an insensitive comment by a White female student about police brutality and profiling in the infamous city of Inglewood, Los Angeles, being about class, not race. This interaction was during the first semester back to in-person instruction during the COVID-19 pandemic, so students wore masks, and the only way to read facial expressions was through their eyes. In this case, the student rolled and squinted her eyes while the White student commented. During the walk between buildings, I casually asked this student and her White female classmate walking with her to be more open in class. After I emphasized the need to express their ideas in the classroom, to not be afraid to ostracize or make other students feel bad (especially regarding uncritical comments), but instead open avenues to argue in a respectful manner, the Black student told me, 'You should not say the n-word'. I was shocked at first. Honestly, I was not expecting it due to the explanations and content of this class. I was able to react quickly and explain, again (because we already talked about it in class), that I *referred* to the word (once) because I needed it for linguistic purposes, that I thought it was weird to avoid pronouncing a word in a linguistics class regardless of its volatility. I also explained how in NYC (at least 10 years ago), a reaction like hers in a sociolinguistics class with an instructor like me would have been very unlikely but that, likewise, I acknowledged that the socio-political context where she grew up (the DC Metro Area) is very different from NYC. In the latter, I explained to her, it is more common for Blacks and Latinxs to share cultural, social, economic and political spaces (at least in underprivileged areas), while in the DC Metro Area, these social groups seem to have what this middle-class Black student called 'boundaries that should not be trespassed'. I am not sure to what extent this is true, but it seems that that was her perception of her surroundings. Perhaps in inner city areas such as Columbia Heights, these borders are more diffused (see Magro, 2020, for identities among urban Latino artists in the DC Metro Area). Nonetheless, I conciliatorily emphasized that I had just *referred* to the word.

Perhaps I should have been more sensitive to this contextuality if I wanted to avoid this conversation and choose another example. However, the purpose of this class was just the opposite. I believe in facing topics such as this one, especially this one, regardless of the levels of discomfort because we need to avoid falling into belief-based attitudes detrimental to the analysis of and action against linguistic racist practices. Omitting these conversations does not help because through them we can learn from each other's perspectives and thus, through their articulation with theory, create knowledge. I end this parenthesis here, acknowledging that there is much more that could be written about the use of this volatile word and how to approach the matter in academic contexts. My approach, obviously, is not the only way to attend to these issues; it is, rather, an example of how I, as a racialized educator with my particular background, usually approach this issue. Each educator should reflect on these topics before approaching them and figuring out from which angle to tackle them. For further discussion and different points of view on this topic, see, for example, Alim (2009), Asim (2008), Autman (2021), Fong and McEwen (2004), Kennedy (2002), King *et al.* (2018), McWhorter (2021) and Smith (2019).

5.7 Unit 7: Language and Identity: Hip-Hop Language

This unit is based on the work of Alim (2004, 2009), Androutsopoulos (2009) and Cutler (2008). Its goal is to articulate the theoretical aspects of identity seen in the previous unit within a familiar and close context that, at the same time, includes voices that are generally silenced, important alternate perspectives, and non-canonical texts and works of art often ignored or disparaged within academic contexts (i.e. Hip-Hop).

This unit starts with an interactive group activity. The first slide projects a photographic collage including headshots of more than 50 classic US Hip-Hop rap artists (see Appendix B, Unit 7, Slide 1). The Prezi application then zooms in on seven of these faces. After each zoom, the students are asked to identify the race of that artist. This activity aims to emphasize the idea that race and language are not natural entities but social constructs that are dynamic and context-bound. The selected artists in this exercise are Fat Joe (Puerto Rican from New York), Drake (African American father and Jewish mother), Fabolous (of Dominican and African American descent), Foxy Brown (who is of West Indian descent, concretely Dougla, a Caribbean people who are of mixed African and Indian descent), DJ Khaled (son of Palestinians), Pitbull (of Cuban descent) and Eminem (White).

In the case of Fat Joe, those students not familiar with him tend to think that he is White or Latino. This is a good opportunity to talk about, as a group, how Latino/Hispanic is often constructed as a racial category by some and as an ethnic category by others, and the sociopolitical implications of these constructions. Within the Latino/Hispanic ethnicity, practices of antiblack discrimination and pigmentocracy are reproduced in a similar way that anti-Hispanic discrimination is found in US society at large. Additionally, the Puerto Rican community in New York has a long history of discrimination, is constructed as *other* and shares leadership in the foundations of Hip-Hop. Thus, it is not the same to be Puerto Rican in Puerto Rico or in a small town in the Southwest of the United States (in which this community is a minority) as in New York, where Puerto Ricans are the largest Hispanic community.

Students are generally able to identify Drake as mixed ('half Black, half White' or 'half Jewish, half Black') since he is a more mainstream artist and most students are familiar with him. The instructor may use this moment to introduce the 'one-drop rule', a historical colloquial term used in the United States that is deeply rooted in African American folk-lore and a tool of racism. This term is used to classify people with some Black ancestry as Black. It is an example of hypofiliation, that is, the automatic allocation of children from a mixed union between members of different socioeconomic or ethnic groups to the group considered to have the lowest status. Thus, following this term, the children of a Black father and a Caucasian mother, or vice versa, will be identified as Black. This rule included individuals with 1/32 of Black blood (Omi & Winant, 1994).

Fabolous is generally identified as Black. Phenotypically, he has a dark brown skin color, and it would be difficult to differentiate him racially from his African American counterparts in this collage. The instructor may mention that Fabolous could identify himself as Domini-can, especially considering racial ideologies within the Dominican com-munity, which will be covered in Unit 9 (based on Bailey, 2000). Unlike other rap artists who claim their Latinity to appeal to a Latino rap mar-ket (e.g. famous Queens MC, N.O.R.E., whose father is Puerto Rican), he does not claim his Dominicanness publicly either, preferring to be considered a Black rapper and adhere to the US general mainstream (in English) music market. This might be due to the value of being Black in the symbolic market of rap music, where being Black grants capital; it could also be due to linguistic insecurity in Spanish. We can only specu-late, but this speculation relates to theory (see e.g. Magro [2016b] for language varieties' value in the linguistic market of Hip-Hop or Urciuoli [1996, 2008] for linguistic insecurity of second-and third-generation His-panics in the United States).

Foxy Brown, whom students immediately identify as Black or African American, leads the discussion toward the dynamics of racial identity in the West Indies and how these integrate into the US racial context. The instructor may explain how some West Indians see themselves as racially different from African Americans. When Foxy Brown broke as an MC into the – by then mainstreamed – second half of the 1990s rap industry, she did not perform her West Indian (or Dougla) identity. Blackness was one of the main marketing tenets of this emerging mainstream Hip-Hop music industry (see Flores, 2000). However, years later, once her popularity was established, she started to make this identity more salient. She started integrating West Indian and (dancehall) reggae flavors into her music and West Indian linguistic features into her rap while, at the same time, she publicly announced her engagement to Jamaican popular dancehall artist Spragga Benz, thus making herself more appealing to the West Indian audience and, probably, working with the music flavors she

loved, but whose adherence to mainstream Hip-Hop marketing parameters was considered as clashing with the understanding of Blackness by
this industry.

In the case of DJ Khaled, students tend to identify him as Latino. The
instruction may introduce the counternarratives that Arabs and African
peoples, due to the long history of interaction and hybridity in the Iberian
Peninsula, are a heavy component of Iberian people's DNA. Therefore,
phenotypically and aesthetically, Hip-Hop Latinos and DJ Khaled are
very similar. Moreover, he could be considered White in countries such
as Spain, in which otherness is often built based on distance from people
that may look phenotypically (although, perhaps, not aesthetically, linguistically, nationally, etc.) like DJ Khaled.

Eminem is invariably identified as White. However, the following
slide displays two juxtaposed pictures of him, one right after his high
school graduation and the other a current one (see Appendix B, Unit 7,
Slide 2). Eminem's change in aesthetics is noticeable. This observation is
used to compare it with similar behaviors in the context of language, as it
is in the case of Cutler's study, in which Eastern European immigrants in
Queens, New York, forged a non-White identity through the use of what
Alim (2004) defines as Hip-Hop language. The instructor may observe
how Eminem's aesthetic change may respond to a need and/or desire to
represent a Hip-Hop identity, which can be linked to one's agency to portray a desired identity. In this case, the roles of who is the listener with the
power to diminish or grant the self-sufficiency and independence of the
speaker are reverted in the symbolic market of Hip-Hop. As it happens
in this unit's case through styling, the speaker may attempt to display a
desired identity (through language and/or aesthetics) but is the listener
who ultimately decides.

Before moving on, the instructor should briefly explain Hip-Hop and
its elements (B. Boying, graffiti, DJing and MCing) and how it has been
conceptualized in academia. To do so, this unit uses Androutsopoulos's
definition of Hip-Hop as discourse. As seen through the lenses of sociolinguistics and discourse analysis, Hip-Hop is understood 'as a "complex
area of practice" (Fairclough, 1995, p. 185), in which social knowledge
and social reality are produced, reproduced, and transformed through a
variety of technologies' (Androutsopoulos, 2009: 43).

Following this text, the slide poses the following questions: who
stated that Hip-Hop was for everyone? Where and when was this stated?
Below these questions, a row of pictures portrays Black and Latino artists from the Bronx, including Crazy Legs (a popular Puerto Rican B. Boy
featured in the classic film *Beat Street* and member of the Rock Steady
Crew); Zulu Nation creator Afrika Bambaataa; and a picture of a group
of DJs setting up a sound system at a Bronx park in the early 1980s. This
slide aims to promote reflection on the Hip-Hop production locus and
stimulate an understanding of racial hybridity in Hip-Hop origins. This

hybridity was determined by a concrete historical and socioeconomic context and the social actors who performed in it, mainly African Americans, West Indians and Hispanics from the South Bronx.

The next slide explains Alim's (2004) definition of 'Hip-Hop Language' as something that goes beyond verbal art, as the language that the artist uses to perform and through which their identities are negotiated and contextualized. It has roots in African American English and is one of the many African American languages. Furthermore, by using the concept of *Hip-Hop Nation Language* (Alim, 2004), it is argued that Hip-Hop is a universal language, a global language – that is, a language that adopts from the mother culture (global phenomenon) and that adapts to the local (what Pennycook, 2009, calls translocality), but is always in dialogue with the 'mother culture', what Alim calls 'the global imprint'. Using the example of different cities (Paris, Madrid and Monterrey), the instructor discusses this process of adoption and adaptation of language choice (e.g. *verlan* in Paris, which is a form of 'Pig Latin' that includes French and Arabic words backward, or the highly slanged Spanish of Madrid or Monterrey), song topics, cultural references and writing and sampling practices, which adapt to each local social reality.

A concrete example I often use to explain lexical translocation is the discussion of the adaptation of the vocative *nigga* as an in-group form of address in US Hip-Hop to Madrid's Hip-Hop language. This discussion is a sensitive matter for many students, and the instructor may decide to use a different example. However, I consider it important to discuss the sociolinguistic reality with a direct approach that helps us question it, deconstruct it, fight it and alter unjust asymmetric power relationships. Based on Allan (2016), the discussion with the students departs from how this word, for erradicationists of the term, is a slur that discredits, slights, smears, stains and besmirches people of Black African descent, no matter what the context. However, the affective quality of a linguistic expression should never be judged without considering its intended perlocutionary effect within the context in which it is uttered. Within the context of Hip-Hop, this term is often used among African Americans (sometimes, too, among Latinos regardless of their race and even among Whites, as we will see in the following unit) to express camaraderie and belonging. However, the racism deeply rooted and intertwined with US history that this word entails does not have a match in the word *negrata* (probably the closest Spanish translation to the slur *nigger*) or even *negro* (which would be the Spanish translation for *Black*). Thus, one of the more credible terms adapted among Madrid Hip-Hop heads in the 1990s that is closer to *nigga* was *cabrón*, a strong slur with a different (and not racial) negative connotation. Those using the phonetical adaptation of *nigga*, or *negrata*, lack credibility and authenticity and sound like they're trying to imitate something they are not. Thus, they tend to be perceived as portrayers of an inauthentic identity.

This unit may conclude with the following exercise aiming to high-light the dynamism of identities. In pairs, students ask each other what they think is their own racial identity. Then, they would work together to find out different contexts (chronological, geographic or social) in which they think their races would permutate and why (e.g. Rose considers herself Black, but in any West African country she would not because …; or Anthony considers himself White, but a century ago he would be considered Italian and non-White because …).

5.8 Unit 8: Language and Identity: Hip-Hop Language, Brooklyn Style

This unit is an extension of the previous one and aims to dig deeper into how language and identity are intertwined through Hip-Hop lan-guage by using Cecilia Cutler's (2008) study as a research-based example. After explaining this to your students, the first slide reads, 'What in the h… does the last unit have to do with Eastern Europeans?'

In Cutler's study, young (16–18-year-old) Eastern European immi-grants in NYC were confronted with the novel problem of a racialized America because, in their countries of origin, race was not a central aspect of their identities. Thus, the instructor aims to explain what it means to be White in the US based on how Whiteness is constructed: the opposition of White versus (*other*) minoritized racialized groups, i.e. non-White. To do so, the slide displays three sources: 'How Jews Became White Folks and What That Says about Race in America' by Brodkin (1999), who makes a historical review of different groups that at a certain point in the history of the United States were not considered White but now are; Bailey (2000), who investigates the issue of race in the Domini-can diaspora; and Ibrahim (1998), who discusses how Africans become Black once they arrive in Canada. To illustrate Ibrahim's study of race as a dynamic social construct that, regardless of its empirical fragility from the biological point of view, has a rigorous explanatory power from the social point of view (as argued in Chapter 3), the instructor may use as an example Chimamanda Ngozi Adichie's *Americanah* (2013). In this best-selling novel, race is articulated from the point of view of a Nigerian woman who becomes Black only upon arrival to the United States. This is a good moment to let your students from immigrant backgrounds express their perceptions of race and how it was articulated in their regions of origin (or their families) in contrast with US racial identities. When doing so, it is important to be sensitive regarding participation in these issues, since some students from recent migrant backgrounds may not have protected status.

This is followed by an analysis of the covert prestige of Hip-Hop and African American English for White youth as a rejecting mechanism of hegemonic White masculinity (based on Bucholtz, 2001). The slide – titled

'Why Hip-Hop?' – presents the following bullet points aiming to explain why the youth in Cutler's study chose *Hip-Hop language*:

- The defiant symbolism of Hip-Hop is attractive to youth.
- Interest in Hip-Hop from a point of view that considers Black as exotic.
- Hip-Hop as an alternative entry point to American culture.
- The use of African American English to project a Hip-Hop identity.
- Symbolic resistance to processes of racialization.
- Crossing as a tool to explore and embrace new ethnicities (Rampton, 2009).

Crossing may be explained with an example of how, in London, youth of South Asian and Jamaican descent style each other's speech traits (sometimes stereotypically magnifying them) to symbolize camaraderie and in-group belonging.

Before the final discussion, the next slide displays a text over two pictures aiming to explain how the participants in Cutler's study used these Hip-Hop sociocultural styles as:

- Identity act (through crossing).
- Non-affiliation with African Americans per se but indexing their attitudes and qualities through clothing; values such as authenticity/credibility ('keepin' it real'); language, whether verbal (the study analyzes linguistic features as in the monophthongization of /ay/ diphthong in rhyme>/rahm/ or discourse/lexical features such as the use of 'nigga' as an in-group form of address) or non-verbal (e.g. gestures or handshakes); participation and lifestyle; cultural hierarchy that favors Black and proximity to Blacks and Latinos to establish authenticity and participation (girlfriends, friends, etc.).
- Political act to confront preconceived notions of race and language.
- Rejection of racism: resistance to that social categorization, which opens a door for many different identities; different degrees of otherness/affiliation such as attraction to Black culture, negative reactions when considered White (as in the case of the young Bosnian Muslim in this study); reacting against parental racism and distancing themselves from Whiteness because this is linked to racism; projecting a Latino identity (aesthetically).

The first picture underneath this text is a movie poster in which a White Spiderman without his mask stares defiantly at NYC from the top of an uptown skyscraper. The second photo is Ice Cube's *AmeriKKKa's Most Wanted* album cover. In this picture, African American MC Ice Cube appears defiantly on a city street, dressed in black and with a crowd of young Black men dressed in black street clothes behind him fading away on the horizon. Although the analysis of this photographic juxta-position could provide material for a unit in itself, the instructor may use it to illustrate overt and covert prestige and its meaning in the perception of youth in North American cities. Urban youth see themselves more as Ice Cube, despite media efforts to portray a hegemonic image of a young White male with superior capacities controlling the city from above.

The final discussion starts with the following questions to be approached in pairs/small groups: do you think the informants in this study are 'keepin' it real'? How do you think the intersection between the global and the local is manifested in these young people? Have you ever tried to 'talk Hip-Hop'? When and why? After a few minutes, the group shares their thoughts. Due to time constraints, a lot of what could be said in this type of group discussion is going to be left out. However, the goal is to raise CLA and let the students reflect on these issues, regardless of whether they can share as much as they would like to or not.

5.9 Unit 9: Language and Identity, Part 3: Language and Negotiation of Ethnic/Racial Identity Among Dominican Americans

This unit is based on Bailey's 'Language and Negotiation of Ethnic/ Racial Identity Among Dominican Americans' (2000). Its goal is to go beyond hegemonic ideas on race perception in the United States and delve into the role of language as a tool to resist US racial classifications.

First, the instructor introduces the social and historical context in which this study was conducted: a Dominican community in Rhode Island in the year 2000 (see Appendix B, Unit 9, Slide 1). The instructor mentions different aspects that included the sociocultural characteristics of Dominican immigration according to race, such as the fact that African descendants make up nearly 90% of the contemporary Dominican population (Torres-Saillant, 1998: 126); the topic of the construction of otherness among Dominicans (i.e. the Dominican ideology of Haitians being Black while Dominicans are not); US Dominicans' resistance to abandoning the Spanish language (Nguyen & Sanchez, 2001); and the socioeconomic status of Dominicans in the United States (Dominicans are an economically disadvantaged community). Moreover, the instructor will review the history of Dominican immigration, which originated with the consolidation of Rafael Leónidas Trujillo's dictatorship and his violent death in 1961, the subsequent Civil War and American Invasion in 1965, the consequent political instability and the sugar cane industry crisis during the 1980s (Bissainthe, 2003: 128). To conclude this contextualization, the instructor should review some of the racist attitudes linked to inherited hegemonic ideologies, such as Trujillo's idea of 'mejorar la raza' (improving the race). Obsessed with stopping Haitian immigration, Trujillo received Spanish and Jewish immigrants with open arms;

groups that, ironically, were despised and scorned in Europe for their racial characteristics. Trujillo's obsession with racial whitewashing also included his 1937 Haitian massacre, in which between 4,000 and 15,000 men and women of Haitian descent were annihilated at the border. One of the tests utilized by Trujillo's mob to identify their victims as Haitians is a tragic example that exposes how language and identity intertwine. Haitians were forced by Trujillo's men to say the Spanish word 'perejil' (parsley). Haitians, Kreyol speakers, pronounced this word with a uvular trill (like the pronunciation of /r/ in French) instead of with an alveolar trill. Whenever a person had difficulties pronouncing this word, they were immediately executed (Paulino, 2016).

The next slide displays information extracted from Bailey's study (2000). The instructor explains how Bailey used discourse analysis of naturally occurring interactions in a high school to argue that Wilson, a young Dominican American student who was phenotypically indistinguishable from African Americans (both physically and aesthetically), used language to negotiate and resist ascription to totalizing phenotypic-racial categories. Wilson did this inter- and intra-ethnically. By using language in this ongoing negotiation of identity, individual Dominican Americans in the United States contribute to the transformation of existing social categories and the constitution of new ones where they might otherwise not have existed (Bailey, 2000: 578). Thus, Dominican Americans in this study define their race in terms of language rather than phenotype; that is, they speak Spanish, and therefore they *are* Spanish. This logic is accepted as sufficient evidence for both Hispanic and non-Hispanic peers not to categorize them as African Americans. However, it is necessary to highlight that this topic is more complex than it seems. Because Dominican Americans share with African Americans a political and social status characterized by low income, segregated neighborhoods, underfunded schools and a non-White and Afro-descendant phenotype, many of these Dominican Americans strongly identify as African Americans and thus adopt features of African American English. Just like with African Americans, these linguistic practices function as a language of resistance toward the discredit they suffer from the dominant groups in the United States (Bailey, 2000).

Before moving on to the interactive exercise that wraps up this unit, the instructor displays and explains a summary of the conclusions of Bailey's study (see Appendix B, Unit 9, Slide 4). The ethnolinguistic terms in which members of the Dominican community in Rhode Island think of themselves are frequently in disagreement with racial terms based on phenotypes such as Black or African American, which are applied to them by others in the United States. Thus, Dominican American self-definition of race in terms of ethnolinguistic heritage – as 'Spanish', 'Dominican' or 'Hispanic' – challenges the popular and historical US notions of race in which the Afro-descendant phenotype has always preceded all other criteria – such as national origin, language or religion – for social clas-sification. Unlike other Afro-descendant immigrants, who largely merge into the African American population by the second generation, Domini-can Americans, even though 90% of the Dominican population is Afro-descendant, are successfully reversing in many contexts the historical precedent of Afro-descent over ethnolinguistic identity for purposes of social classification (Bailey, 2000: 555).

At this point in the program, most students should have reflected on the idea that race, despite its historical construction as a discrete and static individual attribute, is a situational and dynamic non-discrete construct contested in different contexts. In the case of Dominicans, notions of race do not differentiate Dominicans in the same way that US notions of Black/White do (see Torres-Saillant, 1998). For Dominicans, Spanish is central to resisting this phenotypic-racial categorization that denies them their Hispanic ethnicity. This is a good moment to intro-duce the instructor's own narrative illustrating the dynamic situational nature of identities with an example based on personal experience, or to let the students provide one. An example I used based on my experience (which I already mentioned in section 3.3.1) describes how my identity was constructed by others when I traveled from NYC to Kenya in 2005 with my wife for her friend's wedding (this friend was a Kenyan of Indian descent). Casually conversing with the staff in the Mombassa hotel where we were staying, the hotel pool lifeguard (a Kisii Kenyan) talked about racial classifications in Kenya and how tribal phenotypical differences were evident to him but not to foreigners. After my wife, an African American, asked him which tribe he thought she came from, he could not tell, but he recognized her as 'a sister', while he thought of the rest of the guests as Indian or White. However, he did not place me in any of these three racial groups. He did not identify me as Black or as White. Latino/Hispanic was an unknown ethnic/racial classification for him. However, based on the racial and aesthetic phenotype depicted by reggaetón music videos – a music genre whose main locus of production was Puerto Rico and became popular worldwide in those days – I was racially classified as 'ragatón' (Kenyans' phonetic render of reggaetón) due to my phenotypi-cal and aesthetical appearance, despite my objections (I do Hip-Hop, not reggaetón!).

This unit concludes with a final activity that uses excerpts from Bailey's study. Printouts of these excerpts are distributed among the students (see Appendix D for the selected excerpts). The students read their excerpt in pairs/small groups, discuss it and match it with one of the following categories:

(1) 'Spanish' as identity.
(2) Highlighting facets of identity through language.
(3) Negotiation of phenotype and identity.

(4) 'He is from Haiti'.
(5) 'I never thought you were Spanish'.
(6) 'You don't look like the guy who plays basketball'.

Next, a group discussion starts focusing on what made them choose their match and how language and identity intertwined in their excerpts. To conclude the unit and help settle the topic, the instructor asks one of their students to read the following excerpts from Bailey's study:

- Language is not just a resource through which individuals construct identities; it is also a medium through which sociohistorical relations of inequality and reified, essentialist categories are reconstituted and reimposed. In the excerpts presented here, Wilson's classmates repeatedly invoke his African-descent phenotype, treating it as relevant to his social identity. When Wilson is presented as Haitian, for example, he has some difficulty in convincing another Hispanic that he is Dominican, despite displays of fluent Dominican Spanish. (Bailey, 2000: 578)
- Language is a medium that affords individual social actors the freedom to highlight various aspects of identity; but communicative behavior occurs in a sociohistorical context in which phenotype has been made to matter – and this association of phenotype with social identity is reproduced in everyday talk and interaction, even as social categories are situationally challenged and transformed. (Bailey, 2000: 579)

5.10 Unit 10: Language Ideologies and Attitudes: Linguistic Indexicality and Iconization in Translating 'Teaching Children How to Discriminate'

This unit emphasizes the importance of indexicality and iconization as analytical tools in the process of linguistic differentiation (Irvine & Gal, 2000). Other examples should work, but the analysis used as an example for this unit starts with Lippi-Green's 'Teaching Children How to Discriminate' (1997). In this analysis, I investigated the discursive construction of social stereotypes in the children's animated film *Madagascar* (Dreamworks, 2005). The focus is on the linguistic and ideological strategies used in translating and dubbing the film into Spanish (in this case, for Spain), particularly through two of the film's characters: the lion and the zebra. The latter is played by an African American actor in the US version and an (Afro) Cuban actor in the Spanish version. The goal is for students to raise their linguistic awareness by understanding how language is used to represent and perpetuate hegemonic ideologies that benefit and harm concrete social groups.

To introduce the analysis of the transfer of American children's animated film stereotypes in the process of translation and dubbing prior to the distribution of these films in Spain, the instructor may start by explaining the sociocultural context into which the film is translated. In this case, the context is Spain, a country that, from the 1990s, due to an increase in immigration, highlighted the visibility of new *others* in addition to those historically constructed from its internal (mainly regional) diversity. To identify the ideologies hidden behind the apparently harmless dubbing of these films, the concepts of indexicality and iconization are used as analysis tools (Irvine & Gal, 2000), concepts that will be explained during the presentation.

After this brief introduction, we may engage the group with the following question: do you know any linguistic stereotypes? As usual, the students are allowed a minute to discuss it in pairs/small groups. After listening to a few answers, the first slide presents the theoretical anchor of this unit with the following quote: 'The stereotype is a political fact, the major figure of ideology' (Barthes, 1975, as cited in Lippi-Green, 1997: 79). This quote is followed by a summary of Lippi-Green's (1997) 'Teaching Children How to Discriminate'. In this chapter, she analyzes the use of language in animated children's cinema, concluding that language is used to generate stereotypes and produce a hierarchization of social reality. Thus, linguistic strategies are hidden under the apparently inoffensive voice of an animal. These strategies serve ideologies that link a particular use of the language to the attributes of a social identity. The instructor may use the graphic representation in Appendix B, Unit 10, Slide 2, to explain this relationship.

Next, the instructor explains the phenomenon of indexicality, that is, when a sign points to (or indexes) some object in the context in which it occurs. In the context of this study, we are talking about nonreferential meaning, such as when a speaker's linguistic features indexically signal their race. Then, the instructor explains the semiotic process of iconization, that is, 'the attribution of cause and immediate necessity to a connection (between linguistic and social groups) that may only be historical, contingent, or conventional' (Irvine & Gal, 2000: 37). Since the definition provided by the authors may be complicated for undergraduate students to understand, the instructor may explain it using an example such as the following, from the animated Disney film *Dumbo*. In this film, the African American English linguistic features of the crows represented as 'lazy' and hedonistic are made to be – and are subsequently interpreted as being – iconic of the speakers' identities, therefore associating a 'lazy' hedonistic behavior with African Americans and vice versa. Thus, people who speak like the crows in that movie must be lazy, and the crows must be lazy because people who speak like that are lazy (in this case, African Americans).

Following the explanation of these key analytical concepts, the instructor explains the relevance and consequences of the investigated phenomenon. That is, consequences on the social, emotional and cognitive development of the child population (they learn how to be racist at an early age); linguistic ideologies and postcolonial ambitions linked to a pan-Hispanic agenda (racism and neocolonialism are reproduced within the political project of the Europeanization of Spain, in which Spaniards become the normalized White while Latin-Americanness and Blackness are otherized); and, thinking beyond, the consequences for bilingual/translingual transcultural children of African American and Spanish descent who are exposed to these racist ideologies twice in two different sociolinguistic contexts.

The instructor should double-check whether the students are familiar with the corpus of this study (in my experience, all the students are familiar with *Madagascar*). If so, it is not necessary to explain its sociohistoric context or its plot. Nonetheless, it is important to highlight the economic and mediatic magnitude of this film, which reached millions of children worldwide. This is followed by a presentation analyzing the film's two main characters (Alex the lion and Marty the zebra) and how they were translated and dubbed into Spanish – what they indexed, and what was iconized in these processes.

To do so, the instructor first explains that a semiotic analysis of any given film's plot may offer multiple interpretations. A critical interpretation for the current analysis is that *Madagascar* presents a world in which the social order, the status quo, is established and normalized, contained within a neoliberal social order where everything has its place and everyone plays their role. In this social order, asymmetric power relations are sustained through consensus and the rejection of conflict. Therefore, according to this vision of the social world, it is necessary to remain under some internalized rules, under a 'common sense' system, without thinking of alternatives (in this case, being captive in a zoo). Otherwise, the social actors in this story would expose themselves, as it happens in the film, to the catastrophic consequences of receiving complete freedom when their true natures emerge. Because when this happens in the film and the social actors are presented as fully free, and the system that holds the social order into place – and keeps those relationships of subordination without contestation – fades away, the consequences of (what the scriptwriters believe to be) the natural status quo are amplified. That is, the scriptwriters portray this (believed) natural order with all its power and without any restrictions or rules because, according to the ideology reproduced in the film, we are like this by nature; it's the survival of the fittest, and the lion is, by nature, fitter than the zebra.

Although the lion keeps a privileged position in captivity (because the scriptwriters may have ideologically internalized the concept that he deserves it by natural right, a popular idea), he maintains a cordial 'civilized' relationship with the zebra. The lion does not need to eat the zebra because, in our society, there is a whole industry in place that provides him with steaks without the need for him to hunt and eat his zebra friend. Only 'civilization', that is, a neoliberal society portrayed as captivity in a zoo, can offer a safe and secure natural order of power relationships between the different and diverse social actors without violence. This is imposed by an apparently mutual agreement and consensus by the actors, although it is really imposed by those holding the power to run the zoo. When this system is questioned, disaster occurs. In other words, the film represents an ideology that normalizes the belief that such a system benefits both the dominant and the dominated.

After this semiotic analysis, the instructor argues how these ideologies are iconized in the film through the four main characters. Although all the characters were linguistically iconized through a wide range of linguistic features, Marty the zebra was the more salient case due to the actor's ethnicity and language variety. Although in this section, this analysis is presented in detail for readers to grasp an understanding of the processes that interplay when translating animated films, when offering this analysis to students, instructors should summarize and present the following information however they consider more effective based on time restrictions and the students' level, and adapting the input to the students' linguistic abilities by simplifying/exemplifying the terminology. As in the rest of the units, some content may be explained in the students' L1, and others in L2, but always keep in mind that the outcome goal is for the student to understand this content.

In the original (US English) version of the film, Alex is voiced by the popular comedian and actor Ben Stiller, who describes himself as half Jewish and half Irish Catholic (Wills, 2009). Alex is the most famous animal at Central Park Zoo. Nicknamed the King of New York (a modern version of the king of the jungle, and including the pun of New York City seen as a 'concrete jungle'), he is an urban, civilized, funny-looking version of an animal that in 'real life' is commonly credited with being the fiercest and most dominant of its wild surroundings. Alex loves steaks, but he does not know they come from animals until he is meat-deprived for two days after being shipwrecked on the island of Madagascar. Alex is happy at Central Park Zoo, where he is a star. Thus, when they are shipwrecked, he is the one who most firmly proposes to return to captivity. Alex's language variety is Standard American English (with some dialect features of New York Jewish English), a variety of English associated with White, middle-class individuals. Lippi-Green (1997) already argued that what has been constructed as standard English is used to give voice to main protagonists in animated films playing a positive role. Heroes and heroines have been iconized since the beginning of spoken animated cinema, with attributes such as power or physical beauty, economic, social and/or cultural capital, sexual availability, goodness versus evil and other attributes related to playing a positive role (Lippi-Green, 1997).

In the Spanish version, Alex is dubbed by Sevillian actor Paco León. It can be argued that the choice was made based on how the iconization of a language variety contextualized in US culture – that is, the standard English used by Alex, and the interpretation of the linguistic ideologies that this iconization entails – is translated into Spanish culture.

The American Alex is a sensitive lion, tolerant, friendly, fun, a 'good vibes lion' – not the classic American hero stereotyped as tough, serious, with heroic characteristics, those attributes corresponding with the stereotype of an 'alpha male'. However, Alex does have the potential to be fierce if the boundaries of what is socially accepted are blurred, as when they are shipwrecked in Madagascar.

The Spanish Alex, likewise, is a sensitive, tolerant lion (he can tolerate because he is in a privileged position that grants him the power to tolerate), sympathetic, a 'good vibes' lion. The Alex represented by Paco León does not represent the classic Iberian male stereotype with all the personality attributes that this entails (arrogance, intransigence, explicit nationalism, authoritarianism, machismo, rigidity, rudeness, etc.; that is, the generally traditional version constructed in Spain of a Spanish 'alpha male'). But like the American Alex, he has the ability to be fierce and dominant, and he brings back his privileged dominant authority (granted by nature) when there is a departure from the established social order. Thus, the iconization of the social categories discussed in Ben Stiller's Standard American English finds a parallel in Spain through Paco León's standard (central-north) Spanish and its corresponding iconization. Interestingly, Paco León's native Spanish linguistic variety is Andalusian Spanish, which is a stigmatized/inferiorized variety (Rodríguez-Iglesias, 2016). Nevertheless, his performance of standard (central-north) Spanish is flawless.

Although humorous, these types of roles aim to normalize a certain ideology of what a typical and exemplary Spaniard should be in 21st-century Spanish society, including both flaws and virtues. This particular way of being, this image portrayed of an exemplary Spanish citizen is reproduced in different media – such as television series, entertainment programs, news, sports broadcasts, cinema, theater and literature – in which this language is institutionalized and repeats the same structure, the same meaning and often the same words, turning the stereotype into a political fact, the major figure of ideology, as Barthes (1975) explains. This representation of what it is to be a 'normal' Spaniard is linked to a democratic neoliberal, implicitly nationalist, modern and sensitive personality who rejects conflict, especially violent conflict, but who in his own way is brave, with a certain degree of formal education (although he avoids showing it because it would be associated with pedantry), and always portrayed as sexually attractive and available but with an aura of humility which does not allow him to be conscious of it. All this is iconized through speech, non-verbal language, dress and other symbols that build this identity, this prototype of a modern Spanish male citizen to whom, in Bourdieu's (1991) terms, symbolic capital is granted through its legitimization in mass media.

The linguistic features iconized in these social and personal categories are those of the central-north Peninsular Castilian Spanish used by the middle class (see Hualde *et al.*, 2010), avoiding those traits that diatopically appear in the same regional variety but diastratically are characteristic of the working class: elision of intervocalic /d/ at the end of the word, aspiration of coda /s/, nasalization of /n/, rhotacism and those intonations influenced by regional linguistic varieties used by both national and international migrants that generally compose the substratum of the working classes, mainly Andalusian and Extremaduran Spanish (Hualde *et al.*, 2010). In this regard, the actor is impeccable; he perfectly styles the middle-class center-north Spanish despite being originally a speaker of the Andalusian variety of Seville, as mentioned earlier.

If time allows it, this is a good opportunity to expand on these issues by mentioning how a microlinguistic analysis of an interview, carried out to promote *Madagascar*, reveals that Paco León's daily speech shows those features characteristic of Sevillian Spanish, including aspiration of /s/ coda, rhotacism and seseo. However, while performing the role of Alex, Paco León does not produce any of these features, even differentiating /Θ/ from /s/. However, when humor or ferocity appears (the wild part of the animal), these linguistic features appear. During these moments in the film, the actor relaxes his effort to suppress those 'inappropriate' features characteristic of those less prestigious varieties, thus representing an ideology of linguistic purism and linking the less privileged social classes with the linguistic features that are opposed to what is normalized as speaking Spanish 'correctly', that is, that particular variety of Spanish spoken in the north-central peninsula. The linguistic attitudes toward these southern dialects – and sociolects of the working class – of Peninsular Spanish are negative. This is so despite their covert prestige (Labov, 1972) and is linked to the rejection of those social categories they index: the rural, the marginal urban, lack of formal education, low socioeconomic status and the vulgar. These attitudes are linked to the behavior of the lion when his wild side appears, when he loses control and moves away from the civilized order. Thus, these linguistic features index wild, uncivilized, violent behavior while being associated with these disadvantaged social groups through a process of linguistic iconization. This process is translated from what similarly happens in the US version of the film when Ben Stiller performs an angry wild lion. In those instances, he uses linguistic 'street' non-(White) non-'standard' English features linked to the speech of underprivileged and stigmatized socioeconomic groups in New York, such as working-class African Americans or Latinxs.

Following this analysis, we can look at Marty the zebra. In this case, linguistic ideologies linked to pan-Hispanism, as well as the attitudes toward certain varieties of Spanish and what these varieties index, play a decisive role in the process of iconization. In the original version, Marty is portrayed by the famous African American comedian and actor Chris Rock, who is well-known for his performances in international films and comedy shows, where he displays an excellent command of AAVE (a stigmatized variety of English). A brief semiotic study of the zebra versus the lion shows us an asymmetric status relationship in the animal kingdom between these two animals; lions are dominators while zebras are subordinates. Colloquially, which is how I usually explain it to my students: the zebra is usually portrayed as a somewhat purposeless animal whose main function is to serve as food for the mighty lion, who is portrayed at the top of the food chain. Zebras are simply grazing, doing nothing, unemployed and displaying hedonistic behavior, while the lion reigns over the jungle. Among the connotations that the zebra indexes in this film, we have the following: it is not a donkey or a horse, neither white nor black; motivated by a survival instinct; food for the predators of the savannah, of which the lion is king; driven by the pursuit of a quiet and pleasant life; useless, but sociable and funny. This is how Marty is represented graphically and linguistically (see Appendix B, Unit 10, Slide 5). This character is dubbed by Alexis Valdés, a well-known Cuban comedian. He has a BS in Engineering, and he can speak formal normative 'standard' Cuban Spanish, something that I personally witnessed during an informal conversation with him in New York in 2005. Moreover, Valdés can perform different varieties of Peninsular Spanish, as he demonstrated in his performance in the film *Un rey en La Habana* (2005). However, to dub the zebra, Valdés performs a variety of Afro-Cuban Spanish.

This analysis points toward the idea that the distributors of *Madagascar* in Spain did not hire Valdés solely for his tone of voice, his phenotype or his interpretive and humorous capacity, but for his capacity to perform linguistically an Afro-Cuban identity with all that this identity indexes. In this way, the casting crew for the dubbing of this film demonstrated sensitivity when it comes to recognizing different varieties of American English, at least enough sensitivity to translate Alex using Paco León, and Marty with Alexis Valdés, thus constructing cultural parallels and revealing a problematic element through the use of language and those ideologies that the chosen varieties index. Hence, Alex's use of a 'standard' variety of English corresponds to the central-Peninsular middle-class Spanish styled by Paco León; Marty's AAVE corresponds to Valdés's colloquial register of Afro-Cuban Spanish. This Cuban variety is even stylized by Valdés in an over-performance of these linguistic features to mark its salience (something that is observed when comparing other interpretations of the actor performing a Cuban role) and thus indexing the Blackness of the zebra. Some of these linguistic features are *seseo*, aspiration or elision of /s/ coda, gemination and, more saliently, the characteristic intonation of the Cuban Spanish variety that indexes the speech of Antillean Afro-descent in the Spanish imaginary.

While in the United States, the zebra is Black and the lion is White, in Spain, the lion is constructed as a peninsular 'White' male (constructing Spaniards as White is going to be contingent on the historical and geo-political context), and the zebra as Latin American, Antillean/Caribbean and Cuban, a country commonly stereotypically constructed by Span-iards as a land of 'mulattos'. Moreover, there is a semiotic relationship between the zebra, who is neither white nor black, and the mixed race of Valdés, who is racially categorized by most Spaniards using the rac-ist term 'mulatto' (etymologically, from mule, the animal resulting after crossing a horse and donkey). It should be emphasized to the students how all these social categories are iconized through language and how this iconization links a particular ideology to those varieties of Spanish spoken by Spanish-speaking Antilleans. In a racial spectrum in which racist categories represent a hierarchical order, this otherness is con-structed as the opposite pole to Spain's 'us' in a continuum where other Latin Americans are in between and others are closer to this imaginary 'us', such as some Argentines or Chileans whose countries' populations may be perceived as less 'other' due to their 'Whiter' phenotypes.

Thus, the zebra's speech indexes Blackness, linguistic impurity and the 'other', attributing a negative connotation to it. The iconization of Caribbean Spanish, a stigmatized variety in itself, places it in a relation-ship of subordination and inferiority with respect to the prestigious vari-ety, the central-north Peninsular Spanish, reproducing and perpetuating a circularity. In this circular process, pan-Hispanic postcolonial ideolo-gies create an 'other' in Spain's society (the Latin American immigrant), who uses varieties of Spanish represented as inferior and without sym-bolic capital. This 'other' is inferiorized and, without symbolic capital because they are represented as incapable of speaking 'properly', must be subordinated to the group that 'owns' what is ideologically promoted as the prestigious variety.

Concluding, following Bourdieu's (1991) idea of linguistic markets, *Madagascar*'s writers use the prestige (or symbolic capital) of differ-ent linguistic varieties to perpetuate hegemonies and asymmetric power relationships. *Madagascar* and its dubbed version in Peninsular Spanish exemplify how, in Barthes's (1975) terms, bourgeois society imposes its values through specific cultural materials. To facilitate students' compre-hension, *Madagascar*'s creators created a 'funny-speaking' zebra and a 'normal-speaking', 'well-articulated' lion, and this is how it is intended to be perceived by their young audience. However, these ways of speaking, these linguistic varieties that are linked to very particular speech commu-nities, are iconizing concrete social categories that reflect an ideology of what is to speak 'correctly' or 'normal', and what is to speak 'incorrectly' and 'funny'. By adapting the attribution of these forms of speech as an index of concrete social groups to Spanish society, and by iconizing concrete ideologies with concrete linguistic varieties, Spanish children learn to discriminate as American children do.

Finally, to link these processes of indexicality and iconization to a glotopolitical context, the instructor may explain how these linguistic processes analyzed in *Madagascar* may be rooted in sociopolitical and historical factors. For example, the demographic changes due to an incoming flow of immigrants to Spain during the 1990s turned Spanish society from a relatively homogeneous society into a more heterogeneous one. This factor, as well as Spain's recent acceptance into the European Union (1986), along with a reinterpretation of pan-Hispanism in the neo-liberal economic context – with the commoditization of the Spanish language as (economic and cultural) capital and an instrument of attempted economic expansion and recovery of international status (see Del Valle, 2007a) – has incurred in the development of aggressive ideologies aiming to build and impose a national identity constructed in contrast to the recent arrival of 'others'. Thus, Spanish economic and political elites promote a discursive narrative aiming to portray a more 'European' representation of Spain (Ochoa de Michelena, 2007; Toasijé, 2009) with all the privileges this identity would entail. This agenda would seek to increase the status of a Spanish identity in European and global markets while simultaneously breaking apart from the Africanity of Spain as (historically) self-perceived by Spaniards and perceived by other European nations, with all the negative ideological connotations and stigma unjustly ascribed to this identity (such as phenotypically, aesthetically, economic and cultural underdevelopment). All this will demonstrate to students how language, language ideologies and language attitudes intertwine with politics in concrete ways.

To finish this unit, the instructor will ask students to work in groups to identify and explain a case of racist iconization in an animated film they have watched.

5.11 Unit 11: Language Ideologies and Attitudes Toward Bilingualism

This unit aims to shed light on language ideologies – such as homogeneism (Blommaert & Verschueren, 1998) – and attitudes regarding bilingualism and issues of languagelessness (Rosa, 2019).

The first slide introduces an image of US President George Washington with the following question: what is the official language of the USA? (see Appendix B, Unit 11, Slide 1). Surprisingly, not all students are aware that the United States does not have an official language. To emphasize the political nature of language, we may ask students to browse and discuss the reasons behind the decision of the 'founding fathers' not to establish an official language when building this nation, when the important role that languages have played (and play) in the construction of national identities is widely known.

Usually, students tend to justify this decision with 'the official version', that is, the 'founding fathers' understood it was an issue of individual freedom. After allowing students to provide their answers, we may hear some of them linking this decision to political reasons. If that is not the case, we may remind students of the relationship between language and identity and its importance during the process of nation-state formation, and how the geopolitical situation during the independence of the colonies played a determining role in the 'founding fathers' opting out of an official language. The instructor may explain that colonists came from a varied array of countries, and the American revolutionaries of English descent sought support not only from the German and French settlers in America but also from France and Germany. The Continental Congress even translated key documents into French and German. As it turned out, French and German forces were instrumental in the fight for independence (Marshall, 1986; Ray, 2007).

Next, we may highlight the following two notions to review the relationship between language and identity: the dynamism and dependence in time and place of both the notion of language and identity (that is, the perception of ourselves changes with our community of practice, allowing us multiple identities over the years or even within the same day); and Goffman's (1963) idea of the self as constructed entirely through discourse, thus making our language choices of paramount importance to our identity construction. We may go back to examples from Unit 3 about language standardization in Spain and the role this process played in the construction of Castille and its surrounding kingdoms as a nation-state unit. This is a good moment to ask students to provide other examples of the relationships between language and nation construction.

The following slide presents this excerpt from Gibson (2004):

[Being bi/multilingual] in the wrong languages is seen as an impediment to integration and hegemony, which is equated with harmony, although Phillipson (1999) has pointed out that there is 'no straight correlation between a single language such as English and positive ascriptions such as progress, peace, international understanding, or the enjoyment of human rights.' (Gibson, 2004: 99)

After one of the students reads the text for the class, we ask them to discuss examples in groups to illustrate this fragment. This task is usually difficult for students because of their unfamiliarity with linguistic maps outside of the United States (and sometimes even within the United States). If we need to provide help, as an example, we may talk about the socioeconomic and linguistic characteristics of Switzerland (a multilingual, peaceful and economically developed country) compared to those of Ireland (a relatively monolingual country with a history of violent conflicts and economic struggles). These simplified examples extracted from Phillipson (1999) usually help students to think about similar examples in their contexts.

The following slide shows a glass of water with oil and a text explaining homogeneism (see Appendix B, Unit 11, Slide 4). According to Gibson (2004), this text argued that the United States, a nation of immigrants, has always feared new arrivals (for illustrative examples of the xenophobic history of the United States, see Crawford, 1992; as well as Daniels, 1990; Reimers, 1998; Ross, 1994, as cited in Gibson, 2004). This has been due to the common belief that an increase in the numbers of a group translates into an increase in power, which threatens the status quo established by those groups who had arrived before. Also, Allport's (1979, as cited in Ochoa, 1995: 223) statement is used to explain the relevance of social status in the regulation of prejudice: 'It is not a person's status in society that is important. It is rather the sifting of his/her status upward or downward that regulates prejudice'. This quote is followed by: 'When certain subordinate groups free themselves from a subordinate position imposed by tradition and improve their situation in relation to others, there is most likely conflict' (Allport, 1979: 217, as cited in Ochoa, 1995). These quotes are used to explain how the majority reacts by establishing policies and laws favoring themselves when they perceive a loss of power, such as in the case of English Only policies. The instructor should point out that, although attempts were made from the early days of the republic to standardize the English language in the United States for both practical and lexicographic purposes, 'no movement aimed at making English the official language of the US emerged till 1981' (Ray, 2007).

To illustrate the dynamics of the CLA classroom and how we can integrate students' knowledge into our programs, let us see the following interesting debate that arose between two students during my first implementation of this unit. A Hispanic student (Cecilia) expressed that the use of English in the political-administrative institutions of the United States responded to a practical question rather than a matter of power. Cass, a White female, immediately responded that the issue was not just speaking a single language, but which language was used and why that language and not another. Cass articulated her argument using the United Nations as an example. She explained that in that organization, multiple languages are used as official vehicles of communication. Cass also stated, 'Why can't the same be done in the United States Congress so as not to privilege one group over another?' (Cass, comment in class).

This interaction is also representative of, in the case of the Hispanic student, how a low CLA may drive us to reproduce those hegemonic ideologies that oppress and harm us and, in the case of the White student, how CLA may help us fight injustice and help others raise their CLA regardless of privilege. Since then, I have integrated this discussion into the unit as follows. The instructor may poll the students, giving them the following options: (1) English is used in the political-administrative institutions of the United States for practical reasons; (2) English usage in the political-administrative institutions of the United States is a matter of power. The students are given a few minutes to discuss this in groups before reporting to the class what they thought and why. Additionally, the instructor may explain that approximately 30 states have laws or con-stitutional amendments that establish English as their official language, and both the US House of Representatives (HR 123, 1996, as cited in Ray, 2007) and the US Senate attempted to establish English as the official language. However, although both attempts were successful, they were short-lived due to inaction in the first case, and to the Democratic Party's opposition to Official English and the Republican Party's reluctance to officially associate with Official English in the second (Ray, 2007).

The following slide presents information (based on Gibson, 2004) on the topic of the ideology of English Only in the workplace (see Appendix B, Unit 11, Slide 6). Among the specific ideas to be discussed, it was argued that English Only regulations in the workplace are generally an attempt by employers to dictate workers' identity, as a way to exercise their hege-mony to reshape workers in the image and likeness of the English-speak-ing employer. This attempt implies a belief in a tacit assumption that it is both natural and preferable to be monolingual. Also, this ideology is used as an example of the process of erasure, 'the process in which ideology, in simplifying the sociolinguistic field, renders some person or activities (or sociolinguistic phenomena) invisible' (Irvine & Gal, 2000: 38). In this case, English Only ideology attempts to hide and erase from the social landscape languages other than English and those citizens who use them. The following example by Johnson (2000: 290) may be used:

Work-related language attitudes can also be founded in cultural notions about national, class, or ethnic privilege. Even characterizing the United States as 'an English-speaking country' presumes the privilege of not mentioning that millions of its residents speak languages other than English. A person with this sense of language privilege believes in the right not to be subjected to varieties other than his or her own. The most common example of this occurs in work situations where bilingual or LEP employees choose to use a language other than English in situations among coworkers (for example, speaking Spanish while making sand-wiches at a luncheonette) or with clients and customers who share the same language background (e.g., speaking Mandarin Chinese with cus-tomers in a computer store). The example [of the] Puerto Rican women in a corporate lavatory being shouted at to speak English or go back home shows precisely this underlying attitude of privilege.

At this point, the instructor requests that students provide their own experiences related to this topic. From what I have observed, introducing the instructor's experiences at this point has worked to help students to be more open to sharing their own. The example I used links with the idea of languagelessness (Rosa, 2019). It reflects the underlying linguistic ideologies prevalent in the US public educational system, particularly recruitment methods in English as a second language (ESL) programs in Montgomery County, Maryland, public schools, in which bilingual students are treated as linguistically deficient and incomplete in both languages. During the first month of classes in kindergarten, my daughter, with a Spanish surname and an African American mother, was selected without notifying us, her parents, to take a test in order to explore the possibility of recruiting her for the ESL program – even though at the time, she was a simultaneous bilingual speaker with a verbal competence in English of 96th percentile/superior in the WPPSI-III test, and we had declared in the school forms that her 'language spoken at home' was both English and Spanish. This five-year-old was set apart and taken to a classroom where she was assessed for her English proficiency. Her classmate/ neighbor across the street, a White Canadian-descent girl with an Anglo surname whose parents declared French and English as 'language spoken at home', was not selected to take this test.

A year later, when my daughter switched to a French immersion program in another Montgomery County school, the same procedure took place. In this case, linguistic ideologies influence linguistic educational policies that take into consideration the ethnicity and race of students to judge who has a 'problem'. Ironically, this systematic view of bilingualism as a deficiency that needs to be addressed and remedied instead of a cognitive advantage, as research supports, is, however, viewed by most White parents as an economic and cognitive advantage to further advance their children's education. This is evident when we look at the high demand for admission in immersion and bilingual language school programs by middle-class White parents. The issue is not being bilingual, but rather *who is* bilingual.

This example usually sparks comments from minoritized students. In previous applications of this unit, examples included punishment for speaking AAVE (e.g. an African American student punished during recess in first grade for using 'I ain't' instead of 'I am not') or Spanish (high school Spanish speakers being recriminated and threatened with disciplinary measures for speaking Spanish with each other).

Next, a slide presents the different names this ideology of homogeneism has adopted, plus its goal. Thus, both the ideology of standard language (Lippi-Green, 1997), as well as the monoglottic or monolithic ideology (Silverstein, 1996; Blommaert, 2005), or homogeneism (Blommaert & Verschueren, 1998), are used to refer to those ideologies assuming that monolingualism can exist and, in fact, does exist and is a necessary component for nation construction. In addition, this ideological framework aims to ensure that society returns to an ideal and romantic vision of its pure and harmonious roots. This romantic vision, in the case of the far right, rejects diversity and, in the case of 'mainstream antiracists', accepts diversity under two conditions: it must be limited in numbers (so the White majority remains in power), and it should assimilate to the White majority's norms (Blommaert, 2020a).

Going back to the example in which a language is prioritized over others, the argument is that there is a danger that these other languages (and their speakers) will be silenced both literally and figuratively. Thus, the same slide also displays the following quote by Lippi-Green:

> SLI [standard language ideology] proposes that an idealized nation-state has one perfect, homogenous language. That hypothetical, idealized language is the means by which (1) discourse is seized, and (2) rationalizations for that seizure are constructed. It is also a fragile construct and one that needs to be protected. (Lippi-Green, 1997: 68)

Following this, the instructor explains that a society with a monoglottal ideology not only denies the existence of linguistic diversity within its borders but will also engage in practices that prohibit such diversity (Blommaert, 2005). Within the US context, when English is the only language allowed, other languages – and the cultures, ideas and persons linked to them – are effectively silenced. This argumentation is tied to the following statement by the Federal Commissioner for Indian Affairs in 1887 when he established English Only boarding schools to eradicate the Navajo language and Native American resistance to the United States government: 'Through sameness of language is produced sameness of sentiment and thoughts' (Crawford, 1992: 48) (see Appendix B, Unit 11, Slide 7).

To conclude this unit, the instructor goes over the following idea. When a single language is prized, and society ascribes positive values to it above all others, speakers of devalued languages may be shamed into abandoning their native tongue. In their quest for a more positive social identity, these speakers may decide to attempt to assimilate linguistically, therefore losing a cultural, social and economic resource: being bi/multi/translingual.

5.12 Unit 12: Stigmatization of Hybridity/ Translingualism: The Case of Spanglish

This unit has a twofold goal: to explain what translingualism and hybrid linguistic behaviors are and to unmask the social reasons behind their stigmatization. To do so, the unit is based on the works of García and Otheguy (2014), José del Valle (2014), Otheguy and Stern (2011) and Otheguy and Zentella (2008).

The first slide poses the question '¿Qué es Spanglish?' (What is Spanglish?) on top of a photo and a still frame from a video recording of the late Bronx Latino MC, Big Pun (see Appendix B, Unit 12, Slide 1). After allowing a couple of minutes for the students' answers, a video of a freestyle of the aforementioned MC is projected. During his spectacular freestyle, an (improvised, memorized or a combination of both) rap performance, Big Pun pulls resources from Spanish to rhyme with both English and Spanish words, which is an exemplary case of translingualism. His language choices, AAVE in which an emblematic use of Spanish is embedded, index his Latino identity as understood by Urciuoli (2008) while asserting Latinxs as an undeniable legitimate group within Hip-Hop culture. The participants, well-known African American MCs such as Mos Def, Cannibus or the recently deceased DMX, display admiration for Big Pun's lyrical skills during this cipher (a sporadic and informal gathering where MCs rhyme in turns, trying to demonstrate their rapping prowess over a beat or acapella), including exclamations of amusement during those parts in which Big Pun rhymes using Spanish resources.

Following this video, the instructor offers an analytical explanation of what Spanglish/Espanglish is based on the studies by Ricardo Otheguy. Although Otheguy uses the term adapted to Spanish, *Espanglish*, instead of the commonly used *Spanglish*, I use both terms indistinctively. Nonetheless, I recognize the political implications of using one or the other. The adaptation, *Espanglish*, aligns better with Otheguy's findings, that is, *Espanglish* as another way of speaking Spanish particular to the US context, or 'Popular Spanish of the USA' (Otheguy & Stern, 2011: 86).

Analytically, Espanglish is not a hybrid language, nor a creole, despite what some authors have tried to argue. Espanglish is, rather, a way of speaking Spanish that has an unfortunate and mendacious connotation (Otheguy & Stern, 2008). Building on the authors' argumentation, the instructor explains that the peculiarities of what is known as Spanglish are parallel to those of Spanish used in Spanish-speaking countries. However, US Spanish speakers are stigmatized in society at large (not within the field of sociolinguistics). To prove Otheguy's point, the instructor explains the similarity of the linguistic processes involved in what is understood by society as an aberrant linguistic practice such as 'Spanglish' and 'real' Spanish.

In the case of localisms or the 'local lexicon of Spanish' (Otheguy & Stern, 2008: 88), an array of local terms corresponds to what Otheguy calls their 'neutralizing term' (Otheguy & Stern, 2008: 88). Although the term 'neutralizing' is problematic per se, if we consider the standard language ideology and what it says about 'neutral' language, it is useful for the purpose of proving this point. For instance, *auto, carro, máquina, coche* and *buga* (different words for car) correspond to the neutralizer *automóvil*; while in what is considered Spanglish, *sóbbuey, metro, under, tubo, subte* and *tren* correspond to *ferrocarril subterráneo* (underground railroad).

Regarding lexical doublets, these do not represent a mixture or impoverish the language; on the contrary, they supply needs created by the expansion of physical and cultural borders. Such is the case of *bildin* – 'a somewhat intimidating structure of many stories, like those found in USA cities' – and *edificio* – 'a more modest construction found more often in their homeland' (Otheguy & Stern, 2008: 88). For a Spanish speaker not familiarized with Uruguayan Spanish, the sentence 'un gurí que pide un chop' will not be understood, not due to the accent or the syntax, but due to the localisms *gurí* (kid, from Guaraní) and *chop* (beer, from German). However, there is no discourse around denying Spanish spoken in Uruguay as a different language from Spanish. Moreover, following Otheguy's argumentation, using words with different meanings also occurs outside the United States. For instance, the common uses in US Spanish of *carpeta* (usually the term for *folder*) for *carpet* (usually, *alfombra*), or using *forma* (shape) for *form* (usually, *formulario*) are comparable to the use in Argentina of *coger* as the colloquial term for having sex, when it usually means *to catch* in other Spanish varieties.

Likewise, those terms in which a different morphology strikes the listener and makes him justify the term Spanglish also occur outside the United States. For example, the use of *terapista* (therapist) instead of *terapeuta* or *financiamiento* (financing) instead of *financiación* have a match in the use of *competencia* (competence) and *competición*, accepted in Spanish-speaking countries other than the United States but sounding equally strange for those who have never heard the word with a different morphology before. All these processes have to do with the distinction between system and use, language and speech, a foundational concept of modern linguistics already familiar to students since Unit 1. It is true that some syntactical resources are lost (which also happens to popular Spanish from other places), but this happens, against the common belief, without adding structures from English. Although some structures may penetrate (which also happens in other situations of language contact, e.g. Spanish and Quechua), this is not generalizable to the whole system. Such is the use, for instance, of gerunds as nominals, e.g. *cocinando es duro*, instead of the infinitive, *cocinar es duro*.

Once again, using multiliteracies to legitimize and introduce into an academic context stigmatized forms of popular culture, the following slide displays a juxtaposition of two humorous photos featuring the king of Spain and the Latin rap group from the Bronx, Terror Squad (see Appendix B, Unit 12, Slide 3). Phillip VI exclaims in a comic speech bubble: 'Hay que hablar como yo, ¡joder!' ('You have to talk like me, fuck!', using the lexical feature *joder*, which indexes north-central Peninsular Spanish). Fat Joe, from the Terror Squad, exclaims: 'Nohtro español tá 'truja'o, better speak English' ('Our Spanish is broken, we better speak English', using terms and written the way it would sound when spoken by Nuyoricans). This is used to argue how, from a social point of view, Spanglish is related to a series of ideologies (Otheguy & Stern, 2011). One is the tendency to separate between the different countries, those born in them and those who are not. Another one is the ideology attempting to separate the different social classes, whose language varieties are acceptable, 'good' and valid, who is allowed to be bilingual and who is not. Lastly, that ideology, which, by connecting to the ideological North American tradition established during the 1950s of denigrating Spanish-speaking immigrants whose language varieties do not reflect the norms of north-central Spain, denies the US Spanish speaker a cultural, social and economic resource: Spanish language in general. Nonetheless, it can also be argued that, despite the efficiency and precision of Otheguy's analysis, reputable authors such as Ana Celia Zentella (1981) defend the use of the term Spanglish as a source of empowerment for a population whose hybrid linguistic behaviors have been historically stigmatized and linked to social class and race in mainstream culture. It is important to emphasize that what some people refer to as Spanglish is, on the one hand (as Otheguy points out) popular Spanish of the United States, while on the other hand, it refers to hybrid linguistic practices which more recently have been conceptualized as translingualism (Canagarajah, 2011; García & Otheguy, 2014).

Thus, the next slide (based on Gibson, 2004) explains that in bilingual settings, the language of racialized minority groups is analyzed as having two components: the 'us' code versus the 'them' code (Gumperz, 1982; Lambert, 1972, as cited in Zentella, 1990), or following Valdés (2000), the high versus low language. Following this traditional explanation, it can be said that the minority language, the 'low language', represents intra-group discourse, connotes intimacy and is mainly confined to the context of the family/home because it suffers from a lower prestige than the 'high' code. The latter represents the most powerful group and is associated with wealth and status, which is related to what is known in sociolinguistics as diglossia (Fishman, 1967) (see Appendix B, Unit 12, Slide 4). Exposing this is not enough. The instructor should ask the students who is profiting from and who is harmed by this sociolinguistic order.

The following slide argues, first, how from an insider point of view (in this case, the US Spanish speaker), Spanish speakers may use Spanish to index themselves as different from the dominant group while simultaneously creating camaraderie with other Spanish speakers. These linguistic choices occur in certain situations and even within conversations. The instructor may explain this through an example in which Latinxs talking within a group that includes English speakers use Spanish to index their Latinx identity, camaraderie and solidarity and connect with other Latinxs within the group through different hybrid linguistic practices. Likewise, the instructor may explain how the use of hybrid linguistic behaviors may be both inclusive and exclusive, and it is useful to create meaning around the idea of 'us' versus 'them', since outsiders cannot easily share in these linguistic practices. To insiders, this is a legitimate form of communication with its own unconscious rules and forms, which serves as an important identity marker for the Spanish-speaking community. As in any speech community, it is a dynamic, evolving symbol of solidarity (Mar-Molinero, 2000: 175).

However, from an outsider's perspective, these hybrid linguistic practices or popular Spanish of the United States may be understood as a deficiency to speak English (or Spanish, or both), while the insiders may see it as representative of their US Spanish-speaking identities. The slide projects the following statement by Morales (2002: 3): 'Spanglish is what we speak, but it is also who we Latinos are, and how we act, and how we perceive the world'. Moreover, we can argue that so much of the discussion of multilingualism assumes that the speakers are equally proficient in all languages. But for many of these speakers, although they have at least a fundamental proficiency in English (or Spanish, if English is their first language), they are not comfortable with the language. Although able to create 'grammatically correct' utterances, they cannot fully express themselves and create their desired identity. To do so, they may rely on their primary language because it is a quicker and more effective communication tool, or as in the case of Big Pun, in the secondary language, since this allows them to mark a desired identity.

To conclude this presentation, the instructor may display and emphasize the following statement: 'For many, language is not a uniform that can be put on when they arrive at work and removed at the end of the day, but is integral to their being, in the way that religion or political affiliation is to others' (Gibson, 2004: 5–6). Spanglish/Espanglish is a way of speaking and a matter of identity. To finish the unit, the students compare their attitudes toward Spanglish before and after this presentation.

5.13 Unit 13: Language Ideologies: Hispanophobia

This unit is inspired by Cobas and Feagin's (2008) 'Language Oppression and Resistance: The Case of Middle-Class Latinos in the United States' and Gibson's (2004) 'English Only Court Cases Involving the U.S. Workplace: The Myths of Language Use and the Homogenization of Bilingual Workers' Identities'. The term Hispanophobia was proposed by Zentella (1997, as cited in Gibson, 2004). With a humorous tone, this unit aims to seek two outcome goals. First, to tinge the theoretical priming made during this program to expose more explicitly how linguistics connects with politics, which specific groups profit from linguistic ideologies and which ones suffer from them. Second, to exemplify how language practices, discourse, attitudes and ideologies can be both a mechanism of oppression and a tool of resistance through the analysis of those strategies utilized for both purposes.

To contextualize this unit, the first time I conducted it, the cover of the visual presentation projected in the center a comic image of the, back then, controversial entrepreneur and presidential candidate Donald

Trump (see Appendix B, Unit 13, Slide 1), which sparked some laughs and jokes from the students and generated a relaxed class environment. The pun was intended, since he exemplifies political opportunism, media guile, bigotry and racial and ethnic prejudice. Days before this presentation, he made his emblematic statement about Mexican immigrants: 'When Mexico sends its people, they're not sending their best. [...] They're sending people that have lots of problems, and they're bringing those problems with us. They're bringing drugs. They're bringing crime. They're rapists. And some, I assume, are good people' (*Time Magazine*, 2015).

The next slide argues how Latinx population growth has become a cause of worry for many White Americans, and even other minorities influenced by this ideological framework which perceives this growth as a threat, as the death of the 'American way of life' and English language (see Appendix B, Unit 13, Slide 2). This White discourse, heavy in rhetoric but short on evidence, masks an effort to keep the preeminence of the dominant group's language over Latinxs and thus supports Whites in maintaining their political and economic supremacy (Cobas & Feagin, 2008). Among proponents of this discourse, the now-defunct, influential Harvard University political analyst Samuel Huntington overtly accused Latinxs of being a threat to democracy and the American way of life (Huntington, 2004, as cited in Cobas & Feagin, 2008). The instructor may discuss the effects of the phenomenon known as fear of the 'browning of America' and Leo Chavez's (2008) concept of 'the Latino threat'. The Latino threat narrative perceives Latinx groups as a dangerous invading force, a constant in both pre- and post-9/11 public discourse, which has increased fear among the White American population regardless of social class. Thus, many monolingual English speakers grant English the capacity of being a symbol of the 'American way of life' because they believe that allowing immigrants to use their native language(s) allows them to reject the 'American values', which will endanger their vision of the United States as a (mainly White) nation.

As a result of this widespread belief that linguistic homogeneity is the best way to achieve a harmonious society, racialized minority languages such as Spanish suffer disapproving public attitudes (Lippi-Green, 1997), and Latinxs are constantly pressed to assimilate or return from whence they came. Supporting materials for the instructor that dig into the historical causes and consequences of the development of this fear and its political roots may be found in Massey and Pren's (2012) study. Massey and Pren explain what happened after 1965, a year often cited as a turning point in the history of US immigration because of a change in policy that resulted in increased immigration from Latin America and Asia. However, due to this change in border policy, the population of unauthorized immigrants from Latin America also rose from nearly zero to 80% of the total in 2012 (Hoefer *et al.*, 2011; Wasem, 2011, as cited in Massey & Prenn, 2012) due to 'a complicated tale of unintended consequences, political opportunism, bureaucratic entrepreneurship, media guile, and most likely a healthy dose of racial and ethnic prejudice' (Massey & Prenn, 2012: 1).

The following slide focuses on the response to this fear by Whites: the racialization of Latinxs/Hispanics and their language while attempting to demean the importance of their language and link it to low intelligence and untrustworthiness (Urciuoli, 1996; Santa Ana, 2002, as cited in Cobas & Feagin, 2008) (see Appendix B, Unit 13, Slide 3). The instructor may highlight that not all White people respond this way and, unfortunately, some racialized minorities also fall for this hegemonic response, including some Latinxs seeking assimilation and/or deploying fractal recursivity (Irvine & Gal, 2000). Nonetheless, Spanish speakers are portrayed in mainstream media and are perceived as the last immigration wave threatening the security of White America, regardless of the irony that 'the exploration of America by Spanish Europeans [has been documented] long before White Europeans' (Castellanos, 1992, as cited in Gibson, 2004); and the greater part of the current US territory was part of the Spanish Kingdom and, later, Mexico until the mid-19th century (Gutiérrez, 2009). The instructor may introduce the counternarratives normally excluded from popular discourse that Latinx culture has been part of 'America' longer than the United States has existed and that, 'whether it is the cowboy icon, mustangs, barbecue, dollar sign, law, or Texas chili', understanding the Latinx experience and the Mexican American heritage is essential for understanding the roots of America's ethnic and racial minorities (Guevara Urbina & Álvarez Espinoza, 2018: 6).

Nowadays, migration, in contrast with previous waves, is seen as an 'aberrant form of human behavior' (Blommaert & Verschueren, 1998: 118). When confronted with neighbors who do not sound/look like them, they must assimilate or return from whence they came (Cobas & Feagin, 2008). This argumentation is followed by the depiction of a photograph of Susan Tulley, a White Southern California resident and President of the Citizen's Committee on Immigration Policy, and her following statement:

> Your heart goes out to people who are just seeking a better way of life. We do have an obligation to help Mexico develop. I'd rather do that than say all you people come here and become my problem. I'm willing to give money to my church to build houses in Mexico. But I'm sick to death of my own children competing in the classroom for a decent education. (Maharidge, 1996: 163, as cited in Gibson, 2004: 9)

Then, the instructor offers Gibson's argumentation:

> Tulley believes Mexican children are receiving an unfair share of the decent (apparently finite) education earmarked for her children, and that

their parents are a burden she must shoulder. It would be much easier to send money through an intermediary and wipe her hands clean, though one has to wonder why she is more comfortable aiding those unknown and far away than her children's classmates. The fear that Spanish speakers are taking away something that rightfully belongs to the English-speaking majority is common across the country. (Gibson, 2004: 9)

This is followed by a humorous photograph of a smiling young Brown boy with a T-shirt reading 'Deport Racism 2016', holding a sign reading 'Deport This' in his left hand and giving the finger with his right under the last sentence of Gibson's previous fragment (see Appendix B, Unit 13, Slide 4).

The next slide, titled 'Resistencia through language' (resistance through language), presents Cobas and Feagin's (2008) findings (see Appendix B, Unit 13, Slide 5). Using different strategies, Latinxs often resist attempts to squelch their language despite their disadvantage – which stems from the power of Whites – in the US linguistic market. When Latinxs are asked to stop speaking Spanish in public spaces on the grounds of being out of place, Latinxs often resist and respond by asserting the legitimacy of their language. Based on Cobas and Feagin's (2008) findings after interviewing 72 middle-class Latinxs in seven different US states, the instructor presents the five main strategies deployed by White people to discourage the use of Spanish by Latinxs and their resistance against such discriminatory, linguistically restrictive and oppressive practices:

(1) Silencing Spanish speakers: outright commands to Spanish speakers to speak English.
(2) Voicing suspicion: protestations that when they speak Spanish Latinxs are talking about Whites.
(3) Doubting English proficiency of Latinxs: skepticism about English proficiency of Latinxs despite evidence to the contrary.
(4) Denigrating the accent: mocking Latinxs' 'accents'.
(5) Ignoring Spanish speakers.

The instructor may offer examples based on her/his personal experience related to one or more of these strategies. Two examples I commonly use are: (1) a few times when my kids and I were interacting in Spanish in public spaces, someone made a denigrating comment loud enough to be heard; as a resistance response, we spoke louder and joked about the racist in Spanish; (2) while studying my master's in education, an elderly White female professor, consistently grading Latinx students' papers lower on the grounds of English grammar issues or plagiarism, was exposed as the racist she was when one of the Latinx students complained – with his *New York Times* journalist credentials in hand (he was an English speaker who did not speak Spanish but had a Spanish name and phenotype). Cobas and Feagin (2008) explain that Spanish is constantly ridiculed by influential Whites calling for stricter control of Hispanic immigrants. Along with this practice, the use of Mock Spanish in asymmetrical power relationship daily interactions is also explained. For example, interactions between White restaurant managers and Spanish cooks, or the ex-president of the United States, Donald Trump, and his subordinated hearers (such as in his frequently used 'bad hombres'), are examples of another extended and common practice among Whites who feel entitled to embed terms in Spanish (with English-influenced pronunciation) within their speech as an assertion of power over their Latinx interlocutors (Barrett, 2009).

Before finishing the presentation, the instructor may explain the following statement by linking it to the idea of hegemony:

> There are no signs of surrender to Whites' anti-Latina discrimination despite their limited resources compared to their White antagonists and despite the fact that ideological elements emanating from the dominant culture may mask for some Latinxs the structural basis of their victimization and thus interfere with their ability to see the systemic structure of their oppression. (Cobas & Feagin, 2008: 408) (see Appendix B, Unit 13, Slide 6)

This unit ends with an exercise in which students identify and match the five aforementioned strategies used by Whites to squelch Spanish to five excerpts of Cobas and Feagin's interviews (see Appendix E).

5.14 Unit 14: 'Appropriateness' and Stigmatization of Linguistic Varieties: Talking Hip-Hop

This unit draws mainly on 'Talking Hip-Hop: When Stigmatized Language Varieties Become Prestige Varieties' (Magro, 2016b), a study on language attitudes in New York City toward Spanish heritage language in an urban context characterized by inequity. In the context of Hip-Hop, this study's results suggest that the stigmatized vernacular variety becomes the prestige variety. This unit has a twofold goal. One is to develop awareness about language attitudes, understood as 'any affective, cognitive or behavioral index of evaluative reactions toward different language varieties of their speakers' (Ryan, 1979: 7), the intricacies of appropriateness (Leeman, 2018) and languagelessness (Rosa, 2019). The second is to introduce students to innovative mixed methodologies in social sciences in general, and sociolinguistics and the field of linguistic attitudes in particular, through the methodology employed in this study: a matched-guise technique with rap followed by a semi-structured interview.

In 'Talking Hip-Hop: When Stigmatized Language Varieties Become Prestige Varieties' (Magro, 2016b), the theories of language stratification and the concepts of overt and covert prestige (Labov, 1966) are drawn on to study both attitudes and linguistic ideologies. In sociolinguistics, prestige is the respect granted to a specific language variety within a particular speech community in relation to other varieties. Labov's theories explain that prestige can be separated into overt prestige and covert prestige. Both are used when changing speech to gain prestige but do so in different ways. Overt prestige is linked to the linguistic practices of the culturally dominant group. Covert prestige is related to membership in an exclusive speech community, rather than in the dominant cultural group. For example, using inner-city language varieties with covert prestige, such as some varieties of AAVE, would grant more 'street cred' than those with overt prestige, such as academic English. Even though the dominant cultural group generally sees the variety with covert prestige as being inferior, using language fitting with the local community would lead to earning respect among those members of the community too.

As Leeman (2018) recommends, instructors should have a solid understanding of the dynamics of appropriateness in academic contexts and be aware of expansionist models, particularly in Spanish HL classes, because these tend to rely on 'appropriateness'-based accounts of sociolinguistic variation (Leeman, 2018). This is a topic greatly discussed among both educators and students and which, in my experience, generates anxiety and dissonance. Such accounts validate non-standard varieties and practices but relegate them to specific settings, such as daily interactions with family or friends. Meanwhile, in academic/professional settings, only the standard variety is considered appropriate under this perspective.

Thus, the instructor must be aware that this is not an issue of different varieties being appropriate for different settings, but the elevation of a variety while demoting and denigrating others and, consequently, the people who speak them (Leeman, 2018). In the same vein, we, as critical educators, must reconsider commonly used analogies such as wearing a bathing suit to a formal wedding when discussing the use of non-standard varieties in academic/professional settings in terms of 'formality'. As Leeman explains, this type of analogy, and the representation of language variation that they embody, portray students' home varieties as simply informal ways of speaking rather than stigmatized varieties, simultaneously ignoring their association with specific social groups. Thereby, negative ideologies that inferiorize non-standard varieties and the people who speak them (representing them as backward and unintelligent) are erased. Like a wolf in sheep's clothing, these approaches to language variation avoid, even denounce, labeling non-standard varieties 'incorrect' or 'unacceptable'. Instead, they attempt to offer a 'neutral' descriptive account of the distribution of varieties by domain, while they only admit standard varieties as valid in academic/professional domains, which are considered high-status domains (Fairclough, 1992b; Villa, 2002, as cited in Leeman, 2018). As a result, users of standard varieties are legitimized in these contexts, while speakers of other varieties are effectively silenced and limited in their access to social and economic power. As a gate-keeping mechanism, this determines who can speak and be heard in high-prestige domains (Fairclough, 1992b, as cited in Leeman, 2018).

But who determines what is appropriate? Are appropriateness norms universally shared? Answers to these questions will highlight issues of power instead of avoiding or eliding them. These questions will also grant agency to speakers in making linguistic choices and, thus, amplifying their possibilities of resistance through linguistic practices. These discussions provide opportunities to challenge notions of appropriateness as part of a fixed sociolinguistic order with which speakers must comply, acknowledging that this order is historically contingent, socially constructed, imposed, accepted as normal and subject to a change in which the student may play a fundamental role.

Likewise, the concept of languagelessness (Rosa, 2019) will allow the instructor to understand and raise linguistic awareness about linguistic attitudes toward bi/multi/translingual speakers depending on their ethnoracial background. While mainstream students who are speakers of the standard variety and can speak more than one language (or language variety) are perceived positively, heritage speakers (or speakers of varieties other than the standard) are seen as incomplete speakers of both the standard and non-standard varieties (see Unit 11: Language Ideologies and Attitudes Toward Bilingualism, in this book).

This unit starts with a slide introducing the goals, methods and theoretical anchor of the study utilized for this unit. Thus, the instructor explains the concepts of overt and covert prestige (Labov, 1966) and the conclusions drawn from García (1988), Zentella (1990), Urciuoli (1996, 2008) and Del Valle (2007b), who argued that Spanish-speaking student youth – mono- or bilingual and belonging to the less privileged socioeconomic strata of New York – perceive their variety of Spanish as less prestigious compared to that imposed in formal/academic contexts following a standard language ideology (Lippi-Green, 1997). At this moment, the instructor may ask their students to discuss in small groups the following questions: do you think that the language variety you speak at home would be valid in this academic context? Why? Do you think the variety you speak in this academic context would be valid at home? Why?

The next slide introduces and describes some of the characteristics of the language varieties of Spanish utilized for this study (see Appendix B, Unit 14, Slide 3). On the one hand, those varieties of Spanish that heritage students – not necessarily being literate in Spanish – brought from the realm of everyday life and family have different dialect features depending on the country of origin. Furthermore, these heritage (or legacy, as I like to call them) varieties also have diastratic features, particular to the socioeconomic and cultural conditions in which these speakers live.[5] It was explained that for methodological reasons, only speakers of varieties of Dominican Spanish from New York were selected for this study in order to have a more homogeneous group in terms of their diatopic features than if there had been students from different national origins. However, it was detailed how these varieties from different national origins coexisting in NYC share what Zentella (1990) has called the interdialect of New York Spanish. In addition, following Otheguy (2011), it was explained that these varieties habitually coexist with English – the language of formality, education and professional contexts – in a situation similar to diglossia (Fishman, 1967), in which Spanish would be the Low variety (the least prestigious, the subordinate) and English the High variety (the most prestigious, the dominant). The explanation goes on to argue that the use of Spanish in public spaces (generally the use of these stigmatized varieties) connotes solidarity and camaraderie among its speakers (Barrett, 2009; Gibson, 2004), which is a practice shared by other discursive communities of other languages, such as the use of AAVE among certain African American communities (Rahman, 2008).

On the other hand, the instructor describes what is understood by Standard Spanish in this study. What is understood by Standard Spanish has different features depending on the region where it is constructed (e.g. academic Spanish used in Peru, Spain, etc.). However, these differences tend to be limited to a few regional dialectal features, such as the use of *vosotros* instead of *ustedes* for the second-person plural subject pronoun in Spain, *voseo* (the use of *vos* instead of *tú* or *usted* for the second-person singular subject pronoun in the Southern Cone and different areas of Central and South America) or the use of /θ/, for instance. Apart from these few differences, these varieties tend to be homogeneous across regions because they are part of a standardized code (the instructor may point out how this relates to Unit 3 and the process of linguistic standardization). Moreover, from a diastratic perspective, regardless of the regional substrate, these varieties index middle-class speakers with formal education. Although the study could have chosen any other, it chose a central-Peninsular variety of Spanish for two reasons: the voice utilized for the matched-guise technique was able to interpret this variety naturally (facilitating the methodology) and, of all the standard varieties of Spanish, due to inherited linguistic ideologies, this variety is perhaps the one that most indexicalizes standardization and accuracy (something that, as explained later, was reflected in the responses of the participants in this study).

To argue how language choices serve as pragmatic tools, instructors can highlight the relevance for this study of how discredited vernacular varieties are used in cultural practices associated with Hip-Hop, creating a space where language transmits identity, affiliation, solidarity and representation of familiar and affective proximity. Based on Flores-Ohlson (2009, 2011), who argues that the use of Spanish in bachata songs is used to express emotional proximity, while the switch to English is used to express detachment, standard varieties of Spanish among heritage students would play a similar role to that played by English in code-switching with Spanish: emotionally distancing the interlocutors.

The next two slides the instructor presents are, first, the hypothesis of this study – in the context of Hip-Hop, the stigmatized vernacular variety becomes the prestige variety – and second, the pedagogical implications for future studies. These pedagogical implications include the effects that CLA pedagogical strategies could have on the psychosocial problems that legacy students usually face, such as linguistic insecurity, low self-esteem and abandonment of Spanish (Urciuoli, 2008; Del Valle, 2007b). It is then argued that, based on the conclusions of this study, it could be beneficial for heritage students to insert into the classroom a discourse about language focused on pointing out the construction mechanisms of language prestige and discrediting. That is, to emphasize what we are trying to make our own students aware of through these SPC units: the socially constructed nature of prestige and how it is not something 'natural' or 'inherent' to any language variety. Another implication that the instructor may discuss is the possible use for pedagogical purposes of their language varieties through cultural materials socioculturally close to the students, as Hip-Hop is in the case of this study, and how all this influences students' motivation. A positive attitude toward language influences motivation, and motivation is linked to the desire to keep learning a language, thus influencing language proficiency (Masgoret & Gardner, 2003; Dörnyei & Ushioda, 2013).

Due to time constraints, the instructor may summarize the methodology of this study. The participants' characteristics may be synthesized as first and second migrant generation Spanish speakers, with different skills in English from very limited to fully bilingual, and taking Spanish in a heritage speakers' class in a New York City public university. Although the Spanish-speaking communities with the highest representation in New York, according to Otheguy (2011), are Puerto Rican, Dominican, Mexican, Cuban, Colombian and Ecuadorian, this study selected only students of Dominican origin because it greatly simplified the methodology and is, after Puerto Rican (which does not need to go through the migratory status process), the second largest Spanish-speaking group in New York. In addition, the study followed the post-stratification variables chosen by Moreno-Fernández (2007): participants between the ages of 18 and 31, of both sexes, of the first and second generations of immigrants and whose parents' socioeconomic levels were low or medium. Aside from these characteristics, these informants had an affiliation or, at least, extensive knowledge of Hip-Hop culture due to the popularity of this culture among the most economically disadvantaged youth in New York.

Linking what was shown in Units 7 and 8 concerning Hip-Hop language, the instructor may highlight how Hip-Hop in Spanish adopts and adapts New York Hip-Hop elements to the Spanish speakers' cultural context and their identity, a global phenomenon based on authors such as Alim (2009), Condry (2001), Pennycook (2007) and Terkourafi (2010). At the time of this study, there was a vibrant Hip-Hop circuit among Spanish artists. As in every local Hip-Hop community, the artists affiliated with this circuit in NYC have created a translocal style community, part of the stylistic whole that Alim (2009: 106) has called 'Hip-Hop Nation Language'. The instructor may review this concept, previously seen in Units 7 and 8:

> Hip Hop style does not impose a homogenized 'one-world' culture upon its practitioners' rather 'the global style community of Hip Hop is negotiated not through a particular language, but through particular styles of language, and these styles are ideologically mediated and motivated in that their use allows for a shared respect based on representin [*sic*] one's particular locality.' (Alim, 2009: 111)

The importance of the idea of authenticity in Hip-Hop (Terkourafi, 2010) and how it is related to linguistic varieties may also be commented on, describing Hip-Hop as 'a culture of being true to the local, of telling it like it is' and 'the constant pull towards localization that this implies' (Pennycook, 2007: 14). Furthermore, these 'street varieties' or 'resistance vernaculars' (as described by Potter, 1995) have achieved recognition and obtained symbolic capital, becoming the variety of prestige, the valid vehicle of expression in Hip-Hop (Potter, 1995). Thus, the use of vernacular varieties in rap could be understood similarly to how Spanish is used as a resistance tool in the public space of the United States. In this sense, Cobas and Feagin (2008) explain how Spanish is used to resist the groups and social values that the standard variety represents. These standard varieties, imposed by a small sector of society (Dorian, 1994, as cited in Cobas & Feagin, 2008), would represent the antagonist values of Hip-Hop as the dominated social group and popular/working-class culture Hip-Hop is.

This last statement may be seen as an uncritical idealization of Hip-Hop and, if time allows, the instructor may discuss the topic of what is understood by Hip-Hop. My 'intention is not, and cannot be, to establish what Hip-Hop is and what it is not' (Magro, 2016b: 18). But my views on Hip-Hop may be useful for instructors not familiar with this insider's view, not only for this unit, but also for future discussions that may arise around the topic of cultural and/or linguistic appropriation, authenticity and Hip-Hop:

Since its origins, especially in the case of rap (but also in Graffiti and Breakdance), there has existed both a collective and individual consciousness which has distinguished between real Hip-Hop artists and 'sell-outs' (those who drop out and betray the ideological values of Hip-Hop because of business goals, whether or not they are met). Already in 1979, The Sugar Hill Gang appropriated and sold the popular raps written by renowned MCs from the emergent Hip-Hop scene of the Bronx, such as Grand Master Caz, to record them and turn them into the prefabricated commercial success that was Rapper's Delight. Although the festive and popular elements have been constant themes in Hip-Hop culture, also, since the beginning, Hip-Hop has had a vindictive element of political and social commitment. In the late 1970s, the Universal Zulu Nation organization made this element explicit, calling for unity, peace, and love as a form of resistance to racism and marginalization suffered by young people from underprivileged neighborhoods in NYC. Many other artists, especially in the late 1980s and early 1990s, proposed more aggressive models of social activism and resistance in their productions. Regardless of the style or political position taken by the Hip-Hop artist, authenticity is the main concept that awards credibility to Hip-Hop productions. An important aspect of this authenticity is the socioeconomic background of the artist. In this sense, the Hip-Hop locus of origin and production is located undoubtedly in underprivileged neighborhoods, regardless of the contradictions that may arise in its artistic content. (Magro, 2016b: 18)

Next, the instructor may finish synthesizing the methodology of this study by playing two of the tracks used in the matched-guise technique and briefly contrasting some of the linguistic features that differentiated the two varieties of Spanish (see Appendix B, Unit 14, Slide 7).[6]

The results of the investigation are presented in the next three slides (see Appendix B, Unit 14, Slides 8, 9 and 10). In addition to confirming the hypothesis, the qualitative results (obtained with the interview) are far more illuminating than the quantitative results (obtained with the matched-guise technique). Another interesting outcome of the investigation was that the participants showed awareness of their use of Spanish and its different dialects, sociolects and registers. The conclusions are summarized in the final slide (see Appendix B, Unit 14, Slide 12) and commented on with the students in a brief question-and-answer session.

Finally, as this is the last unit, the instructor may include the following activity, or conduct it in the next session by itself as a final activity for this program. The instructor displays a fragment of Netflix's episode four of *Master of None* (Ansari & Yang, 2015). This excerpt humorously exemplifies linguistic attitudes and ideologies toward South Asian English (spoken by Hindus, Pakistanis, Bangladeshis and others) in the United States. The strategies that the protagonist of Hindu origin uses to resist these ideologies and attitudes, which result in the protagonist losing a much-needed acting job, unleash fun conversations between the protagonist and his actor friend, during which they reflect on the topic of linguistic iconization and erasure. To finish the program, the students reflect in an open discussion on how the issues examined during the SPC units (language, identity, power, stigma, prestige, iconization, erasure, etc.) are represented in this TV excerpt and what can be done to eradicate racism in TV series and films.

Notes

(1) In my doctoral dissertation, the reader will find a detailed account of how I negotiated and navigated with my department and my students the obstacles to gaining 20 minutes of extra time each week to implement the SPCs.

(2) 'Una ideología es el conjunto de ideas sobre la realidad, sistema general o sistemas existentes en la práctica de la sociedad respecto a lo económico, lo social, lo científico-tecnológico, lo político, lo cultural, lo moral, lo religioso, etc. y que pretenden'.

(3) I recommend *An Introduction to Antonio Gramsci's* The Prison Notebooks – A Macat Politics Analysis *(2016) available in public domain.

(4) These examples based on old Disney movies may be unknown to today's students. I generally use an example based on personal experience while watching *Happy Feet* with my, then, five-year-old daughter. After the leader of the group of penguins with physical attributes such as being overweight and of short stature spoke with English styled as the language variety used by some Latinxs in the USA, my daughter asked me, 'Papa, ¿por qué los pingüinos feos hablan inglés como tú?' ('Dad, why do the ugly penguins speak English like you?').

(5) The term legacy speaker, equivalent of heritage speaker, is inspired by the term legacy preference student, a preference given by some university institutions to certain applicants on the basis of their familial relationship to alumni of that institution. The term legacy speaker aims to grant a positive connotation to these speakers that I attempt to consider privileged instead of inheritors of a linguistic problem.

(6) These tracks are available for free download.

6 Integrating SPCs in Different Curricular Settings

This chapter aims to aid educators in the development and integration of antiracist materials in two different curricular settings. First, I address the development and integration of concrete pedagogical modules in four lower-level Spanish courses of a well-articulated across-sections Spanish program in a US state university. These levels are basic Spanish, intermediate Spanish 1, intermediate Spanish 2 and an intermediate/advanced Spanish 1 composition/grammar course. Second, I examine an interdisciplinary general education class focused explicitly on language and racism in which I had full curricular freedom. This examination includes a discussion of assessment and grading in alignment with the ungrading movement (Blum, 2017; Kohn & Saffel, 2020; Sackstein, 2015).

6.1 Integrating SPCs into the Curriculum of (Spanish) Language Lower-Level Classes

The language program for which I developed the following modules is situated in a big state university on the US East Coast. Half of the student population in this institution does not identify as White (50% White, 16% Asian, 13% Black, 10% Hispanic/Latinx, 6% unknown and 5% non-resident alien). The Spanish program is structured in a sequence commonly followed by Spanish departments in the United States: basic, intermediate, intermediate/advanced and advanced. Each semester, there are multiple sections in the first two levels (basic and intermediate 1), in which most of the students who are required to take credits in a second language are placed. The number of sections decreases progressively as the level ascends. The program is standard across sections but still allows a certain degree of flexibility to instructors as long as they focus on the outcome goals established for each class curriculum, follow the class schedule and the activities in the textbook and rigorously subscribe to the assessments developed and agreed upon by the director, coordinators and instructors. With a more democratic orientation (e.g. all faculty participate in assessment development and selecting textbooks in the lower levels), this program is not under a strict surveillance regime, as in the case of X University's program. However, there are still mechanisms in place to ensure that all instructors follow the class program and that there are not too many disparities in methodological approaches and assessments.

One of the main issues in this program (and in many other departments with a graduate program) is the continuous influx of new graduate students who must teach Spanish language courses as part of their responsibilities. These graduate teaching assistants (GTAs) often do not have a background or experience in teaching methods and/or their academic focus is on areas unrelated to second language acquisition (SLA) (e.g. literature and cultural studies). However, to mitigate this lack of pedagogical knowledge and expertise, the department offers a mandatory class on teaching methods that GTAs must take while teaching their first semester (generally, lower-level Spanish classes). During this class, GTAs not only learn about the teaching methodology followed in this department (a communicative approach) but must also observe classes taught by veteran lecturers who are already familiar with this pedagogical approach and participate in assessment development. The implications of this situation promote a push for a very structured and automatized schedule and guidelines for GTAs to follow.

In this program, the first three levels of Spanish (basic, intermediate 1 and intermediate 2) use the same textbook divided into three semesters of five chapters per level. This textbook follows a solid communicative approach methodology. Within a flipped-classroom approach, it has an online component to help students learn vocabulary and grammar that they put into practice in face-to-face sessions by interacting in pairs or small groups in class. The main issues of this program reside in its content. Although it tries to address issues of regional and situational linguistic variation, social variation is completely omitted. Moreover, in my view (and in some of the students' views), its aseptic materials, which focus on themes like travel, food, celebrations, professions and similar topics that are recurrent in second language (L2) textbooks, infantilize the way university students learn. The neoliberal approach to language as a marketable skill is evident throughout this textbook written by two White American professors. Conversations about race and racism within Hispanic cultures and within the United States are absent in its pages.

These three Spanish levels are followed by two intermediate/advanced courses that function as a gateway for further advanced-level Spanish courses. These include a course in reading and writing and another in advanced grammar and composition, both framed within a prescriptive/normative/standard language ideology. I will provide an example of an antiracist module for the latter.

It is also important to consider that working in more standardized settings is not an excuse for adhering to a racist curriculum. Regardless of the curricular setting, there is always room to implement antiracist strategies within daily practice. These are what I call guerrilla tactics. Such strategies include integrating critical comments and promoting students' reflection during the transitions between activities. Comments based on critical analysis of book contents can help unveil asymmetric power relationships. For example, when seeing structures that present linguistic variation, such as the Spanish present perfect, textbooks tend to draw a dichotomy between a supposed linguistic variety from Spain and another from Latin America. This simplistic view of language variation focused on regional variation displays an asymmetric relationship between the language variety of one country (Spain) and those in the 33 Latin American countries (while simultaneously omitting Equatorial Guinea in Africa). By making it visible, students become aware that textbooks reproduce neocolonial ideologies (in this case, related to pan-Hispanism).

Another guerrilla tactic includes integrating introductory or warm-up activities that include materials addressing issues of representation (such as music or current news). These activities can be a great way to point out the absences of cultural others that they will face while working through the activities in the textbook. For example, a non-mainstream Hip-Hop video playlist that addresses social issues and is racially and gender-inclusive can play during the transition time between classes. The provocative content of the selected videos may spark questions that can be used as a warm-up activity before class starts.

Likewise, some of the textbook activities do not require much effort to tweak in order to integrate counternarratives. For instance, when learning numbers from 100 to 10,000 in basic Spanish, instead of using the usual historical dates celebrating colonists' achievements, a class activity can integrate the dates of successful enslaved people's revolts, which are numerous but are often hidden or approached as anecdotical by mainstream history books (e.g. Haiti's independence in 1804 or Gaspar Yanga's rebellion in 1570 in what is today Mexico).[1] Review days – those classes that some programs offer as 'feel free to use your own materials' to prepare students for a new semester or an assessment – can also be planned from an antiracist perspective by including counternarratives (see the next two sections as examples).

Preparing these materials takes planning and work (although not as much as you may think for some of them), but until a massive structural and curricular change happens, it is our duty as antiracist educators to find the gaps and cracks within our standardized programs to integrate as much antiracist practice as possible. Let's examine four concrete examples of how to do this in a standardized language program.

6.1.1 Which Spanish: An introduction to Spanish for incoming students (basic level)

This is a 50-minute class designed for the very first class of Spanish programs. Although it is adaptable to any level, incoming students to basic Spanish should become familiar with the object of study for at least two semesters, starting on their first day. They are learning a new language; they should know what a language is and what Spanish is.

Theoretically, this lesson is informed by José del Valle's (2014) 'The Politics of Normativity and Globalization: Which Spanish in the Classroom?'; Bonnie Urciuoli's (2008) 'Whose Spanish?'; and Ralph Penny's (2000) 'Standardization' chapter in his *Variation and Change in Spanish*. These readings are recommended for instructors prior to putting this lesson into practice.

There are two sets of outcome goals for this class. The first set is related to the general course's outcome goals: reducing the students' anxiety threshold by starting to know each other and establishing a safe and inviting environment for communication; participating in conversations in different culturally determined situations and showing sensitivity and tolerance to culturally determined behavior acts; becoming familiar with the collaborative method of working in small groups; and knowing their object of study – Spanish – from a historical and sociopolitical perspective. The second set includes antiracist outcome goals: comparing different linguistic varieties to raise critical linguistic awareness (CLA); identifying language ideologies and the discourse associated with them in different sociolinguistic situations; interpreting language ideologies and articulating how they benefit and harm different social groups in different sociolinguistic texts; and demonstrating 'cross-cultural' competence through reflecting, relating, comparing and contrasting different languages, language varieties and language practices from a critical perspective.

The instructor should introduce the plan to the class, emphasizing that they will work toward completing a final task – a group reflection – and that the goal is to know more about what Spanish is. It should also be emphasized that the vehicular language of this class is English, which is an exception in this program, in which Spanish is the vehicular language for at least 90% of class time.

After the introduction, a Prezi presentation will help present the activities. First, the students work in small groups to answer the question, 'Which Spanish are you going to learn here?' After two minutes, the speakers in each group report to the class what they discussed. The students' answers generally include 'Standard Spanish', 'generic', conversational, basic, utilitarian and a few related to regional varieties such as Central American, the Spanish spoken in Spain, etc. The instructor will not provide feedback.

The following question is, 'What is a language?' The same procedure as in the previous step is followed. Based on my experience, students' answers tend to focus on structuralist definitions of language, and a few include anthropological aspects such as community or culture. The infamous definition attributed to Weinreich (1945) is then shown: 'A

language is a dialect with an army and a navy'. A good strategy for talking about the political nature of language is to compare, for example,
Haitian Creole and Jamaican Patois, two languages very similar from a
structural point of view but constructed differently. The former has the
status of an official language, the latter of a 'bad' English dialect. The
instructor may guide the students to reflect on both languages' historical,
political and racial characteristics and how language, power and identity
intertwine in the construction of nation-states and national languages.

Next, the instructor shows a five-minute cartoon video that nar-
rates the history of the Spanish language from a Eurocentric/neocolonial
perspective. The instructor may point out and offer counternarratives
to the video's Europeanizing views, such as when it describes how the
Catholic Kings (both of European descent) expelled 'the Muslims' from
the Iberian Peninsula; or the representation of Muslims as Arabs when
historians agree that the vast majority of Muslims came from Africa and
mixed with the local population for more than 800 years (Toasijé, 2009),
and as a result, the majority of Spaniards are their descendants.

Following this video, the instructor briefly presents how the process
of linguistic standardization works according to Ralph Penny (2000).
The goal of this presentation is to raise CLA about the ideology of the
standard language, how subjective the process is, how it is a process not
based on linguistic facts but on political and economic power and social
prestige, who performs this process and how, who benefits/harms and
who is empowered and inferiorized as a result of it. If time allows, the
instructor may project a map representing the political and linguistic situation of the Iberian Peninsula during the European invasion that resulted
in Castilian, and not Arabic, becoming the official language of today's
Spain. This map shows how the Iberian Peninsula was under African
dominance and/or influence for the greatest part of its history; however,
this narrative has been consistently hidden due to a 'whitewashing'
agenda conducted by institutional and corporate Spanish power groups
(Toasijé, 2009).

Before letting the students complete their final task, the instructor
plays clips from 'Ebonix' (1999), by the late Harlem MC Big L, and
'Habla como Pana' (2012), by Afro-Panamanian dancehall reggae artist, Kafú Bantón. In both songs, the artists deploy a similar strategy
to validate their (stigmatized) linguistic varieties. Big L translates from
mainstream English and mainstream English slang to the sociolinguistic variety he speaks: the AAVE used by most New York MCs, what
he defines as 'criminal slang'. Kafú Bantón translates from mainstream
Spanish to the sociolect spoken by most working-class Panamanian
youth, 'el panameño común' (the common Panamanian, as he explains in
his video's description), the social class to which most Afro-Panamanians
belong. He rhymes 'esto es cultura, no es invención' claiming the creativity of this linguistic variety and advocating for its validity. These videos

exemplify how languages are social constructions, how they have different values in different linguistic markets and how language and race issues are inherent to all languages.

This class finishes with a discussion, first within groups, then reporting on these two questions to the rest of the class: which Spanish? Who benefits or who may be harmed by this decision?

The materials proposed for this lesson can be adapted to the areas of expertise and experiences of each instructor. As a Hip-Hop educator, and considering the interests of many of my non-White students (and plenty of my White students), I tend to use Hip-Hop materials during my classes. Nonetheless, I understand that not all instructors are familiar with or feel comfortable using this type of material. However, when selecting cultural materials within an antiracist approach, we must consider what we know about antiracist pedagogies; that is, we need to integrate a multiplicity of voices and texts that have been historically excluded and stigmatized in academia and other hegemonic circuits such as the mainstream music industry.

For instance, in Spanish classes, instructors may consider music artists such as Shakira, Enrique Iglesias, Calle 13 or Bad Bunny as alternative artists from an Anglo-American perspective. They perform in Spanish in a predominantly English music industry. However, within Hispanic cultures, these are well-recognized mainstream groups fully integrated into the dynamics of hegemonic ideas of culture and race and the logics of neoliberalism and the commoditization of culture. Regardless of the content of their songs – Calle 13 is more socially conscious in their lyrics – they are Grammy Award winners, platinum-selling artists and non-racialized within their Hispanic cultures. Additionally, we should be cautious with multicultural approaches. As explained in Chapter 3, focusing on multiculturalism is risky because it tends to 'depoliticize', 'soften' and in essence water down the critical work needed to promote long-lasting change for racial equity (Irizarry, 2009: 194; Martínez & Welton, 2015, as cited in Welton et al., 2018: 3). Intersectionality is important, and it should be addressed through our materials, but racism is different from sexism, homophobia or other forms of discrimination. As previously discussed, the primary focus should be on race.

6.1.2 Let's introduce ourselves: Identity (intermediate 1 level)

This lesson is designed for the first week of an intermediate 1 Spanish course (the second level of the Spanish program). It can be programmed for two 50-minute classes (recommended) or one summarized 50-minute version (the version presented in these pages). Each semester, the first week is dedicated to introducing the course. The goals related to the class syllabus have to do with this introduction, that is, reviewing learning strategies and past materials in order to reactivate previous knowledge and get into speed for the semester ahead (i.e. getting familiar with the technology used in the course, pedagogical approach, class procedures, ways of interacting, etc.).

These goals aim to lower students' anxiety threshold by helping them meet new classmates and establish a safe and friendly environment for communication; become familiar with the collaborative approach to participation in this course; participate in conversations in different culturally determined situations while showing sensitivity and tolerance to culturally determined behavior acts; deploy learning strategies for SLA; and activate knowledge acquired in the past semester. Finally, by observing their linguistic proficiency and communicative competence, we can identify whether students have been placed at the right level. The communicative goal, and final task, is for students to introduce themselves to the class.

The antiracist goals aim to raise the CLA of the students by linking language and identity. These goals are to establish a safe environment to discuss race-related topics; identify language ideologies and the discourse associated with them in different sociolinguistic situations; interpret language ideologies and articulate how they benefit and harm different social groups by identifying how language, identity and power intertwine; and demonstrate 'cross-cultural' competence through reflecting, relating, comparing and contrasting different languages, language varieties and language practices from a critical perspective.

The lesson is informed by two excerpts from two articles: Magro's 'Resistance Identities and Language Choice on Instagram among Hispanic Urban Artists in da DMV' (2018: 215–219) and Bailey's 'Language and Negotiation of Ethnic/Racial Identity among Dominican Americans' (2000: 555–559). Instructors should read these two excerpts if they are not familiar with theoretical aspects of identity. The class proceeds as follows.

First, the instructor introduces the agenda for the class, explains how this lesson plan fits into the general outcome goals of the class and presents the communicative/linguistic goals (introducing themselves) and the antiracist goals of this class. The class is divided into five segments. The first segment focuses on strategies for language acquisition. It offers a brief review of metacognitive and task-based strategies proposed by this language department that are projected, discussed and exemplified. The first set of strategies is focused on planning and organizing, monitoring and identifying problems and evaluating and managing learning. The task-based strategies are focused on using the knowledge students bring to class (using background knowledge, making inferences and predictions, personalizing, transferring from other languages and use of cognates, substituting and paraphrasing); using their senses (images, sounds, kinesthesia); organizing the information (finding and applying patterns, classifying and sequencing, taking notes, using graphics organizers, summarizing, using selective action); and using a variety of resources such as accessing different information sources, cooperating and self-talk through the tasks.

The second segment of the class is a brief presentation on identity. The instructor projects a slide that summarizes Goffman's (1956) theory of identity as theatrical performance; the multiplicity and multifaceted nature of identities and how these are open to constant reappropriation, recontextualization and transformation (Lee, 2017); the relationship between linguistic form, language use and the ideologies of language; and how identities are restricted/influenced by the symbolic value of various linguistic markets (Bourdieu, 1991). The instructor may offer an example of the relationship between language and identities and, depending on time, leave students to discuss examples in small groups based on their personal experience.

The following three segments focus on the communicative activity. The input for this activity is a three-minute video of Sani Ladan, a young Cameroonian student in Spain, who migrated to this country as a kid by jumping 'the fence' that separates Ceuta (a city in Africa under Spanish rule) and Morocco. Sani Ladan's story is one of success. Despite suffering xenophobia and racism, he became a college student and a respected intercultural professional. Moreover, he is multilingual and is fully proficient in Spanish. However, before the video of Sani introducing himself for an interview plays, students are asked to use the following strategies to try to understand what he says in the video: cooperation, using what they know, clues, predicting and guessing based on context, taking notes, summarizing, focusing on specific information, structures, ideas and keywords. The instructor also shows four guiding questions so the students can focus on identifying specific information: who is Sani? What does he do for a living? How does he identify himself? What does he think about national identities in Africa? After watching the video, the students work in small groups to answer these questions. Then, a speaker for each group presents the information they were able to collect from the video.

In the following activity, the students use Sani's model to introduce themselves to their classmates in small groups. These questions are offered as a guide: what is your name? What do you do (in the university/for a living)? Where are you from? Identities are dynamic and multifaceted: how do you identify yourself? This last question may open avenues for the final discussion. For instance, based on my experience, students avoid the issue of race when self-identifying. Thus, the final discussion could be related to the reasons behind this omission, the construction of racially 'neutral' identities based on nationality (e.g. 'I am American'), the problem with 'non-racist' identities, or discussing how despite this omission, this aspect of our identities plays a major role in oppressing racialized groups, and especially Afro-descendants, in US society. The discussion will be triggered by the students' responses and will necessarily differ on each occasion. As instructors, we should utilize what we know about critical race theory (CRT) and what has been explained in these pages to moderate the discussion.

After introducing themselves within their groups, one student per group will introduce her/himself to the class. Then, the class and the instructor will provide feedback (what was good and what could be improved from a communicative perspective). The class will finish with a discussion on language and identity in English.

Like the previous lesson plan, this one can be adapted to other materials related to asymmetric power relationships, but again, although it is highly recommended to address issues of intersectionality (e.g. through the migratory experience in the case of Sani), racism – that is, discrimination based on race – is the central axis. It is necessary to be aware of multicultural approaches and their tendency to relegate racism to just one more form of discrimination. It is not.

6.1.3 An antiracist scriptwriter's manual: Practicing commands (intermediate 2 level)

This activity is designed as a lesson plan for a 50-minute class or, in its extended version, as a 120-minute module to be divided into two 50-minute classes that add activities aimed at expanding linguistic proficiency within the context of an antiracist activity. This section focuses on the 50-minute lesson version; the extended version is available in the online component. This activity is an additional activity to the one proposed by the textbook I was using when I designed it; concretely, it was framed in a unit about Spanish and professions.

In the previous semester, the students learned how to use the infinitive to create rules. As the next step in their linguistic proficiency scaffolding, the students learn to use commands in this first unit of their semester in this intermediate 2 level. Students prepared for class by studying vocabulary related to professions and reading the grammar about the use of commands in Spanish. They completed a battery of online exercises to practice and start using both the vocabulary and the grammar for this unit. The final task for this activity is to create a manual with antiracist rules for film and TV scriptwriters. The focus is on scriptwriting and how this profession has tended to represent Black women in films and TV series.

This unit targets the following general outcome goals for this course: (1) recognizing and analyzing their own grammar issues in their oral and written production; (2) initiating, maintaining and concluding conversations about social and cultural topics of general interest for the Spanish-speaking world; (3) communicating their concerns, opinions and arguments in Spanish in both written and oral format; and (4) practicing and deepening the use of complex grammatical constructions of daily use in Spanish.

The antiracist goals for this lesson are: (1) comparing and contrasting different language varieties; (2) identifying language ideologies and the discourse associated with them in different sociolinguistic situations; (3) interpreting language ideologies and articulating how they benefit and harm different social groups in different sociolinguistic texts; (4) demonstrating 'cross-cultural' competence through reflecting, relating, comparing and contrasting different languages, language varieties and language practices from a critical perspective; (5) analyzing racist ideologies and attitudes and articulating how they benefit and harm different social groups.

During the class introduction, the instructor should emphasize that the final task is to create a manual of antiracist rules for film and TV screenwriters. The instructor should explain how this activity relates to the unit – and its communicative/linguistic goals (rules and commands) – plus its antiracist goals, while interacting with students about the representation of racialized others in films and TV series.

The instructor then shows a video subtitled in Spanish. This input is an analysis of racist practices against Black women perpetuated by Spanish films and TV series. It focuses on six topics: racialized women as just immigrants; performance of 'accents'; only one racialized woman in the film or TV series; Roxane Gay's concept of the role of the 'Magical Negro'; colorism; and Black women always represented as prostitutes, jail inmates, cleaning staff, field laborers and caregivers. The author of the video, Lucía Mbomío, an Afro-descendant Spanish journalist and writer from Alcorcón, Madrid, speaks a variety of central-Peninsular Spanish with some features of the sociolect of the working-class periphery of Madrid. This language variety, as spoken by an Afro-descendant, helps target antiracist outcome goals 1 and 3. Moreover, the topic of 'accents' and how they are used to indexicalize race and iconize specific racial groups helps target antiracist outcome goals 3 and 4. The general content of the video helps target antiracist outcome 5.

After watching the video, the instructor and students review the six topics and a list of new/useful vocabulary necessary to accomplish the task. The instructor asks the students to provide any other new vocabulary they may find necessary to accomplish their task and add it to this list. After the content of the video has been summarized, the students work in groups to create rules, first using the infinitive (a structure they already used in the past semester). When completed, each group presents its rules to the class, and students take notes of those rules they missed and consider to be important additions to their own manuals. Students may also ask questions and seek clarifications if they think an antiracist rule is problematic from either an antiracist or linguistic perspective (e.g. they could not understand it, or the way it was structured may have changed the meaning of what the rule was meant to say).

The students' suggestions generally aim to amend the problems in the misrepresentation of racialized women that the author of the video explains. Because of their work in groups, the answers that the students share with the class are generally already filtered; that is, they discuss the rules among themselves, finding consensus on what to share. However, some nuances may be missing. The other groups are encouraged to make suggestions, or the instructor can redirect the students to the issue that they are not identifying. For example, in several classes, some students proposed 'no representar a las mujeres racializadas como prostitutas y presas' (do not represent racialized women as prostitutes and jail inmates). However, following what Lucía Mbomío explains, a rule such as 'no representar a las mujeres racializadas solo como prostitutas y presas' (do not represent racialized women only as prostitutes and jail inmates) would capture the issue more accurately because she explains that the problem is not that racialized women appear in those roles, but that those roles are the only ones in which racialized women generally appear in films and TV shows. The author of this video explains that the problem lies in making the part the whole, which is a key issue that expands to the other five topics. To redirect attention to this issue of making the part the whole, the instructor may ask the other groups questions, such as would it be realistic to omit racialized women from these roles? If the students, as sometimes happens, cannot identify this issue on their own, the instructor could introduce the adverb *solo* (only) and ask the students, now with a linguistic focus, how their rule changes and, with a critical focus, the implications of this change in the rule.

Once this presentation ends, the students work to add new ideas, but this time, they turn their previous and new rules into commands. To do so, the instructor may provide students with a table that offers a model for turning a couple of verbs in the infinitive into both affirmative/negative and *tú/usted* command forms. It is at this moment that, in my previous example, the students created new rules, such as 'contrata a mujeres racializadas en papeles como doctora o profesora' (hire racialized women in roles such as doctor or professor). After the students finish, each group presents its new manual. The instructor may provide linguistic feedback while the students are presenting; but it will be during the following and final discussion that the students will reflect and provide feedback to each other on their manuals. If time allows, the instructor can help the students put together a single manual for the class that gathers all their rules.

This lesson plan, as mentioned, may have different extensions, such as turning the commands into recommendations using other linguistic structures. This can be done using another table or in a brief essay (e.g. impersonal *se, es aconsejable* + infinitive, conditional). The students may also justify their rules in relation to the input and own experiences in this essay or an oral discussion in class (this extension is included in the online component).

6.1.4 Writing activities (intermediate/advanced level)

This module comprises two units involving two 50-minute classes (four classes of 50 minutes in total); each unit has a final task. It is designed for an advanced grammar and composition Spanish course. The course has a strong prescriptive orientation and is framed within a normative and standard language ideology. The textbook used for this course focuses on different hegemonic texts, including narrative, journalistic reports and argumentative essays from hegemonically legitimized authors.

In the previous unit, the students focused on the description. In preparation for this first unit, titled 'The Narration', they completed a battery of online self-graded exercises focusing on grammar and the comprehension of a literary text. The final task for this first part of the module is to narrate a text in the first person using the personification of an object as a literary device.

In the introduction, the instructor explains the plan of this module, how it is divided, and the final tasks for each of both units: a narration and a journalistic report. Next, the instructor introduces the plan for the following two classes, where they will first work on analytical exercises about the textbook reading; second, on grammar exercises from the textbook; third, watching Hip-Hop music videos that exemplify the literary personification of an object; and fourth, writing a brief composition in which the students will narrate. The instructor explains the linguistic goals of this unit (narrating using the past tense and adjective relative clauses) and its antiracist goals.

This module targets the following course outcome goals: (1) analyze and produce diverse texts; (2) write with clarity and comprehensibility in different text genres; (3) utilize a written text as a foundation for oral expression; (4) focus on complex grammar structures; (5) write coherent texts by using the writing rules of Spanish with few errors that distract the reader from the content of the text. The antiracist outcome goals for this module are: (1) comparing and contrasting different language varieties; (2) identifying language ideologies and the discourse associated with them in different sociolinguistic situations; (3) interpreting language ideologies and articulating how they benefit and harm different social groups in different sociolinguistic texts; (4) demonstrating 'cross-cultural' competence through reflecting, relating, comparing and contrasting different languages, language varieties, and language practices from a critical perspective; (5) analyzing racist ideologies and attitudes and articulating how they benefit and harm different social groups. The course's outcome goals and the antiracist goals for this class may seem contradictory. However, although one of the goals for this course is to learn grammar rules imposed top-down, this goal provides an opportunity to question why they are learning them; whom these rules benefit/

harm; how they can be used to stigmatize, inferiorize and put obstacles toward education to certain social/linguistic groups; and what other more just worlds can be imagined.

The first class starts with a focus on the activities suggested by the general syllabus, that is, activities about comprehension and analysis of a text they read at home and activities with a linguistic focus on structure. They work in pairs or small groups. The last task is an individual writing exercise based on the textbook but with a twist: students narrate a racist episode they witnessed in their lives. In their paragraph, the students integrate time expressions, use the past tense, and answer where, when, with whom, why, how the place was, how they felt and how this experience changed them. A student shares her/his composition, and the instructor moderates a discussion to promote reflection while integrating concepts related to CRT. Linguistic feedback may be provided after this discussion.

Following this set of exercises, the instructor shows a Hip-Hop video by Nas ('I Gave You Power', 1996) in which this MC personifies a gun. The instructor should warn the students that the language in this video may be offensive. Depending on the class culture and the climate established in the class, the instructor may decide to play the clean version of this song. However, this warning can lead to a sociolinguistic discussion. Although the language in this video can be considered offensive and vulgar in certain contexts, in the language variety in which it is written – Hip-Hop language (Alim, 2009) – this lexicon and linguistic features are a normalized form of expression and the usual communication vehicle in that context. Although it is a stigmatized and delegitimized language variety in the academic world (like the community that speaks it), in the symbolic market of urban music, its value is inverted, and it becomes the prestigious variety (Magro, 2016b). There is also room for a discussion about the violence implicit in this song and how, as is usually the case with Hip-Hop, it just represents with all its rawness the living conditions of many underserved Black and Latino US neighborhoods. It could be also worth mentioning how, whenever Hip-Hop materials address or reproduce issues of violence, there is a tendency in academia (and mainstream in general) to place the focus on them without addressing how, generally, these issues respond to the internalization of ideologies of violence that are normalized in mainstream media (e.g. action, police, war, epic or mafia films). This topic can also open up avenues for critical discussion of gun laws in the United States. Whenever time allows it, I use one of my own experiences to start a conversation about a topic related to all this: the racism surrounding who has the right to carry firearms. I usually start by positioning myself: I am against the use of guns at any level. However, I remember the first time I was in New York City in 1992 and how there was a big polemic around the banning of the poster for the film *Juice* (1992). In the original poster for this movie, the actor and MC

Tupac Shakur appeared with a gun in his hand. The poster was cropped out to leave the gun out of the poster. Just a few months earlier, actor Bruce Willis had appeared in the poster for his featured movie *The Last Boy Scout* (1991) carrying a gun in almost the exact position as Tupac Shakur. The poster for the latter film was not banned.

Going back to the discussion about linguistics, the instructor can briefly introduce students to what is meant by Hip-Hop language and Hip-Hop Nation language, how local communities worldwide adopt it and adapt it to their languages and sociocultural context through a process of translocalization (Pennycook, 2007) and how this phenomenon manifests in the different varieties of Spanish (and other languages). To exemplify this, the instructor may play fragments of 'Kool Kaín' (a Spanish rap song by El Meswy, 2000), in which the MC does a personification of another object (cocaine), or 'Libertad' (2014), in which Chilean female rapper, Anita Tijoux, personifies freedom. In this way, it is shown that Hip-Hop, discrimination, exclusion and otherization are not unique domains of American culture and, in the same way, certain social groups and their cultural/linguistic practices are often excluded from pedagogical materials in the Spanish-speaking world. Moreover, besides offering good examples of creative writing and personification as a literary device, these songs help to legitimize cultural productions and communities often excluded from academia. These videos promote the empowerment of racialized students and reflection among White students on who is harmed by/benefits from attitudes linked to the standard language ideology.

To finish the first unit within the module, the students work on their final task: a narration in the past tense about an object in the first person, that is, personifying it. The instructor may suggest that this object can be abstract, such as police brutality, racism or xenophobia, or something concrete, like a water polo ball on which to project their thoughts on racism.

In this particular course, paragraphs are shared in a forum on the course's online platform. Students are asked to provide feedback to their classmates. At the beginning of the next class, the instructor may choose one composition and provide feedback, discuss the reasons why the author chose their objects and link this discussion to the subversiveness of literature and art as political positioning proposed by authors such as Gabriel García Márquez (who wrote the input text for this unit in this course's textbook).

The second part of this module focuses on the journalistic report and the journalistic opinion letter. The final task of this module is to send an opinion letter to a newspaper. After finishing the first part of the module, the students prepare for this module by reading, at home, a text about the journalistic story in their textbooks.

Before starting with the procedures, the instructor introduces the plan for this unit, which is designed to complete a final task. During this introduction, the instructor may refresh the linguistic and antiracist goals for this second unit of the module (same as in the last unit). The first activity is to watch a video about the structure and characteristics of the journalistic report. At the end of this video, there is a comprehension quiz that the students complete. Once the students are familiar with the theoretical components of the journalistic report, the instructor plays two journalistic video reports. The two videos I selected were *Graffiti tour en Medellín* (Lucía Mbomío, 2018) and the first five minutes of *Nora and Margarita* (*Nadie nos ha dado vela en este entierro*, 2020). The first video talks about an initiative to empower disenfranchised youth in a working-class neighborhood of Medellín through graffiti and how this 'dangerous' neighborhood (especially after Pablo Escobar's capture and killing) became a tourist site. The second video focuses on two Black women living and working in the shantytown of Atochares (Almería, Spain). In this settlement, around 500 people with an irregular migratory status from different countries in Africa live without running water, with tapped electricity and sharing houses made of wood and plastic (even during the COVID-19 pandemic). About a tenth of them are women who not only suffer these inhuman conditions but also live under constant threat and fear after attacks conducted by far-right groups.

After watching these two examples of a journalistic report, the students choose one, and they answer an analytical questionnaire in their textbooks, mainly about how this report answers the fundamental questions of a journalistic report.

The textbook offers a rubric for the opinion letter. After students work on how to outline the structure of their letters and work on their final task, the instructor may present the different options for publishing their letters. Depending on the country of origin of the video they selected (Colombia or Spain), and in order to let the students analyze in which publication they have more chances to be published depending on their letters, the instructor may discuss how the different newspapers align with the political agendas of political parties from right to left and economic interests such as big corporations, banks, etc.

At this point, the students start writing their opinion letters. First, they work on their scripts. Second, the students exchange scripts and provide feedback to each other following a rubric. Third, the students start writing their first draft. Once again, they exchange their drafts and, following a rubric provided by the course program, provide each other with feedback. Finally, as homework, they work on their final letter, which they publish on their online platform; after the instructor provides feedback, they send it to their newspaper of choice to try to have it published.

6.2 SPCs in an Interdisciplinary Class

The following antiracist pedagogical proposal is not a Spanish language learning course, but a general education interdisciplinary sociolinguistics seminar for undergraduate students interested in antiracism and language teaching. Although this course is focused exclusively on sociopolitical contents (SPCs) and therefore allows more time to delve into the field of critical sociolinguistics, it expands on the same SPC units and principles as the examples previously proposed in this book.

This seminar is designed for incoming humanities majors, particularly those seeking a degree that will allow them to teach any language (including both first language [L1] and L2) at any educational level. However, by expanding on the depth of the readings and work, it can be easily adapted to different levels, including graduate courses. This course is anchored in a critical interdisciplinary approach – sociolinguistics, applied linguistics, Hispanic applied linguistics, linguistic anthropology, sociology, social psychology, race studies, Latinx studies, language acquisition, education, Hip-Hop studies and antiracist pedagogies – that emphasizes the social, political and ideological dimensions of language. As in the previous pedagogical proposals, its objective is to raise CLA, but in this case, the program does so through the learning and implementation of antiracist language teaching methods in the language classroom. The students learn to do this through socially receptive pedagogies that incorporate their experiences and consider the need to include those of their future students and promote change toward equity within and outside the educational environment.

The seminar is designed backward, building knowledge and skills to complete a final group project that is presented in class (see Appendix F for this project). By the end of this seminar, students are able to develop and/or integrate didactic antiracist materials designed to raise linguistic awareness among language students and promote social change through targeting and challenging language ideologies that perpetuate inequality and iniquity. Divided into three modules – introduction to sociolinguistics and research methods in the arts and humanities, language ideologies and antiracist pedagogies – and a total of 25 units, each unit of this seminar focuses on both theoretical and practical approaches to sociolinguistics. When I first designed this course, it was for a 16-week seminar with two in-person sessions per week, 75 minutes per session.

There is an asynchronous module preceding each in-person class. In each module, students are expected to review a set of assigned readings, videos and music, which they respond to via questions designed to engage with the readings, or with a small assignment to reflect on and apply the readings to a real-life situation. Each of these readings, with its assignment, is expected to take students two to three hours twice a week before each in-person class. The theory is complemented with short lectures and different hands-on class activities that help to identify and analyze, from a critical perspective, different linguistic ideologies, attitudes and practices partaking in the perpetuation of asymmetrical power relationships.

The nature of this seminar pushes students to take an active role in their learning process. They do this by engaging and collaborating with other students and the instructor regularly, both in live sessions and through group work and activities such as reflection journals in which they read and comment on each other's reflections. All assessments, including in-class discussions and participation, are accompanied by detailed instructions and an assessment rubric. The assessment focuses on content. Thus, to be completed, some activities offer an oral (video) or written (essay) format as an option. Evaluation following linguistic academic standards and normativity is discouraged. Students are not penalized or corrected as long as they can perform and show that they reached the outcome goals for their tasks.

Aligned with the ungrading movement in higher education (Blum, 2017; Kohn & Saffel, 2020; Sackstein, 2015), rather than in grading, sorting or judging, the focus is on learning. The goal is students' growth through bidirectional meaningful feedback and establishing an exchange of ideas between all the members of the course horizontally and centered on the student rather than the instructor. Thus, feedback on assignments and class activities is provided by both the instructor and classmates, and both must be taken into consideration to review their work. The goal is not to 'label' each student with a letter at the end of the semester but to make sure that their antiracist CLA grows and they achieve the course's outcome goals, encouraging students to come out of their shells by lifting prescriptive measures that may inhibit written and oral expression of their ideas, thus facilitating their engagement with their learning process all while upholding academic rigor.

The students' assessment method for this course increases their motivation to do well by making expectations clear, lowering their stress and giving them agency in determining their strengths and weaknesses while reflecting on their own learning processes. To do so, the rubrics are simple guidelines focused on the expected quality standards related to the content of their work. Based on Blum (2017), the goal is to focus student attention on the work itself and engagement with the feedback loop (provided by students and instructor) by removing elements, such as hyperspecific long rubrics, which may end up being distractors. As I mentioned earlier, feedback about prescriptive grammar rules is minimized. Thus, the goal is to build metacognition and self-evaluation skills and give students pathways to grow in their learning over time. Growth is an important component of this approach because, as discussed, not all students start these classes with the same base level.

Simultaneously, the discussion about the intertwining of the grading system, 'academic writing' and cultural hegemony is promoted in the classroom: who benefits and who gets harmed by these systems deeply rooted in academia? As a metagoal for this course and aligned with authors such as Blum (2017) or Sackstein (2015), this approach to assessment and grading aims to promote awareness about how colleges promote credentials, obedience, cultural gatekeeping, access to education and the sorting of haves and have-nots, but not necessarily learning. Likewise, the class as a whole discusses and questions the privileges, accessibility and social mobility that the handling of the standard linguistic varieties grants and its intertwining with race, and what can we do to resist and change these ideologies with what we know about language, identity and power.

For a long time, every semester, in every class, I have claimed that I would get rid of grades if it were up to me. I do not think the obsessive fixation on grades above all else is helpful for learning. Grades are not a good motivator because they are extrinsic motivators, and, as I explained in this book, intrinsic motivation (doing things for their own sake) is often blocked by this extrinsic motivator and the fear of the negative consequences attached to it. Grades inhibit risk-taking. I agree with Blum (2017) that the uniformity that grading provides does not take into consideration the differences among students regarding experiences, goals or levels when they enter our classes. I also agree with her that grades do not provide adequate information. In Blum's (2017) words:

> If the purpose of grades is to convey a student's accomplishment, adequacy, excellence, compliance, effort and/or gain in learning, then they fail. Is a student who enters already knowing a lot and continues to demonstrate knowledge at a high level, but then misses an assignment because of a roommate's attempted suicide and ends up with a B-plus, the same as someone who begins knowing nothing, works really hard, follows all the rules, does quite well and ends up with a B-plus? What information is conveyed? What about someone who loves biology and excels in those classes, but who loathes history, bombs in history classes and ends up with a 3.0 GPA? Compared to someone who muddles through every class and a similar GPA, yet with no passion, excellence or highs or lows? What do we learn from the GPA? What does a course grade mean?

Although I'd rather work with guidelines, suggestions and established parameters rather than 'rules', I agree with Blum that grades do not serve a just purpose. Nonetheless, although, like Blum (2017) or Sackstein (2015), I have tried to get rid of as many grades as possible, at the end of each semester, I end up submitting grades for each student. I do not believe in this system, but it is imposed on us instructors by our institutions. It would require a big systemic change to get rid of grades completely, and I believe that this is a fight that students should take on themselves. In the meantime, assessment strategies such as the one in this course have worked well in my classes by helping me know my students better and develop a closer relationship with them. I also noticed a change in student focus from 'what the professor wants' to the task at hand, and, especially, a drive toward curiosity and enjoyment when they learn new concepts that they can relate to real-life situations, and the enthusiasm for learning conceptual tools that allow them to express what they did not know how to put into words before starting this class.

Nonetheless, this grading system also has its problems. It does not work as well with unmotivated students or those with poor self-evaluating skills (although motivated students with poor self-evaluating skills grow in this area). Also, this system means more work for students. However, this work seemed to me more rewarding and enjoyable than, for instance, having to explain a rubric repeatedly or grading multiple assignments and, in the last one, not identifying much growth.

This course has eight objectives aligned with its different assessed assignments:

(1) Demonstrate 'cross-cultural' competence through reflecting, relating, comparing and contrasting different languages, language varieties and language practices from a critical perspective.
(2) Identify language ideologies and the discourse associated with them in different sociolinguistic situations, including films, news, music, daily interactions and textbooks.
(3) Analyze how language, identity and power intertwine in different types of texts, such as films, news, music and textbooks.
(4) Interpret language ideologies and articulate how they benefit and harm different social groups in different sociolinguistic situations, including films, news, music, daily interactions and textbooks.
(5) Develop and implement, in a real course program final project, pedagogical tools to increase students' linguistic awareness in language classes.
(6) Reflect on your own linguistic awareness development and agency throughout the course.
(7) Be familiar with diverse research methods in the arts and humanities.
(8) Analyze racism as a form of historical and systemic discrimination in the United States and internationally that may intersect with other forms of power and oppression.

At the end of each module, students complete an entry in their reflection journal by answering questions aiming to link the theory seen in the seminar and their personal experience. After the first module, these questions are:

(1) Have your views about language changed since you started this class? How? Relate to personal experience(s) (400 words).
(2) Considering what we covered in class, first, copy and paste your first definition of racism (week 5) and, second, write a reviewed version of it.
(3) After posting your reflection, you will be able to read what your classmates wrote and will be asked to comment on two of their posts (from two different people and no more than 50 words). What more can you add to their thoughts? Do you agree? How does their reflection compare to yours?
(4) Reply to any comment you may receive from your classmates.

The questions after the second module are:

(1) Reflect on your linguistic behavior on social media and briefly answer these questions (400 words): think about your linguistic choices on social media. Do you use linguistic performance to portray a particular identity(s) on social media? Which identity(s) and how do you do it? Why do you think you do this? How does this compare to the linguistic strategies of Hispanic urban artists in da DMV?
(2) After posting your reflection, you will be able to read what your classmates wrote and will be asked to comment on two of their posts (from two different people and no more than 50 words). What more can you add to their thoughts? Do you agree? How does their reflection compare to yours?
(3) Reply to any comment you may receive from your classmates.

At the end of the semester, along with their projects, students complete a final reflection:

(1) How did this class affect your views about language, race, racism and antiracism? Relate to your personal experience(s) and make connections with race–language–power relationships. If you are a White student, you may reflect on how this class impacted you, stressed you, benefited you or made you face your privilege and how you will use what you learned to fight racism, become a better person, etc. If you are a student of color, you may reflect on how this class impacted you, stressed you, benefited you or empowered you and how you will use what you learned to fight racism, gain allies, protect yourself and others, become a better person, etc. 400–600 words. Be concise, precise and insightful.
(2) After posting your reflection, you will be able to read what your classmates wrote and will be asked to comment on two of their posts (from two different people and no more than 50 words). What more can you add to their thoughts? Do you agree? How does their reflection compare to yours?
(3) Reply to any comment you may receive from your classmates.

The rubric used to establish parameters and provide feedback to each student is as follows:

Reflection Journals Module 3 Final

Criteria	Ratings			Pts
General content	**40 to > 32.8 pts** **Meets expectations** Student makes an effort to answer briefly and concisely, justifying his answer using class materials and personal experiences. Comments on classmates' posts	**32.8 to > 26.0 pts** **Approaching** **expectations**	**26 to > 0 pts** **Does not meet** **expectations** Does not answer, or answers with no justification	40 pts
Language ideologies	**20 to > 16.8 pts** **Meets expectations** Based on the readings, the student's reflection identifies and/or interprets language ideologies and articulates how they benefit and harm different social groups in different sociolinguistic situations	**16.8 to > 13.0 pts** **Approaching** **expectations**	**13 to > 0 pts** **Does not meet** **expectations –** **limited** The student is unable to reflect, identify and/ or interpret language ideologies	20 pts
Analysis	**40 to > 33.6 pts** **Meets expectations** The student analyzes how language, identity and power intertwine and provides an example(s) related to his/her experience(s). The student is able to reflect analytically about her/his critical linguistic awareness development, his/her antiracist persona and how the class impacted him/her when comparing his/her awareness before taking this class	**33.6 to > 26.0 pts** **Approaching** **expectations**	**26 to > 0 pts** **Does not meet** **expectations –** **limited** The student is unable to reflect on how language, identity and power intertwine	40 pts

Total points: 100

Some of these final reflections will be discussed in the next chapter, along with an analysis of six cases from an advanced Spanish language class participating in a course that integrated SPCs.

Note

(1) This is an activity I developed for a Kahoot game: https://create.kahoot.it/share/adivina-la-fecha/d4880403-aef6-4186-8616-fdcfc9a5bd11.

7 The Students Talk: Testimonials from Participants in Antiracist Programs

In an effort to provide a vision of our outcome goals regarding antiracist critical linguistic awareness (CLA) and how this CLA manifests through students, this chapter will first analyze six case studies in an advanced Spanish class and then provide the testimonials of four students after completing the Language and Racism seminar described in the previous chapter.

As this book has already explained, one of the pivotal axles in the field of critical applied linguistics (CALx) is the effort to establish links between local uses and practices in language learning and the broader context of social processes and discourses in a scenario of sociohistorically situated asymmetric power relations. In Pennycook's (2007: 169) words, the goal is '[to draw] connections between classrooms, conversations, textbooks, tests, or translations and issues of gender, class, sexuality, race, ethnicity, culture, identity, politics', not only to describe these connections but to promote change in inequality through practice – that is, through sustained criticism and direct action. Framed within this perspective, intricately linked to a critical pedagogical approach, the aim is not only to illuminate the student/educator but also to transform through radical pedagogy the existing relations of power inequalities in our society, which are also reproduced in the classrooms (Giroux, 1983).

While there is a link between CLA and a rise in students' motivation – which is also related to a rise in linguistic proficiency (Magro, 2016a) – CLA, additionally and more importantly, tries to transform students by promoting reflection on the elimination of these inequalities, wealth and privilege and creating an open and self-critical community of inquisitive citizens within their pedagogical and cultural contexts. In this book, these pedagogical and cultural contexts are higher educational institutions, one private (X University [XU]) and the other a state research university.

This book has examined the role of language in producing, maintaining, challenging and transforming asymmetries of power, discrimination, inequality, social injustice and hegemony in relation to race and its intersection with other aspects such as ethnicity, class, migrant status, gender and more. For authors such as Talmy (2010: 129), this is the focus of CALx, which aligns with Leeman *et al.*'s (2011) idea of CALx as a tool to help students gain a critical understanding of how language is interwoven with social and political structures. Furthermore, this book has explained and provided examples of how this can be applied in language classrooms to transform students by helping them see the context and political standing of Spanish in the United States – and other languages throughout the world – in a new light. This is done by providing students with tools of inquiry and analysis to understand how educational practices materialize hierarchies and power structures over students through the current ideologies of monolingualism and languagelessness (Rosa, 2019) in the US education system. Thus, these tools help our students understand how language is intertwined with power, identity and the results of the asymmetric power relations that language conveys; this is how we help raise CLA in our students and its links to antiracism.

In this concluding chapter, I inquire about how this CLA manifests from an ethnographic and holistic perspective. I aim to shed light on the extent to which there was an ideological transformation in each of the selected cases. While doing so, I investigate why, as has been argued, content related to the sociopolitical nature of language is effective in influencing motivation and what makes this content special compared to other possible content. Likewise, aligned with Norton (2012), the following analysis understands that a vision of the learner as a binary being (such as aware–not aware, motivated–unmotivated) is not sustainable within a qualitative framework since these affective factors are generally socially constructed, changing over time and space and, quite possibly, coexisting in a contradictory way within the same individual depending on the context. All this theoretically justifies the need to analyze the various social, historical and cultural contexts – which include issues related to race, resistance, inequity, ethnicity, class, iconization of different linguistic varieties and linguistic history – of the cases I selected in the first section of this chapter. I did this by granting agency to these students, as different authors propose (e.g. Attinasi, 1983; Duff, 2012; Leeman, 2005; Willis, 2004). This is done to gain a deeper understanding of what happened to their CLA and motivation, to see how they negotiated or even resisted it.

I organized the cases into two categories: students of an advanced Spanish as a second language (L2) course and students from a Language and Racism seminar.

7.1 SPCs for Advanced Spanish Students

The following analysis focuses on six case studies of students who participated in a sociopolitical content (SPC) program in an advanced Spanish course as part of my doctoral dissertation (Magro, 2016a).

These students underwent a weekly 20-minute class focused on SPCs. During this investigation, CLA was assessed by two semi-structured interviews (one at the beginning of the semester, another at the end) and an artifact designed to collect CLA data (a final exam), which was utilized to triangulate with the interviews. The interviews, organized in three segments around three topics (attitudes toward different linguistic varieties, ideologies about Spanish in the United States and attitudes toward US Spanish speakers), were compared among the participants at the beginning and end of the semester, within their group, and with the control group. The final exams were analyzed by identifying emerging and recurrent topics and links between them. The differences between the emergence and recurrence of these themes between the (semi)experimental and the control group were interpreted, and the possible causal relationship that they could have with a change in CLA was investigated. It was concluded that the (semi)experimental group underwent a notable change in their CLA with respect to the control group. Although this was expected, since the experimental application aimed to increase CLA by integrating these SPCs in class, the most important objective of this analysis was not so much to observe *how much* – something that would otherwise be very problematic from a methodological point of view – but *how* these weekly 20-minute SPC sessions influenced the CLA of the participants. The following sections aim simply to provide a panoramic qualitative view of the ways in which these SPCs influenced CLA (which is linked to antiracist awareness, as explained in the first part of this book) and motivation, and how CLA manifests through participants in this type of program (see Chapter 1, section 1.5, in this book). The points made about motivation, although apparently tangential to the focus on antiracism in this book, are included in this discussion due to their importance for language learning. Added to the ethical reasons for including antiracist pedagogies in language learning, positive changes to motivation and other factors – such as self-perception of students' aptitude – and how all these interact with students' background, past experiences (such as studying Spanish abroad) and the teaching/learning experience provide additional arguments to include pedagogical approaches such as this one in our classes.[1]

These cases are divided into four categories, based on the students' previous experiences with language learning: (1) Hispanic heritage speakers; (2) non-Hispanic heritage speakers; (3) students who attended study abroad programs; and (4) mainstream students (students raised as English monolinguals). This organization is a result of considering, during the analysis, the experiences with Spanish that the participants had prior to this advanced class. The participants' previous experiences learning second languages influenced each student differently, especially in their initial motivation levels and their attitudes toward learning Spanish. Therefore, they were grouped in this way with the intention of attending to this variable. The goal of this section is to illustrate how SPCs influence CLA and motivation toward L2 learning.

I selected the six most representative cases of each category among the 18 participants who were part of the experimental group (for a complete analysis of the 10 cases originally selected, see Magro, 2016a). In the first category, the case selected allows us to dig into how the complexity of the concept of heritage language (HL) speakers interacts with the application of SPCs.

For the second category (non-Hispanic heritage speakers), the case selected offers a great opportunity to address how the inclusion of SPCs may influence these students. Although they do not share the same HL as the one learned as an L2, they feel identified with those asymmetric relationships of power suffered by many Hispanics in the United States because they can relate to issues of linguistic racialization and share parallel experiences regarding their linguistic backgrounds, migrant stories, discrimination due to ethnicity and/or race, etc.

Within the third category (students who attended study abroad programs), I selected the more salient case of motivation and two problematic cases with the intention of including those not-so-successful cases. The study of this category grants an opportunity to look briefly into study abroad programs as a powerful motivational factor, how this motivation may be impaired by the instruction received once they return to their home university, and the influence that the SPCs had to recover, maintain or increase motivation. We will also look into how individual differences such as self-perceived aptitude, attitudes, and conservative political positions may interact with this pedagogical approach.

The fourth category comprised the largest group in the class. These students declared that they only learned Spanish as an L2 in a school setting. They did not declare themselves as speakers of another language, which students grouped in the other three categories did. The case selected, Leah's, is a success story, a great example of a student who started the course highly motivated and whose motivation increased further by raising her CLA.

A cursory glance may give the appearance that no cases of students offering resistance to this pedagogical approach have been selected. There were none, other than the two cases selected in the 'students who attended study abroad programs' category. The fact that no cases of resistance to this program were found in this investigation does not mean that they do not exist and may appear in other classes. I am aware that some instructors may be worried about what to do with those students who reject antiracist pedagogical approaches. There are no formulas, since cases may be very different and the result of different factors (political differences, expectations, racist attitudes, etc.). The way I approach these situations is by taking into consideration that 'nunca llueve al gusto de todxs' (we cannot please everyone). While those resisting these pedagogies are generally those more in need of them, we must be aware that no matter how hard we try, we will not be able to reach everyone every time. In my experience, these students tend to quit the class, but we must also take into consideration that students quit classes constantly for diverse reasons. Similarly to how both instructors and students need to learn how to deal with policies that do not please everyone, such as grading, Eurocentric or aseptic contents, instructor-centered instruction, etc., students and educators need to learn how to deal with pedagogies that promote a more ethical and just world for everyone and not just a few.

7.1.1 Jonatan, a Spanish heritage speaker

It is out of the scope of this book to discuss in depth the issues associated with the construct of a heritage language. Nonetheless, before examining Jonatan's case, it is necessary to briefly review what is understood by HL speakers and what we understand by it in these pages from a critical perspective. There is an enormous body of publications and controversy surrounding the definition of the term heritage speaker/language/learner/student and, indeed, different terms such as Spanish speaker/user, native speaker, legacy speaker (Magro, 2018), etc., have been proposed as alternatives. I see this lack of agreement among scholars in the HL field as the result of trying to respond to different theoretical positions, which, in turn, respond to different ideological positions on the matter. In this sense, the perspective taken in this book assumes a speaker-centered heteroglossic position very similar to that offered by García and Otheguy (2015: 645), who focused on 'translingualism' (García & Li, 2014) with regard to those students traditionally labeled as heritage. However, in this book, I use the term heritage language speaker (HLS) for purely practical reasons, this type of speaker being understood as 'individuals raised in homes where a language other than English is spoken and who are to some degree bilingual in English and the heritage language' (Valdés, 2000: 376).

Despite disagreement on the term, what it seems commonly agreed on among scholars in the field, and central for this work, is that these students usually present particular psychosocial characteristics such as linguistic insecurity, issues of self-esteem and attitudes toward learning what has been constructed as the formal code. These characteristics are all influenced by, and/or are the result of, linguistic ideologies, attitudes and practices (Urciuoli, 2008; Del Valle, 2007b). These psychosocial characteristics differentiate HLS from L2 students who, regardless of their linguistic proficiency in the L2, never had the HLS experience in the United States and the process of racialization that this entails. Likewise, HLS are perceived as incomplete speakers in both languages by both their peers and their instructors through a process of languagelessness

(Rosa, 2019). Very often, they suffer the consequences of discrimination as a result of linking their hybrid linguistic behaviors to stigmatized
social classes to which representations produced by mainstream society
adhere to negative social stereotypes such as disorder and chaos, lack of
productivity, danger, crime or illiteracy. Thus, these characteristics turn
HLS into students with different needs, both linguistic and psychosocial/
cultural, from those of L2 students.

Jonatan is an archetypical example of an HLS in the United States.
The son of Salvadorian migrants, he was a 19-year-old native of a small
industrial New Jersey town on the periphery of New York City. The
racial composition of the town, famous for a race riot during the 1960s,
is predominantly Black (50% according to the 2010 United States Census)
and Hispanic (40%), a percentage that doubled in the last decade and
that maintains that trend (the 2000 United States Census reported 20%
Hispanic). His father was a construction worker, and his mother was
employed as cleaning staff. Their home income was between $20,000 and
$40,000. Jonatan identified himself as poor/very poor in the question-
naire the students took when they started the semester. Considering their
economic situation, the highest education his parents reached (his father
completed high school, his mother just elementary school) and having
attended a public high school of over 1,300 students which was classified
at the lowest rank levels in its state, Jonatan's story may be considered
one of success after being able to obtain a scholarship to study at an
institution such as XU.

Jonatan's linguistic background also fits the typical profile of Hispanic heritage students in the United States. Bilingual, though dominant
in English, Jonatan received informal home instruction in Spanish from
his mother, and he is comfortable communicating in Spanish in what has
been constructed in the field of language acquisition as 'informal/col-
loquial registers' or 'home varieties'. Phonetically, he sounded like any
native speaker from El Salvador, although he showed some features of
Spanish in contact with American English typical of US Spanish speakers
(see Otheguy & Zentella, 2008). His vocabulary was rich and diverse,
although from time to time, he code-switched by embedding English
terms which in most cases were not *crutchlike switching* (Zentella, 1997);
that is, he knew the term in Spanish, but for other reasons, he used
the English term. His hybrid linguistic behavior also featured syntactic
structures influenced by English characteristics of Spanish in the United
States, such as the use of the gerund instead of the infinitive (e.g. *me gusta
cocinando* instead of *me gusta cocinar*). Jonatan's greatest difficulties in
this Spanish course had to do with complying with the standard variety
and academic register imposed on students if they wanted to succeed in
this Spanish program. These issues were mainly related to spelling (e.g.
pías instead of *país*), integrating formal sentence connectors (such as
sin embargo, no obstante, en consecuencia) and the use of the Spanish

subjunctive, which in this department was an index of achieving an inter-mediate high–advanced low proficiency level.

Like many other HLS in the United States, since Jonatan first enrolled in the New Jersey public school system, he was subjected to a subtractive bilingualism that bans and penalizes the use of Spanish. In our interviews, and even in an intervention in class, Jonatan shared that he was punished several times for speaking Spanish at his former school. I contacted him to invite him to talk about these incidents in my office. During his visit, Jonatan admitted that he had never thought about these issues until we discussed them in class in one of the SPC units. He had never considered why he had stopped speaking Spanish, and he admitted that he did not think it was of much use until he realized that almost all his 'gringo' classmates were taking Spanish classes. When he decided to enroll in Spanish, he did not do it just because it was an academic requirement; he also did it because, according to him, he knew that he would be finan-cially rewarded in the job market. He blamed not being more proficient in Spanish on the educational system because, especially in high school – both due to teacher and peer pressure and despite his mother's insistence on continuing with his Spanish studies – Jonatan stated that he limited the use of Spanish to home and did not find any practical use for it; on the contrary, in his words, 'they had made me believe that it would hurt my English' ('me habían hecho creer que me dañaría con el inglés', Jonatan).

Jonatan was involved in various Latina university cultural associa-tions and appeared to be interested in political activism. Perhaps this, coupled with his linguistic experiences, favored how his CLA seemed to have been abruptly awakened; his sensitivity toward these issues increased rapidly from the early stages of this program. For example, after two SPCs, Jonatan sent me a humorous video about linguistic varia-tion in the Spanish-speaking world along with a text in Spanish explain-ing that he had accidentally found this video clip and thought it was closely related to what we discussed about linguistic variation in class.

A few days later, Jonatan asked to come back to my office to review one of his essays, but before we could start, he brought up an incident that had occurred on campus that week. His visit seemed motivated by this incident rather than his essay, and he was visibly upset. Jonatan began by explaining that he had just witnessed at XU what had been discussed in class regarding subtractive bilingualism and the criminaliza-tion of the use of Spanish in public places and in educational contexts. A professor teaching a massive class (about 750 students) – Introduction to Economics, a course in which, according to Jonatan, she taught, legitimized and glorified capitalism – sent an email to all her teaching assistants and students requesting the exclusive use of English in class. Jonatan reported to the researcher that the incident originated as a result of his addressing one of these assistants in Spanish during this class. Jonatan (dominant in English, as he admitted) explained to me that he did not do it due to issues with English on his side, but rather because he realized the assistant had trouble expressing himself in English and he wanted to facilitate the interaction. Jonatan admitted that he did not know that these assistants came from different countries, and this one, in particular, was of Hispanic origin and an English learner. After knowing this, he only intended to help him and make him feel more comfortable. Jonatan claimed that he was more upset than he would have been had he not known about these issues. He was now aware that this restrictive policy of his home language had occurred throughout his life, and a behavior that should be rewarded was, once again and in a different context, banned, punished and silenced.

During our final interview, he also acknowledged that, even though his mother insisted that he enroll in a bilingual public school when he started high school, he refused because he had been convinced that it would harm him in the long term and have negative effects on his English proficiency ('me habían convencido de que eso me dañaría al largo plazo y afectaría mal a mi inglés', Jonatan). He said that he could be speaking Spanish perfectly ('yo ahorita podría hablar español perfectamente', Jonatan). But instead, he expressed, he had to attend class with those who could be the children of the very same people who persuaded him to abandon the study of Spanish. This infuriated him. He argued that he was now aware of the link between these events and a monoglottic ideology trying to maintain the status quo in the face of 'what you explained in class, professor, about the Hispanic threat' (Jonatan, my translation). Later on, in his final exam (which was used as an artifact to collect data), Jonatan effectively argued this idea of the Latino Threat. He did so by connecting the elites and power groups as those responsible and greatest beneficiaries of alarming certain sectors of public opinion by capitalizing on the fear of the loss of Anglo culture through the threat that Spanish poses to American monolingualism. During that same visit to my office, Jonatan also recounted a trip he had taken the prior weekend with some friends to Niagara University, a small university whose population, he said, was 90% White. He explained that bilingualism in the United States is a problem, but at least he felt fortunate that where he lives, it is recognized as such. However, in areas such as Niagara University, 'it is assumed that only English is spoken, they do not even consider it as a problem, it is taken for granted' (Jonatan, my translation).[2]

This awakening of his CLA was accompanied by a positive change in his motivation. When he first started the semester, his only motivation was of an instrumental type (Gardner & Lambert, 1972); that is, focused on external material rewards such as a higher salary in his future job or to complete the requirement for his undergraduate major program. In the first motivation questionnaire he took at the beginning of the semester, he was the third least motivated student in his class. He was quiet and reserved, needed to be motivated to participate and was consistently late for class. After the first couple of weeks, a change was observed in both his behavior and his attitude. He was one of the first students to arrive in the classroom. He was constantly participating on his own initiative and seemed enthusiastic about the class.

At the end of the semester, when asked 'Have you on the whole enjoyed or not enjoyed studying Spanish in this class, and how do you think your experience has affected your motivation?' Jonatan replied, 'I have enjoyed it, because it was a fun class. Genuinely enjoyed walking into the class' (Jonatan). This can be attributed to his experience with SPCs because, when asked if something had happened during the semester that influenced the way he felt about his Spanish classes, he replied: 'The professor making me realize that Spanish has different forms, and at the end of the day not everyone follows the book fully' (Jonatan). When asked, 'How would you describe your present state of motivation for learning Spanish, and have you experienced any motivational changes over the past semester?' Jonatan replied: 'Pretty high. I'm more motivated to learn how to fix the small things'. In the final interview, when asked what he meant by 'small things', he implied that he was referring to the mismatch of his linguistic variety with that studied in class, which he understood was useful to be successful in more formal settings such as certain professions, but that he no longer thought that he spoke 'bad Spanish' (Jonatan).

Thus, this increase in Jonatan's CLA appeared to influence his linguistic security, an indirect effect of SPCs observed with this HLS, and that has repercussions for avenues of investigation. In relation to increasing linguistic security, it should be noted that cognitive theories of motivation already pointed to the need to create a climate of acceptance that stimulates students' self-confidence and encourages them to experiment and discover the target language, allowing them to take risks without feeling ashamed (Dufeu, 1994: 89–90).

This change in Jonatan's motivation was accompanied by a change in his linguistic proficiency throughout the course, which improved remarkably (see Magro, 2016a, for more details). Jonatan's main linguistic concerns had to do mainly with the implementation of 'advanced grammar' and, above all, with the written format. In this sense, his linguistic progression paralleled his awakening of CLA and his increase in motivation. In addition, Jonatan increased his positive perception of studying Spanish both in the quantitative data collected with a final survey and in the qualitative data during the interview – 'It was the right decision!' (Jonatan). He attributed this to the novelty of studying language from a critical perspective, and how the contents related to the sociopolitical nature of language helped him to understand in more depth the ideologies linked to the different uses of language(s) in the United States.[3]

Jonatan's CLA at the end of the semester seems high when compared to other HLS in the section that did not receive SPCs such as Abelardo, who comes from an affluent family, the son of Cuban immigrants residing in Miami, and self-identified as White Hispanic and moderate Republican (a staunch supporter of Marco Rubio and radical opponent of Donald Trump). Although Abelardo is quite a critical student despite the dissonance his criticality constantly causes when confronted with his political ideology, he fails to analyze why Blacks are the group that statistically shows the most positive attitudes toward bilingual education (the students receive a statistic that shows this data in their final exam's prompt). He simplifies the problem down to a question in terms of Whites versus Hispanics, completely disregarding Blacks. Abelardo's first counterargument is, as is repeatedly the case in both the semi-experimental and control group essays, about some social groups complaining about the cost of these programs. Similarly to Jonatan's (whose ideology is rather antagonistic to Abelardo's), Abelardo's rebuttal focuses on the fact that 'en vez de comprar una [sic] avión de ataque que cuesta alrededor de mil millones de dólares, poderíamos [sic] usar ese dinero como una inverción [sic] para nuestro futuro' (instead of buying a war plane that costs about a billion dollars, we could use that money as an investment for our future [Abelardo]). Jonatan also advocates for a more education/health-oriented use of federal budgets and argues that, as long as there is money for weapons, there is money for bilingual programs ('mientras haya dinero para armas, hay dinero para programas bilingües', Jonatan). Moreover, in another counterargument, Abelardo identifies the opposition to these programs as a threat to the White, Anglo-Saxon and Protestant culture of the United States ('blanca, anglosajona y protestante de los EE.UU.', Abelardo). However, he refutes it superficially, without establishing relationships between power groups and hegemonic ideologies, arguing that that sentiment is pure racism and stupidity ('ese séntimo [sic] es puro racismo y estupidez', Abelardo) and harms 'our global image' (Abelardo, my translation). Thus, Abelardo reproduces the recurrent idea of the United States as a world power and leader with an image that 'we' need to protect to keep that position of global power. In contrast, Jonatan effectively connected in his argument the elites and power groups as those responsible for and the greatest beneficiaries of alarming certain sectors of public opinion with the fear of the loss of Anglo culture through the threat that Spanish poses to US monolingualism.

Abelardo's lack of awareness could be associated with his political views. However, the lower awareness when compared to the semi-experimental group can also be perceived in students of the control group that showed consciousness about different topics related to social justice. For instance, Stacey, who showed this critical awareness during the debate activities in class (both groups participated in debates as part of the standard curriculum), leaves Blacks out of the equation completely when analyzing the data source. Most of the students in the semi-experimental group were able to associate race, language and the diverse reasons why Blacks could be more favorable to bilingual programs (solidarity with another minority, sharing spaces and even addressing Spanish and African American English inferiorization by standard English speakers). Stacey creates a White versus Hispanic opposition and justifies her support of bilingualism primarily by the majority support of the US population as a whole for bilingual education (which appears in the data offered in the prompt). It is true that she recognizes Whites as the group in power and argues that the lack of bilingual education is one of the factors in school failure among Hispanics in the United States. However, Stacey compares Hispanics to students with special needs, building her argument around the idea that a lack of English language ability is equivalent to having a physical or cognitive impairment. Thus, she reproduces similar thinking to what other students in the control group argued in their essays, which never appeared in any essay of the experimental group: 'Un niño no puede decidir a tener una disabilidad [*sic*], ni puede decidir la lengua de los padres que aprende en la casa como primera lengua' (A child cannot decide to have a disability, nor can he decide the language of the parents that he learns at home as his first language [Stacey]).

In contrast with Jonatan's views on bilingualism after taking the SPCs, and with his classmates in the semi-experimental group, for Stacey, as frequently occurs in the control group students' argumentations, bilingualism refers to immigrant students learning English without having to abandon Spanish (additive bilingualism), without taking into account that many bilingual programs today are aimed at L1 speakers of English, either in full immersion programs or in two-way bilingual/immersion programs.[4] Once again, the main counter-argument in the control group (those who did not take SPCs) does not focus on power relations and language, but rather on the cost of these programs for the government. Stacey refutes in a similar way as it has been done in almost all the essays that used this counterargument, arguing about the banality of investment in bilingual programs if we take into account the benefits described in source 3 (this source of the final exam prompt stated the benefits of a bilingual brain).

Jonatan is a good example of the effectiveness of SPCs in increasing CLA, motivation and linguistic competence in an HLS. Although he stated that he did not want to take more Spanish classes at XU, this decision was justified by the shortage of attractive, practical or relevant classes for what he perceived as his needs in the labor market and/or his intellectual education. It is understandable that for a Latin American student like him who shows a critical conscience, any attempt he may perceive as an imposition of materials with neo-colonizing dyes may provoke resistance. That is the impression he gave when asked if he was interested in the classes offered for his next level of Spanish at XU: an Advanced Oral Proficiency class focused on environmental and social sustainability in Latin America, and a few literature classes focused on Golden Age literature and the Enlightenment in Spain. He said that he would have liked to take more classes but was not interested in those offered. He showed interest and directly inquired via email about a class with similar contents to those reviewed during the SPCs.

However, despite having no intention to continue studying Spanish at XU, his attitude toward studying Spanish, and toward Spanish itself, changed. The analysis and interpretation of all the data obtained from Jonatan and his decision to study Spanish abroad confirmed this conclusion.

7.1.2 Kyra, a non-Hispanic heritage speaker

Kyra's case is one of the most salient in terms of the explicit evidence it offers on the connection between the inclusion of SPCs and an increase in her motivation, with its consequent influence on the development of her linguistic competence. Nonetheless, the focus in this section will be on her CLA.

Kyra was a 19-year-old student whose parents were migrants from India. She was born in a US Mideast city and self-identified as Asian by writing 'Indian' after checking the 'other' box in the first questionnaire at the beginning of the semester. She declares herself as *middle-income level* (yearly household income between 100k and 150k USD). Both her parents graduated college and were employed in the banking industry. Her town in Pennsylvania, based on the 2000 US Census, was mainly White (more than 70%) with a solid Hispanic population (20%). However, based on the 2010 US Census, the Hispanic population had almost doubled, becoming almost 50% of the total population of her town. Kyra mentioned that, in her former school, she interacted in Spanish numerous times and that Spanish was frequently used in public spaces. Additionally, probably based on her phenotypical appearance (brown skin, dark hair and eyes), Spanish speakers tended to address her in Spanish, a language that she started studying in high school and, as she reflected, was very useful and had many opportunities to practice outside of the classroom.

Kyra was a serious and assertive student with a kind personality. She started the semester with a high participation that increased throughout the semester. From the beginning, Kyra showed a critical attitude and an interest in political issues, perhaps with a more liberal ideology than what most students at XU – who were generally more conservative liberals than Kyra and self-identified as Democrats – usually demonstrate. When asked, 'How would you define your political views? Did your political views change during this semester? If so, how?' Kyra replied, 'Not quite, I was very liberal, and I remain very liberal' (Kyra). Her ideology, experience as a second generation of immigrants and linguistic background are factors that most likely influenced the rapid development of her CLA, which already seemed quite developed at the beginning of the semester.

During our first interview, Kyra showed that she was already familiar with sociolinguistic variation while acknowledging the diatopic, diastratic and diaphasic dimensions of language. When asked if there was a correct/appropriate way of speaking Spanish, she answered that 'everyone speaks in a different way and there is no correct way to speak because it is a reflection of culture and society' (Kyra). Both terminologically and in her explanations, Kyra demonstrated a more developed CLA than her co-participants in this research. However, during this first interview, she reproduced the recurrent idea of Spanish from Spain versus Spanish from Latin America:

> there are different dialects and different regions, like in Spain they use the 'vosotros' and they don't use the 's' and 'z' sound as much, and throughout South America they have different ways of speaking, and they also have like formal Spanish and informal Spanish, and they speak it differently in villages than in towns, and that kind of thing. (Kyra)

After analyzing the last interview, both in the tone of her voice and in her answers, as well as in her non-verbal communication, Kyra showed more confidence than in the first interview. She was more concise and clear, she knew how to explain herself better regarding issues related to the sociopolitical nature of language, and it could be perceived that some doubts had been clarified. For example, when asked if she believed that all Spanish speakers used the same type of Spanish, her answer was: 'noooo [laughs], there are dialectical differences, and in the level of formality' (Kyra). She also no longer reproduced this idea of Spain versus Latin America, and it was not as much her answer as how she responded using a sarcastic and jovial tone to reproach the researcher for asking her a question whose answer was too obvious after taking this class.

Another example of her increased CLA at the end of the semester appears when discussing variation in English. For Kyra, from the first interview, there was no wrong variety of speaking English. However, while in the first interview, she used references to her personal experience and that of her parents to provide examples, in the final interview, she said: 'English is spoken across the world and there are different ways and interpretations of speaking English, I don't think there is a correct way though' (Kyra). Taking into account the brief informal conversations that took place with this student regarding the ideas of language and power, this affirmation was interpreted as how Kyra was able to synthesize sociolinguistic variation under a perspective that understands language as the social construction it is.

Furthermore, her final exam denoted a high linguistic awareness through, for example, the recognition of the inclusiveness of bilingualism in the face of the exclusivity, marginalization and stigmatization associated with monolingualism, or with phrases such as 'el monolingüismo es una enfermedad curable' (monolingualism is a curable disease, my translation) (Kyra).

Regarding the link between her CLA and her motivation, she offers evidence by arguing explicitly about it in her questionnaire answers. When asked, 'Has anything happened this semester that has influenced the way you feel about your study of Spanish?' Kyra answered, 'The socio-linguistic lessons definitely made me want to continue learning more about Spanish and languages in general' (Kyra). When asked about her decision to take this class and participate in this research, her answer met the transformative mission of this study by opening to new perspectives: 'I think taking this particular section of Spanish was one of the best decisions I made in choosing classes. The research has opened me up to different perspectives and allowed me to learn more in general' (Kyra). She again mentions SPCs as a determiner for her increase in motivation during the program when answering, 'Is there any activity or activities to which you attribute any increase in your motivation toward language learning? (Please make a list if any and explain why)': 'Learning about sociolinguistics, focus on fluency rather than particular grammar and vocab, using different forms of Spanish, so I'm prepared to use it in real life' (Kyra).

On the one hand, it is suspected that being simultaneously bilingual in Gujarati and English (which she declared as her first language) and declaring Hindi and Spanish as her second languages – 'I understand Hindi and am learning Spanish' (Kyra) – has great explanatory power when interpreting how exposure to SPCs rapidly increased her motivation. From the beginning of this course, Kyra showed great interest in these topics (e.g. she often expressed her interest to the instructor, asked questions after the presentations, participated frequently and started discussions in class). Therefore, the effectiveness of SPCs in raising the CLA and motivation of heritage students is something that should be taken into account when developing curricula for classes with minority racialized student populations (what in the United States has been called 'culturally diverse students') – that is, students who are ethnic and/or racial minorities, heritage language speakers (or speakers of English varieties other than White American English, such as AAVE or Chicano English) and whose experiences very often connect identity and language to asymmetric power relations.

On the other hand, Kyra's motivation questionnaires had a lower score in the desire to continue taking Spanish classes at XU than in the rest of the categories. Her response to 'How would you describe your present state of motivation for learning Spanish, and have you experienced any motivational changes over the past semester?' is representative of the problem that the Spanish department at XU presented and which Jonatan also commented on: 'I would like to continue learning Spanish, but not with the current classes offered next semester. I would like to learn about more relevant social issues' (Kyra). Nonetheless, her motivation in wanting to use Spanish in her daily interactions increased, which was one of the transformative goals of the SPCs – that is, wanting to interact with the Latina population of the United States. It also increased in the category of wanting to learn through cultural activities.

Kyra requested a recommendation letter from me for a study abroad program in Chile three months after the semester ended. This program, she wrote in Spanish, was based on cultural identity, social justice and community development, themes that she said we discussed in class. After being accepted, she left a note in my mailbox, in which she attributed her motivation to apply for this program to the SPC units in this class. However, despite her interest in minoring in Spanish, she decided not to do so because of the assessment system that the XU Spanish program used. She thought this system was not appropriate for learning a language:

> I hopefully will find a way to do it in like a non-academic setting just because school and grades is like more stressful than it is like, then you feel like you are learning because everything is about getting assignments and hopefully, I will be able to do so but we'll see. (Kyra)

At this point, I would like to make a brief point about traditional cognitive approaches to SLA. From these approaches, the evaluation and monitoring of the learner's linguistic competence development is a fundamental component. However, from my point of view, this system, as applied in this program, frustrated the student, especially when their placement at a certain level was closer to the lower threshold of that level, generating resistance and demotivating them to the point of leading students to abandon Spanish. This means that the grades, regardless of students' effort, are always lower than those of students whose score on the placement test places them closer to the upper threshold. Kyra's complaints support the arguments posed by the ungrading movement previously discussed in this chapter.

The insistence on quantifying linguistic behaviors is also highly questionable from other epistemological points of view, especially from sociocultural approaches to SLA. While these scores can give us an idea of where the student is in terms of her linguistic proficiency as understood by a particular department, the researcher does not believe that they should be equally applied. Under the American university framework and its inclination to quantify everything, it is considered essential to award a grade. In this sense, a line of research is opened to investigate the development of an equitable, more motivating and decolonized evaluation system based on students' progress/growth from the beginning of the semester to the end regardless of what is understood by language proficiency in each language program.

Kyra also asserted her frustration in finding stimulating Spanish classes; otherwise, she would have continued. She also said she would sign up immediately for a sociolinguistics class: 'Yeah, if you teach it, I will take it next semester' (Kyra).

This last comment may reveal underlying factors regarding Kyra's motivation, such as the instructor. There is not enough evidence to determine if the instructor was so motivating due to having the opportunity to teach SPCs or if it would have happened with any other content. However, as the instructor of this course, I admit that I was excited and highly motivated to teach this content, and this excitement and motivation probably transferred to some students. In that case, a reasonable question could be: is it enough for the instructor to teach whatever material they are excited about to motivate students? This probably would help increase motivation; theories of motivation thus inform us. There is no reason to think that a well-articulated L2 class with content such as, to take a fictitious example, 'Spanish football in the 21st century', would be ineffective at increasing motivation if the instructor feels passionate about the topic. The question would be what the educational and transformative function of the content is and how this is articulated in a language class and the academic needs of students. In the case of SPCs, both the educational and transformative functions, as well as their articulation with language, are evident. In the soccer class example, it might or might not be, depending on how the content is articulated critically and with the linguistic goals.

In sum, Kyra quickly and effectively developed a CLA that, according to the evidence collected, seemed to have influenced the increase of her motivation and, consequently, her linguistic competence, which, as expected, increased significantly throughout the semester. Kyra was one of the most salient examples in this research of how learning about the sociopolitical nature of language increases CLA and how this CLA influences student motivation. It is very possible that her personal experiences as an HLS, her second generation migrant-descent, her linguistic profile and her race/ethnicity were determining factors that facilitated her predisposition to internalize this kind of content – a phenomenon that seems common among this type of speaker, as Magro (2016a) details. As in the previous case, these individual characteristics of this group of students should be taken into account when designing a specific curriculum.

7.1.3 Julian, a student who attended a study abroad program

I selected Julian's case because it is a good example of how a positive study abroad experience can influence motivation and receptiveness toward SPCs. The relationship between Julian's CLA and motivation is inconclusive because he assessed his motivation with the maximum score at the beginning and at the end of the semester. Moreover, when asked at the end of the semester, 'How would you describe your present state of motivation for learning Spanish, and have you experienced any motivational changes over the past semester?' he stated, 'I came in with a large motivation to learn and it remains very strong' (Julian).

Julian was a 21-year-old White student from Boston placed in this advanced Spanish class after taking a course in a study abroad program in Chile. With a yearly family household income between 150,000 and 250,000 USD, he declared himself to be in the higher middle-income rank of the questionnaire. He declared English as his first language. Although he did not declare a second language in the questionnaire, his Spanish language proficiency at the beginning of the semester was similar to that of a heritage student like Jonatan (except for some phonetic differences). That is, he had some difficulties with the registers demanded by this course, but he displayed advanced proficiency in more natural conversations (he was one of the few participants who decided to do all his interviews in Spanish).

He was an extremely outgoing, good-natured and active student who seemed to enjoy interviews. He considered himself to be a liberal Democrat on national politics and conservative on international politics and national security matters ('demócrata liberal en cuanto a política nacional y conservador en cuanto a política internacional y asuntos de seguridad nacional' and 'domestically liberal, believer in offensive realism in international affairs' [Julian]). Although he showed a neoliberal ideology through his comments in class, he also demonstrated sensitivity toward issues of social injustice from the beginning of the semester. In class, he was very participative, especially during the debates, but perhaps because his level was a little above the rest of the students in terms of his oral speech (and he himself thought so), he was frequently distracted during class by other materials that he read on his computer.

Julian's CLA, however, increased during the semester. For example, at the beginning of the semester, Julian had a stereotypical vision of Spanish speakers in the United States as people with little round faces, Mexicans, browner ('caritas redondas, mexicanos, más morenos', Julian). In his final exam, his essay started by stating that the issue of bilingual education is a political and controversial one between the races in the United States ('La pregunta sobre la educación bilingüe es una política y controversial entre las razas en los Estados Unidos', Julian). By the end of the semester, he was able to effectively articulate the existing conflict regarding language and racial identity in the US and how the opposition against bilingualism had to do with the fear of Whites of losing their identity.

When asked about the effect of SPCs on him, he recognized that he knew there were different ways of speaking before we started the

204 Part 2: When, Where, How

semester, but he did not know how to see this from a scientific perspective ('pero no sabía cómo es posible ver esto de una forma científica como tú lo hiciste', Julian). However, in contrast with the heritage speakers discussed earlier, it could be inferred that this was not that interesting for him. He stated that the relationships between language and power were revealing, but the example he provided had to do with how it was difficult for him to understand jokes in Chile due to a lack of pragmatics and how, now, thanks to the SPCs, he had a greater knowledge for interpreting the different subtleties of the language. This is relevant for the analysis because we can see how after being exposed to SPCs, Julian's idiosyncrasy and personal background as a White, wealthy US male differs from the insights provided by the HL speakers I discussed earlier. This also intersects with his motivation.

As stated earlier, it was not possible to draw any clear conclusions regarding the effect of his CLA on his motivation because, as he stated, he started very motivated and kept that motivation. However, it is interesting how the motivation of this fervent Democrat defender of neoliberalism and believer in offensive realism in international affairs was mainly instrumental and oriented toward gaining professional advantages. When asked, 'Have you any further ideas or experienced any changes in your ideas about future career plans? If so, do you think these have had any impact on the way you feel about studying Spanish?' he answered, 'I'm going to be a diplomat so I will probably get ample use of my Spanish' (Julian).

When inquiring about his history with Spanish regarding the motivations that led him to study it, he replied that in high school, he did not have much interest in learning Spanish and did not put much effort into it at all. But when asked about what made him study Spanish at university, he mentioned an interest motivated by the acquisition of knowledge about Latin America, an area he saw as a job opportunity and for which he needed Spanish.

In sum, although there is no evidence to draw conclusions about how CLA influenced Julian's motivation, it can be stated that his CLA increased, his motivation remained as high as when he started the semester, and he was grateful for having expanded his knowledge about the sociopolitical nature of language. Nonetheless, as discussed in this book, those experiences and ideological frameworks aligned with Julian's White privilege result in qualitatively different insights compared to those of HL speakers.

7.1.4 Dealing with opposing political views: Jacob, another student who attended a study abroad program

Jacob, 19, was a White practicing Catholic student (he was part of a Catholic university organization) and the only student who declared himself several times during class as a Republican and a conservative (at the end of the semester, he stated, 'I am a conservative Republican and still am'). He was born in a small, conservative, Christian-oriented US southern town that has six private Christian high schools. The 2010 census declared this town approximately 65% White, just over 25% African American, and less than 2% Latino. His parents finished their secondary education, and the annual income that Jacob declared was between 100,000 and 150,000 dollars. His mother was a housewife (with the sense of humor that characterized Jacob, he declared in the questionnaire, 'domestic engineer'). He thought of his family as *higher middle-income level*, something that, taking into account the place of residence, could make sense (it would not be considered the same socioeconomic status [SES] residing in a big city such as New York).

Jacob had a peculiar sense of humor; he was participative, especially during the debates we had in class, activities in which he seemed to enjoy adopting the most conservative side of each topic. He was the only student who was often late to class and the only one who received a formal warning for being at risk of failing class due to truancy. His assignments were of very poor quality (when he turned them in), and he left several assignments unturned during the course for which he was penalized on his grade. His attitude was that of a student who, due to having acquired some proficiency in Spanish in Chile, just came to 'take a walk'. That is, he may have thought this class would be an easy and comfortable way to maintain a good GPA. However, he admitted to me during a walk after class that he thought he knew more Spanish than he actually did and realized too late that he underestimated the class and should have worked harder during the semester. He admitted that after this course, he realized that his linguistic repertoire was very limited and only functional in informal registers in a concrete region (Chile). This comment shows his recently acquired awareness of the different dimensions of language. In his final exam, he showed how these materials not only influenced his knowledge of sociolinguistics but also his CLA regarding language and racism. He started his argumentation stating that 'it would be very beneficial if we prioritize bilingualism as a talent and not a characteristic of race and exclusion' ('sería muy beneficioso si priotizáramos [*sic*] el bilingüismo como un talento y no una característica de raza y exclusión'). He understands the relationship between the bilingualism of a great part of the Hispanic population (and most likely of all speakers of languages other than English in the United States, from what his later comments imply) and the stigmatization and exclusion of Hispanics in the United States. In his counter-argument, to refute the argument of '[esos] derechistas que creen que el bilingüismo peligra la unión de la población estadounidense' ([those] right-wingers who believe that bilingualism endangers the unity of the American population) (Jacob), he explains that he does not believe that bilingualism should be something exclusive to English speakers, but for all residents of this country who use public education ('el bilingüismo es únicamente dado a los angloparlantes, sino a todos los residentes de este país quien [sic] usan la educación pública') (Jacob), presenting a more equitable view of the relationship between English and the other languages of the United States. He goes on to argue that for Spanish speakers, German speakers, Mandarin speakers and so on, English is a foreign language and should be taught as a second language to them ('los hispanohablantes, alemánhablantes [sic], hablantes de mandarín, el inglés es un idioma extranjero y debería ser enseñado como un segundo lenguaje para ellos') (Jacob).

However, his CLA clashes with his ideology. My analysis interprets that Jacob's Republican ideology emerges when he declares that the purpose of a bilingual education is to teach English to immigrants and another language to English speakers ('el propósito de una educación bilingüe es enseñar inglés a los inmigrantes y otra lengua a los angloparlantes') (Jacob), thus advocating for an additive bilingualism framed in an assimilationist project in which English remains the 'pseudo-official' (Jacob) language of the United States. Jacob argues that *our* language would still be pseudo-officially English, but each of us could speak a second language ('todavía nuestra lenguaje [sic] sería inglés (pseudo-oficial), pero cada uno de nosotros podría hablar un segundo idioma') (Jacob). However, his speech on bilingualism is in stark contrast to the representatives of the Republican Party's speech (including their bilingual candidates at that time, such as Marco Rubio, who embraces Spanish, or Ted Cruz, who does not). Jacob is one of the few students who identified the hiatus in bilingual programs in the 1999–2003 period when no other participant in the control group commented about this data in the statistics offered in the prompt of this final exam. He attributes this hiatus to what he defined as the 9/11 disaster ('desastre de 9/11') (Jacob) and said that with this statistic we can see the assumptions between race and language embedded in the minds of many Americans ('con esta estadística podemos ver la gran asumpción [sic] entre la raza y la lengua que hay en la mente de muchos estadounidenses') (Jacob). Thus, Jacob establishes relationships between language, race and ideology. He ends his argument by expressing his belief that the integration of bilingual programs can be an important factor in the dissolution of racism ('la integración de programas bilingües puede ser un factor importante en la disolución del racismo') (Jacob). With this statement he recognizes, as other students did, the power of language policy as a promoter of social change.

But it is in the analysis of his motivation that things become more complex, and it is necessary to attend to the individual characteristics and behaviors of this type of student during the course. I believe that conservative students such as Jacob offer a greater challenge than progressive students, who generally come to our classes more open-minded and with a higher critical awareness. Also, as we will see in this case, sometimes these self-identified conservative/Republican students may contradict their own (claimed) ideological positions. Providing a safe space to express ideas without inhibiting our students (always within certain parameters of respect and promoting facts over beliefs in our discussions) helps to unveil ideological contradictions and promote fruitful discussions in class.

Despite his apparently lazy, unkempt appearance and careless attitude, Jacob seemed to enjoy the class and openly expressed his opinions, being one of the most participative students. This could be interpreted as a sign that his opposing views to the majority of the class were not inhibited by a hostile climate, and he did not feel intimidated or rejected. This is something to which special attention was paid during this program: creating an open climate of acceptance where students felt comfortable and sure of themselves to express different opinions and experiment with the language, something that other authors, such as Dufeu (1994), have suggested in order to suppress inhibition.

When discussing topics that could generate dissonance for him, such as the legalization of drugs, the right to carry weapons or free borders, he did not always adopt the conservative side as expected of his claimed ideology. He sincerely defended, for example, the legalization of marijuana (not other drugs), something that made the researcher suspect that Jacob claimed to be a conservative Republican more out of dogma and family tradition than out of ideological agreement with what is generally understood in the United States as being a conservative Republican.

Regarding his motivation, at the beginning of the semester, he was satisfied with his decision to take this course – 7 out of 7 points on the Likert scale of a quantitative questionnaire aiming to assess motivation (for a complete analysis, see Magro, 2016a). At the end of the semester, he was equally satisfied. Likewise, his desire to take more classes at XU, very low at the beginning of the semester (2 out of 7), increased by one point (3 out of 7). However, his motivation for his desire to learn through cultural activities dropped two points. Likewise, his desire to travel to other countries also dropped two points in both. However, Jacob's motivation regarding his desire to learn Spanish through daily interactions and his desire to work or volunteer remained equally high (6 out of 7). These last two areas have to do with the transformative function of an antiracist pedagogical approach in the language classroom, which promotes the interaction of L2 learners with the Hispanic population within the United States instead of focusing on the generally idealized and exoticized Spanish-speaking population abroad. In Jacob's case, similarly to Julian's, it seems that since the beginning of the semester, he frequently crossed what Schwartz (2014) calls the third border – the social, psychological and physical border separating working-class Hispanic populations (allegedly chaotic, disorganized, dangerous, etc.) from the mainstream population within the United States.

Already in the first interview, Jacob commented on how he had different relationships with Latinos in his church and in his neighborhood (he lived in Columbia Heights, a predominantly Latino neighborhood in Washington, DC), something that at the end of the semester had not changed. In this case, both Jacob's experience in Chile and his religious beliefs (he argued how, in his church, racial differences were diluted under a single faith, everyone was different but equal in the eyes of their Lord, etc.) allowed him to use Spanish with the US Latino population outside an academic context. Jacob seemed sincerely interested in the relationships between language, power and identity after this program ('I am glad I took this class to satisfy the requirement and the social linguistics part was very interesting') (Jacob), but he does not show a genuine motivation to continue learning Spanish formally ('I'm not that much more motivated to learn Spanish, but I am more interested in general social linguistics') (Jacob). He thought of a general sociolinguistics class as an advanced Spanish content class taught in Spanish. Even though he admitted to having enjoyed this class – 'I have enjoyed this class very much' – he explains right after that, 'The teacher made the experience though, the content at times was too political for me and honestly, I am just not that interested in the Spanish language' (Jacob). This leads us to reflect on the limitations of this pedagogical approach to increasing motivation when the student is convinced, from the beginning of the semester, that learning Spanish in a university department such as XU's is not the best way: 'When I am in Chile, I become a much better Spanish speaker because I have to be to survive' (Jacob). Jacob was one of those students in this program who confessed that they could not find interesting classes after completing the advanced level. He stated that 'learning [Spanish] in a natural context is the best method' (Jacob).

To illustrate these limitations and the extent to which exposure to SPCs within an antiracist perspective influenced Jacob's motivation, the final interview offers the following data. When asked in this interview what his motivation to learn Spanish was, after a long silence, Jacob broke it with a '¿más?' (more?) (Jacob). The exchange was as follows:

JM: ¿Más?, ¿menos? Después de esta clase, ¿igual? (More? Less? After this class, the same?)

Jacob: ¿Igual? (The same?)

JM: Igual. (The same.)

Jacob: Eh ... .

JM: ¿Estabas muy motivado al empezar? (Were you very motivated when you started?)

Jacob: No. No estaba muy motivado al principio y ahora estoy un poco más motivado, pero no mucho ... (No. I was not very motivated at the beginning and now I am a little more motivated, but not much ...)

When asked why he was a little more motivated, the participant stated 'sólo porque [two seconds pause], sí, el sociolingüismo era lo más importante que ayudó, pero el idioma en sí mismo, eh, no sé, no es una [five seconds pause] ... No sé, cuando viví en Chile sí era [...] si vivo en un país hispanohablante quiero aprender español, si vivo en Alemania, lo mismo, quiero aprender alemán, pero sí, eso' ('just because [two-second pause], yes, sociolinguism was the most important thing that helped me, but the language itself, uh, I don't know, it's not a [five-second pause] ... I don't know, when I lived in Chile it was [...] if I live in a Spanish-speaking country I want to learn Spanish, if I live in Germany, the same thing, I want to learn German, but yes, that') (Jacob). The student seems to admit that he does not really like learning languages in an academic context and that his motivation is increased by learning them in a natural context. However, it seems that learning about the sociopolitical nature of language did help him maintain an interest in this class. His behavior and habits improved notably during the second half of the semester (no absences, punctuality, more quality and quantity of homework delivered and even his appearance and hygiene improved).

However, Jacob's comment reveals a failure of this pedagogy's critical social change mission to promote a view of the US Spanish speaker as a 'real' Spanish speaker. In other words, Jacob does not seem to consider that the United States is also, in addition to being an English-speaking and many-other-languages-speaking country, a Spanish-speaking country. While it may be true that he has fewer opportunities to use English in other countries, it is also true that in certain communities within the United States, the use of English is very restricted, and this could allow him to argue that if he is in a Spanish-speaking area he should want to learn Spanish the same way that if he lives in Germany he would want to learn German. This can be interpreted as an influence of his conservative ideology, which, as discussed in his essay in the final exam, demonstrates a view of the United States as an English-speaking country. Remember how Jacob argued that 'el propósito de una educación bilingüe es enseñar inglés a los inmigrantes y otra lengua a los angloparlantes' (the purpose of a bilingual education is to teach English to immigrants and another language to English speakers) (Jacob), thus advocating a bilingualism that, although additive instead of subtractive, is part of an assimilationist project where English continues to be the 'pseudo-official language' (Jacob) as explained earlier in this section.

Jacob's language proficiency was very similar to Julian's at the beginning and at the end of the semester (like Julian, he conducted both interviews in Spanish). Jacob showed evidence in the acquisition of structures that were not part of his linguistic repertoire at the beginning of the course (construction of hypotheses through the use of the imperfect subjunctive, development of his vocabulary, construction of complex sentences, connectors, etc.). It is suspected that this progress probably would not have occurred if the student's motivation had not been maintained through the integration of the SPCs in the program.

Jacob's case is complex. However, this pedagogical approach, despite Jacob's beliefs, political perspectives and ideology at that time, influenced his critical linguistic awareness, and it seems that, according to him, it at least helped him to maintain his motivation by increasing his linguistic proficiency, an area in which he recognized growth. In a case like this, according to my experience as an instructor with similar students, what could have easily ended in Jacob's academic failure in a demanding program such as XU's, and perhaps uncomfortable situations and tensions, ended up better than it could be expected.

7.1.5 A difficult case: Margarita, another student who attended a study abroad program

Margarita, a 19-year-old White student from New Jersey, the daughter of a teacher and a social worker with an income between 80,000 and 100,000 dollars a year (she declared her SES as middle-income level), called herself by the Anglo version of her name (since the students' names are fictitious to protect their anonymity, the equivalent would be Margaret). However, in class, she was called by her official name, Margarita. This preference (or possible rejection of the Hispanic nature of her name) was a fact that could have links to her low motivation and negative attitudes toward Spanish, which she took – as she acknowledged in the second interview when asked about her motivation to take this class at the beginning of the semester – to meet an academic requirement ('I have to take Spanish, that was my motivation') (Margarita).

Margarita was the most unmotivated student of the two sections from the beginning of the semester. In fact, her data could not be included in the quantitative analysis of motivation because she did not answer all the questions and seemed to answer them without reading them. She did not seem interested at all in these topics, and her participation was limited to achieving the minimum requirement to receive the extra credit for participation in this research. For example, when asked about her political ideology ('How would you define your political views? Did your political views change during this semester? If so, how?'), she answered with a simple 'no' (Margarita). Her case deserves particular attention to investigate what happens when unmotivated students are exposed to content that deals with the sociopolitical nature of language to increase antiracist awareness.

While the first interview was completely apathetic, a change was noted in the second, as revealed in the qualitative analysis of her data; e.g. 'the research section of class motivated me a lot because I was interested in the topics of class' (Margarita). In the last interview, she also confessed that she would never have thought of these types of issues related to the sociopolitical nature of language and that she enjoyed studying language from this point of view. Let us delve into what happened in Margarita's change in motivation and critical awareness, when the Spanish class at the beginning of the semester was no more than an imposed and apparently tedious requirement for her. This analysis will help to clarify the importance of the intertwining of motivation, CLA and aptitude in language learning while taking into consideration the experiences and attitudes toward language learning of the student.

Margarita was the only student in this research who rated the Spanish courses and program as 'average'. However, despite being a student who was clearly dissatisfied with the Spanish program at XU, she made it explicit in the interview that her interest in Spanish had increased after this class. She responded to 'How would you describe your present state of motivation for learning Spanish, and have you experienced any motivational changes over the past semester?' with 'I don't have that much motivation because I have a hard time in Spanish. My motivation has improved this semester but I still feel like learning languages is very hard for me' (Margarita).

Being exposed to antiracist materials during class had a notable influence on Margarita's attitude toward the study of L2 in the classroom, which she considered an ineffective way of learning languages at the beginning of the semester. Margarita had been in a program abroad, living with a family in Barcelona, and argued that immersing oneself in a Spanish-speaking country was the only way to learn Spanish. At the end of the semester, Margarita still thought: 'I would like to continue studying Spanish but I am not sure if a classroom setting is the best way to learn for me' (Margarita). From this statement, it could be interpreted that the increase in her CLA through antiracist materials was probably not enough to increase her desire to continue learning Spanish in an academic setting. When asked, 'How do you now view your decision to study Spanish at SPAN-2006? And your participation in this research? Was it the right or wrong decision?', she replied: 'I am glad I continue my studies but I am not sure if I will continue after this semester. I really enjoyed the research portion of class. I thought it was very interesting and would love a class focused solely on that material' (Margarita). Margarita, like other students in this research, expressed to me that the Spanish department did not offer useful or attractive classes for students in the higher levels of the Spanish program.

At the beginning of the semester, Margarita's demotivation manifested itself daily through her non-verbal communication (yawning, stretching her arms, staring blankly, etc.). She also showed a lack of participation in oral tasks in class, a low quality of her written and oral assignments and even a lack of motivation to participate in the investigation of which the SPC units were part. Had it not been for the information I gained through this investigation, I would have suspected it was something personal, or that she opposed my points of view on racism and other political aspects. She met all the deadlines of all her assignments from the beginning because, as she explained, she was aware that this would help her maintain the minimum required grade to graduate from her program (C+).

But as the semester progressed, a change was noticeable in terms of her motivation, as well as an improvement in her language proficiency, although the latter was still below the rest of both groups (she finished the semester with the lowest mark). Margarita's lack of motivation at the beginning of the semester can be explained from different theoretical positions. On the one hand, from a cognitive approach, Weiner (1992) proposed three main conceptual systems related to motivation: (1) the attribution theory, which explains that what we consider to be the causes of our past successes and failures affects our expectations and, through these expectations, affects our performance; (2) learned helplessness, which occurs when students are convinced through their past mistakes that any attempt to change the situation is useless; (3) self-efficacy, which has to do with the opinion that students have regarding their ability to carry out a task, what Ehrman (1996: 137) defines as the degree to which the student thinks he or she has the aptitude to face the challenge of learning.

However, despite this initial demotivation, after analyzing Margarita's case in depth, it seems that the inclusion of SPCs was pivotal to increasing her motivation during the course. When asked, 'Is there any activity or activities to which you attribute any increase in your motivation toward language learning? (Please make a list if any and explain why)', Margarita replied: 'The research section of class motivated me a lot because I was interested in the topics of class' (Margarita). The fact that the SPCs dealt with topics that were interesting even for the most unmotivated student in both classes provides more evidence in favor of including this type of content in language classes. Margarita seemed destined for academic failure in this class, but she did better than in previous classes at XU. Although she only went from a series of C− in previous classes to a final grade of C+ in this class (her best mark in her Spanish career in this program so far), in the final oral and written exams she received a B. Marks aside (which were required and emphasized by this department), I observed a noticeable improvement in her oral and written skills in daily activities and interactions as well as from a qualitative perspective focused on communicative skills.

Margarita's response to 'Are there any Spanish-related tasks, conditions, or situations where you feel your motivation is higher than usual, and if so, why do you think this might be so?' was: 'Talking about the differences in dialect and origins of language and culture were [sic] very interesting' (Margarita). Note that in the final interview, she insists that her motivation to learn Spanish remains the same and makes it clear that she is referring to learning Spanish in the classroom because she considers herself a student with cognitive difficulties in learning Spanish ('I think I have trouble learning Spanish') (Margarita). However, evidence shows that her motivation increased, at least during particular moments of the instruction. After declaring, 'I really loved the sociolinguistics topics' (Margarita), Margarita argues that 'it was like I was more motivated to be in the class when we talked about sociolinguistics topics than when we were following the book' (Margarita).

Margarita's perception of her aptitude opens possible avenues of research in SLA on students' beliefs about their aptitude to learn languages – that is, their self-efficacy (Weiner, 1992), and how the articulation of content that is relevant for the student (in this case, SPCs with a focus on antiracism) can influence attitudes toward learning and, over time, perhaps change the student's negative perception of his or her own aptitude.

Although, according to Krashen (1981: 19), aptitude and attitude are two variables that are related to the acquisition of an L2 but are not related to each other (for example, a learner may have a low attitude and a high aptitude or vice versa, or have both high or both low), the self-perception of aptitude influences the attitude towards the study of an L2. Researchers in the study of communication, a highly relevant area of study for language teaching, argued more than four decades ago that 'the overwhelming conclusion from both research and theory is that the perceptions one has of self significantly affect attitudes, behaviours, evaluations, and cognitive processes. In classroom research the concept an individual has of self has also played an important role' (McCroskey, 1977: 79).

As a language instructor, it is not the first time that I have faced a case like Margarita's, in which the frustrations resulting from their L2 learning experience in a standardized program result in the student's belief that they have a low aptitude for learning languages. If Margarita had been placed in the previous level Spanish course offered by XU, her linguistic proficiency at that level would have been higher. This would have had psychosocial benefits for her. Moreover, if instead of having been placed in intermediate Spanish when she started Spanish at XU, she had started in basic Spanish, her experience with Spanish during her time at XU would probably have been perceived as more successful by the student, since in this program so focused on marking, her grades would surely have been higher. According to Little (2007), 'when meeting with success, participants also improve their perception of self-confidence' (in Muñoz, 2012: 155). In Margarita's case, it is very possible that her placement upon entering the Spanish program caused her not only to develop negative thoughts about her aptitude but also to be stigmatized by teachers and peers as a student with low aptitude.

In conclusion, the interpretation of the evidence obtained from Margarita makes us think that the inclusion of the SPCs with an antiracist focus and the consequent development of her CLA influenced her motivation enough for the student to be able to finish the course with the minimum outcome linguistic skills required by XU's Spanish department and, fulfilling the transformative mission of this research, with a different perspective on language, providing evidence that she understands language as a social construct related to identity and asymmetric power relations. This happened despite the initial impression she gave me at the beginning of the semester. Her attitude, without knowing anything about her experiences and feelings about her aptitude, would have led me to think that she was not interested in anything I had to say in class. Added to the ethical reasons to include antiracist pedagogies, we should take into consideration the additional benefits (motivation, attitudes, self-perception of aptitude toward language learning) of integrating antiracist pedagogies such as this one in language classes.

7.1.6 Leah, a mainstream student

Leah was one of the best examples of how SPCs raise CLA, motivation and linguistic proficiency when a student already starts the program with high motivation.

Leah was a 19-year-old White student of Jewish descent born and raised in a suburban area north of New York City. This area had a strong Hispanic presence (40% based on the 2010 US Census). She was the daughter of a doctor and a nurse and saw herself as a higher middle-income level, declaring an income between 100,000 and 150,000 dollars a year. A kind, pleasant student, somewhat shy but friendly, she frequently participated in small group activities but not as often in front of the whole class. Always focused during class and an exemplary student regarding her academic responsibilities, Leah seemed deeply invested in SPCs from the beginning of the program. In addition, as corroboration of her high initial motivation in the first questionnaire, she was taking a service-learning class offered by the Spanish department by helping with extracurricular hours of work in a mainly working-class Hispanic urban bilingual school.

Her CLA at the beginning of the semester was low. For example, when providing examples of the different types of Spanish, she offered the standard, simplistic juxtaposition of Spanish from Spain versus Latin American Spanish. However, at the end of the semester, Leah shows a change when she explained that there are 'different forms based on regions, like Castilian Spanish in Spain or, in Latin America, Chilean, Argentinian ... Also like in formality, kind of what you have in English, there is more street Spanish' (Leah). Her response denoted a change, although it could not be expected (nor was it intended) that with 12 units of 20 minutes per week, the participants would develop a theoretical knowledge at the level of, for example, a graduate student, and provide explanations using the terminology provided by theory.

When inquiring about the quality of the change in CLA observed in Leah, upon reaching the part of the interview regarding attitudes toward variants of vernacular English, she was asked if she believed there are incorrect or inappropriate ways of speaking English; she answered, no. Digging into her response, after a long pause, Leah answered, 'There isn't a right or wrong way, but I understand that in the education systems, English is taught differently than the way people usually use English in the streets' (Leah). Although she doesn't use precise terminology, she understands that languages have a specific normative component that is promoted from academic/formal contexts, as opposed to linguistic varieties that do not resemble this norm and are used in other contexts. To make sure that we are discussing sociolects and not registers/styles, notice how instead of the singular 'the street', both the interviewer and Leah used the plural 'the streets' (as in Gang Starr's rap song, 'Code of the Streets'). This use of the plural indexes the culture of US urban centers to set the conversation around sociolects and not registers, which could be, for instance, how two friends who are White doctors would talk to each other over drinks in a bar.

During her final exam, she immediately identified racial differences in the graphics provided and was able to link language learning, in addition to its instrumentality in the job market as most of the students did, to respect and tolerance toward different others ('otros diferentes') and a more cultural and open understanding of the world ('una comprensión más cultural y abierta del mundo') (Leah). Moreover, Leah effectively linked bilingual education to progressive ideas about immigration and discrimination. Her essay advocating for bilingualism had a tone that included numerous exclamations, and she concluded by admitting that there are many other advantages that she cannot cover for reasons of space.

Like 13 of the 18 participants in the semi-experimental group, Leah attributed to the SPCs her satisfaction with taking this class in her answers to the final questionnaire:

I am so happy with my decision to take this class and participate in this research. Learning about sociolinguistics has opened my mind to thoughts I never had before about society and language. After (almost) completing this class and research, I am excited to further my knowledge in both the subjects of Spanish and sociolinguistics. (Leah)

When asked at the end of the semester, 'How would you define your political views? Did your political views change during this semester? If so, how?', Leah answered,

I would describe my political views as very liberal. While I still would consider myself liberal, I believe this class opened my mind up to some very interesting perspectives that I wouldn't necessarily have considered before because of how 'radical' they were, but now I see great potential in them. For example, opening up the border between the US and Mexico. (Leah)

Leah's increase in motivation (she had no intentions at the beginning of the semester, but she declared a major at the end) was explicitly attributed to the class content: 'I am very motivated to learn Spanish and I think even more so over this past semester than I was before because of the class content' (Leah). Also, her proximity and service to the Hispanic community were reinforced by this class: 'This class helped to reinforce the fact that even in the United States, the benefits to studying Spanish are enormous' (Leah). This idea appears again during the last interview when she admits that she is

very motivated to learn Spanish for two different reasons. I think firstly, because in this country, like ... Everything we've talked about in these units has made me realize how important it is to be able to communicate with Latinos here, and also, yeah, I definitely want to do something with Spanish, to be a skill I can use. (Leah)

Leah went further and stated that many participants in the semi-experimental group whom she talked to felt the same way, and their motivation to learn Spanish to use it mainly in study abroad programs changed toward using it within the United States. She wanted 'to apply the things I'm learning in class to more "real-life" situations' (Leah). She also stated that the SPCs helped her see language through a different lens, and this increased her motivation.

Definitely, because this is something that I never really learned about before or talked about, and, in language is so important, like, is so many different layers to it, that when you are just learning it sometimes it's hard, and I think is hard to, like, really believe what you are learning in class relates to society and the world and this component definitely helped me reflect why am I actually studying Spanish. (Leah)

As expected, her linguistic proficiency increased throughout the semester, but the transformative change needs to be highlighted. At the end of the semester, she left a note in my mailbox thanking me for the opportunity to participate in this research and how critical sociolinguistics had provided her with a new perspective on her studies and how she could make a difference in her country. A semester later, she wrote me an email from her study abroad program in Chile when she learned that I would not be teaching a sociolinguistics class that I had proposed to my Spanish department. In this message, she wrote that she had made a written complaint to the Spanish department because she considered courses other than literature necessary, and many other students were also upset about it. She thanked me again for the SPCs and explained how useful they were even in Chile, where she discovered a strong division in the way people used the language based on social class. In her letter, she even detailed differences in phonetic features and how immediately people associated them with their social class, race and neighborhood while simultaneously prejudging them. Leah also informed me about her engagement in discussions in which she attempted to make her interlocutors aware of these issues.

Leah's case was a good example of how SPCs increased CLA, and CLA influenced her motivation and linguistic proficiency. More importantly, Leah's advocacy for underrepresented Hispanic communities within and outside the United States, due to her CLA, portrays the ultimate transformative mission of SPCs in the language classroom.

7.2 Participants in a Language and Racism Class

I would like to end this monograph with a few reflections that students wrote at the end of the semester in a sociolinguistics seminar focused on language and racism. Selecting these was a difficult task because of most students' great responses to this reflection. Thus, I tried to select those reflections that I thought were more insightful and representative of the different sociocultural and racial groups of students in this seminar.

After reading the following reflections, the reader may wonder how typical these 'success stories' are. It would be interesting to discuss those students whose voices could have been more resistant to the course. However, in this particular course, of 25 students, 22 were 'success stories'. Two students dropped this class around the fourth week, and another one struggled through the course. The first two students (male, White) who dropped the class were friends and played together on the university football team. Their football practice overlapped with the time of this class, and after talking to them about why they were falling behind, they admitted that they enjoyed the content of this class but they could not keep up with the work. The other student, a Jewish White male student, struggled through the course because of the restrictions imposed due to the COVID-19 epidemic. His motivation was very low, and he did not seem to be able to adapt to the new learning context (meeting in class via Zoom). He claimed to enjoy the readings, probably to please my ears, but he rarely completed any of the activities. Perhaps in this case, the issue was a mismatch between his and my expectations for this class. Incoming students taking a general education class in the humanities may sometimes idealize these types of classes as easy/low-work classes. This class was rigorous and demanding, and most of the students understood this from the first day of class. In the case of this student, perhaps – and this is my impression after talking with him several times – the topics that this class addressed were not relevant enough for him to put in all that work. His focus on passing the class and grades is something that I should have paid more attention to. I should have emphasized to him the focus on growth and the (un)grading approach of this course, but – and this is a common issue – when you have another 50 students to attend to during the semester, it is ideal but not always possible to dedicate so much time to a particular student.

This does not mean that resistance to antiracist approaches is non-existent. As was discussed in section 4.2 of this book, resistance may come from racialized or White students alike because hegemonic ideologies permeate all social groups. This resistance may come in many forms. Explicit resistance is the most salient, but less common. Silence as a form of resistance (Willis, 2004) or frequent complaints about feeling uncomfortable about discussing or being exposed to certain topics are the most common. One of the objections from instructors trying to implement an antiracist pedagogical approach that I heard is the fear of failure due to this resistance by students. Most of these objecting voices show insecurity about having the necessary tools to handle these situations. First of all, I think that we should bring that pressure down by admitting that success is not always possible. This is a fact regardless of the type of class or whether we are implementing an antiracist approach or not. Effective instruction depends on multiple factors, sometimes beyond our control. Even the most experienced, beloved by students and successful educators have stories that can confirm this. I believe that we should always aim and try our best to achieve our goals and receive positive feedback from our students. I do not refer so much to the feedback received through final course evaluations, but rather to receiving feedback that demonstrates their growth and the ways in which the students reached the course's outcome goals. Likewise, the fear of not being able to accomplish this should not be able to stop us from taking risks. We cannot ask our students to take risks if we are afraid to take them. I personally did not have many negative experiences implementing an antiracist approach, but I can talk about at least one. Allow me to introduce a parenthesis here to discuss it since, as I said, there were no voices of resistance in this seminar, but I would like to somehow address this topic of students' resistance.

I have been teaching a Spanish for the professions class for more than five semesters. This class is titled Spanish and the Law. When I first started teaching it, I used to joke that the only thing I knew about the law was how to run from it. Jokes aside, and considering the fact that I had to become familiar with different legal systems and languages, I was faced with a dilemma. The movement toward language learning for the professions is a problematic matter for me because it falls within what Flores (2017) calls 'language-as-a-resource' and responds to neoliberal pressures. As I already argued in this book, schools ultimately do what they are supposed to do, what they are designed for: to maximize the production of technical knowledge while deprioritizing ideological considerations other than those naturalized by hegemonic economic and political institutions. However, I also believe that these classes, depending on the institutional context, the approach and their critical axis, may be very useful for improving the experience of speakers of languages other than English in the United States. That is, these classes can be oriented to providing language skills to sell products to Latinxs or, on the contrary (or even additionally), to provide better services or much-needed help.

The class we (my department director, the undergraduate studies director and I) designed in my current department adheres to the latter orientation and has a strong critical axis focused on race, migration, gender and linguistic discrimination. As you can imagine, the expectations and motivations of the students coming to a Spanish and the Law class may be very different, and the approach in this class has clashed with some while empowering others. When we first started, most of the students took the class to complete a requirement for their major in Spanish. Later on, students from departments other than Spanish, especially criminology, started to join. These students' goals were very diverse. Thus, some students wanted to use Spanish and the Law for their professional futures as members of law enforcement, human rights attorneys or real estate agents, to name a few. Other students wanted to use it to be able to help family and friends with legal issues, especially related to immigration. Regardless of race/ethnicity, you could find students with any of these future goals.

One semester during the pandemic, I had the worst experience since I first started teaching in college in 2013. One male working-class, undeniably Hispanic student of Mexican descent was taking this class because he wanted to become a police officer. Apparently, his humble background and his being a first-generation student would have made me think that I would share many ideological points of view with this student. However, he was a rigorous Catholic, devoted Republican and fervorous defender of the 2nd Amendment (the right of the people of the United States to keep and bear arms). This is not an excuse, but having this class via Zoom and not being able to be in person with each other did not help address these issues and use them to open class discussions to articulate the content of the class, as happened many times with other similar students that I encountered in this class in previous semesters. This student dedicated most of his time to using the private chat room in Zoom to 'talk trash' about the content of the class and the instructor with his classmates (as reported by another student).

The dynamic of the group became toxic, and I was not able to completely redirect it. Everything became worse after I proposed a debate activity. In this debate, students had to virtually imagine themselves in 19th-century Texas and discuss legal issues related to slavery, the racialization of Mexicans and the conflicts with the Comanche Nation. They were asked to choose one of the four main groups inhabiting Texas at that time: Whites, Mexicans, African Americans and Comanches. After they returned from their private chat rooms, the Mexican student expressed discomfort with this subject. He did not explain why but acted as a spokesperson for the class. After reflecting on what went wrong, I believe that the activity was not properly explained, and that was my responsibility. Some African American students may have felt that they did not want to revive the issue of slavery from such a close perspective. It seems my instructions gave the impression that they needed to choose their own racial group in the debate when that was not the case. However, I admit that my dislike toward this particular student and the fact that he acted as a spokesman when he rarely participated in the class prevented me from reflecting on what went wrong and where the misunderstanding was and put me on the defensive. The issue could have been easily avoided with an apology and reintroducing the instructions of the activity or simply changing it for another. Instead, I went into a controlled tantrum, but still a tantrum, about the world not being a comfortable place and how they could think this activity was insensitive but how explicitly defending carrying guns while being against abortion and, simultaneously, supporting the death penalty; supporting Donald Trump while being the son of Mexican migrants who crossed the US border without documentation; and blaming racism on the people being discriminated against because of their laziness were comfortable topics, but not this debate.

We are educators but also humans; these situations happen. However, they have to do more with ideological resistance than with antiracist approaches. Students' resistance may appear at any level with any content; let it appear at least for an ethical cause. Also, use these situations to reflect on and think about better approaches than mine in this example. Now, let us go back to the students' reflections in a seminar focused on language and racism.

The critical applied sociolinguistics hybrid seminar where I collected these reflections is addressed to incoming majors in the humanities (and I use the present tense to describe it because it is still being offered as I write this), particularly those seeking a degree that will allow them to teach any language (including both L1 and L2) at any educational level. It is anchored in a critical interdisciplinary approach – sociolinguistics, applied linguistics, Hispanic applied linguistics, linguistic anthropology, sociology, social psychology, race studies, Latinx studies, language acquisition, education, Hip-Hop studies and antiracist pedagogies – that emphasizes the social, political and ideological dimensions of language. Its objective is to raise CLA through the implementation of antiracist language teaching methods in the language classroom. The students learn to do this through socially receptive pedagogies that incorporate their experiences – and those of their future students – and promote change toward equity within and outside the educational environment. Each unit focuses on both theoretical and practical approaches to sociolinguistics. The theory is complemented with short lectures and different hands-on class activities that help to identify and analyze, from a critical perspective, different linguistic ideologies, attitudes and practices partaking in the perpetuation of asymmetrical power relationships with a focus on racism. By the end of this seminar, students could develop and/or integrate didactic antiracist materials designed to raise CLA among language students and promote social change through targeting and challenging language ideologies that perpetuate inequality and iniquity.

The 16-week seminar in which I collected these reflections was conducted online due to the pandemic. With a backward and flipped-classroom design, the students worked toward a final project, and they prepared for each class on their own before each class meeting. Two 75-minute in-person sessions per week were preceded by an asynchronous module. In each of these modules, students were expected to review a set of assigned readings, videos, music and other media materials. After completing them, they were expected to respond online to a series of questions designed to engage with the readings, or with a small assignment to reflect on and apply the readings to a real-life situation. Each of these readings, with its assignment, was expected to take students two to three hours twice a week (before each in-person class). Students were pushed to take an active role in their learning process by creating multiple opportunities to engage and collaborate with other students and the instructor regularly (both in live sessions and through group work and activities).

The seminar scaffolds theoretical knowledge in three pyramidal modules. Module one, 'Introduction to Sociolinguistics and Research Methods in the Arts and Humanities', has a duration of seven weeks; module two, 'Language Ideologies', lasts four weeks; and module three, 'Antiracist Pedagogies', is a three-week module. The last sessions were dedicated to questions and answers about their final projects and their final project presentations.

The assigned activities were designed to trigger our class discussions from a student-centered perspective. These were available online in our course digital space. This was done from the first day of class. Before coming to class, the students needed to read the syllabus and introduce themselves with a quick video in which they were asked to answer the following questions: 'Who am I? What are my interests (personal, educational, professional)? Why am I taking this class?' The following day in class, the class as a group discussed the syllabus and attended to concerns, questions, suggestions and comments. For the second class, after reading Ralph Penny's (2000) introduction to language variation, the students were asked to submit a reflection journal talking about which aspect(s) of language variation interested them and why. I watched the videos before class in order to address concrete topics during my brief presentation. This presentation summarized and answered questions regarding theoretical issues. During and after the presentation, the students worked in group class activities and/or discussions related to this class' topic, and were always encouraged to share personal experiences and how they related to theory. Following a similar approach to this book (first building on theory to, later, address praxis), as the seminar moves forward, activities that include content focused explicitly on racism are progressively introduced.

An example of this type of activity focuses on racial identity in the Dominican Republic and the Dominican diaspora and its relationship with language. Before class, the students read Torres-Saillant's (1998) 'Tribulations of Blackness'; the reading is followed by a YouTube video by Godfrey, an American comedian of Nigerian descent ('I Am Not Black, I Am Dominican'). Finally, they prepare three questions for class about race in the Dominican Republic and beyond. These questions, which I read before class, allow me to organize class discussions based on the students' interests and inquiries. One goal of this class is to acknowledge the dynamism of race and its dependence on (spatial, temporal and social) context. The work of the students in class, who discuss a selected number of the questions they posed previously to coming to class, tends to show a wide range of levels of identity awareness regarding these issues. Hispanic and Black students who have lived in shared spaces are familiar with Godfrey's generalization regarding Dominicans' insistence on denying their Blackness when phenotypically they look Black and are of African descent. White students are generally clueless about this issue. However, through their interactions in groups, they learn about this topic and are able to relate it to identity theory. Sometimes the outsider perspective of White students is as illuminating as Black and Hispanic students' insights regarding this topic. Their connections to different theoretical aspects are also illuminating because, based on their personal experiences, their focus differs. For instance, a Black female student whose parents migrated from West Africa articulated this issue to her experience of 'becoming Black in America', while a White female student related it to the theory of cultural hegemony and how mainstream media has a negative effect on the perception of Blackness and how, in consequence, Dominicans may avoid being identified as Black. A Black male student commented on how he used to hate it when some Black Dominicans did this because he felt that they were ashamed of their Blackness, but now he understands that the problem is deeper and more complex and also relates to the construction of the 'Black Haitian' other in the Dominican Republic.

Another activity based on the ungrading movement that worked well in this course was 'Write your own definition of racism *here* [in our digital space] and bring it to class'. This happened in week five after reading the first ten pages of Bonilla-Silva's (2003) chapter 'The Strange Enigma of Race in Contemporary America'. Approximately half of these definitions omitted the element of power and rather defined racial prejudice, despite Bonilla-Silva discussing these elements in his text. For example, a White female student stated, 'Racism is discriminating against and having preconceived notions about a person or group of people because of their race'. Other answers implied the element of power. A highly motivated White female student wrote, 'systematic oppression of a minority group perpetuated by the dominant racial group of a region; can be seen in a multitude of ways such as reduced educational opportunities, mistreatment based on certain features, microaggressions, violent crimes, etc.'. We discussed these definitions in class. All voices were heard, and the students had time to discuss the definition on their own. Additional questions were introduced by the students and the instructor in order to place the focus on the element of power in racism. For example, we discussed whether people of color can be racist – and, if so, in which situations – or inverted racism. Toward the end of the semester, the students revisited their definitions of racism and were asked to change them, if they felt they needed to, and explain the reason for their changes or why they did not change their first version. This exercise is an example of the activities in this course that helped open a window into the students' growth during the semester while promoting the students' agency in their learning.

Other activities were more oriented to daily experiences, such as recording a brief video (one to two minutes) explaining a case of racist iconization in an animated film they watched after reading a text extracted from Lippi-Green's (1997) *Teaching Children How to Discriminate*; or, after reading an excerpt from Cobas and Feagin's (2008) *Language Oppression and Resistance: The Case of Middle Class Latinos in the United States*, and watching a recording of New York attorney Aaron Schlossberg raging inside a restaurant in New York City and aggressively addressing its employees regarding their use of Spanish and threatening to call immigration officers on them, the students were asked: 'Have you ever witnessed a racist scene similar to those in this article? Think about it and bring it to class. If you haven't, search on the internet, choose one, and bring it to class'.

These are some examples of the working dynamics in this course that I hope help the reader visualize how the relationships between language and race are addressed daily during the semester within an antiracist approach. The following texts are five samples selected from the final reflection that the 25 participants in this seminar wrote at the end of the semester. In them, the qualitative differences in CLA between racialized students and White students are noticeable. These differences at the end of the semester were influenced by their previous life experiences and how they were linked to the contents they were exposed to during this seminar. As we have seen in these pages, living as a racialized individual in the United States makes us think and develop an awareness that White people do not need to because, as I explained, Whites are not racialized; they do not need to think about race every day. However, as can be interpreted in the sample by an African American male student, racialized individuals are also exposed to the internalization of the very same ideologies that harm them. Nonetheless, the following samples support the idea discussed in previous sections: differentiated instruction for racialized and White students/educators must be taken into account. Thus, I would like to end this book with these (unedited) testimonies from our protagonists, our students.

Puerto Rican female student:

> Race, along with all of its implications and language, were never aspects in my life that I could afford to ignore. My heritage obligated me to be aware of how they benefited/harmed me in different contexts and situations and how they affected people's perceptions of me. Therefore, before this class, I was already aware of the role of race and language in my life, yet I was surprisingly ignorant of the true extent of its effects. Being a bilingual individual who lived most of my life in Puerto Rico made me incredibly insecure in both languages. The variety of Spanish used in Puerto Rico is deemed inferior by other Latin Americans and even worse in the U.S. Additionally, English is my second language, which meant I couldn't pronounce some words 'properly,' and no matter how hard I tried and practiced, the accent wouldn't go away entirely. Thus, I believed both languages I spoke were not good enough and felt linguistically inferior to other Spanish and English speakers. Similarly, I never identified with a specific race because my heritage is primarily a mix of White, African, and indigenous, which meant I fit into all/neither of those categories simultaneously. Regardless of my racial identity, I knew black and darker-skinned people faced racism I would never be able to understand genuinely; still, I believe my experience with racial and linguistic discrimination has helped me better empathize and fight with them against racism.
>
> This course has changed my perceptions of language, race, racism, and anti-racism for the better. I am no longer as linguistically insecure as before, and when I find myself thinking the way I used to, I remember that prestige and 'proper' language are merely social constructs designed to further privilege and benefit the power group. Unfortunately, not everyone knows this and consciously or unconsciously continues to foster these harmful ways of thinking; however, I am now well equipped to create consciousness on the issue using theoretical explanations and concepts to present a well-constructed position. I can now view language as an essential part of my identity without devaluing any aspect of it because, in the end, it makes me who I am. Even though I

am still required to use 'proper' language in the academic and professional setting, I consider the power relations at play and advocate for change whenever the opportunity arises. Concerning racism, I am now knowledgeable of the importance of power/privilege in racial issues and how much of a difference it actually makes. Advocating against racial issues and other forms of oppression was one of my passions since I was in middle school, but this course has equipped me with the theoretical information necessary for perceiving things differently and allowed me to interpret my life experiences in a way I wouldn't have been able to before. The class has been enlightening because it further demonstrated how much I have yet to learn and improve. It also allowed me to consider other viewpoints from individuals with opposite experiences and lives to mine, which reshaped some of my opinions and judgments while fortifying others. While I may not be a victim that needs to be saved, that doesn't mean that it's my responsibility alone (or any other minority's, for that matter) to fight against racism, especially in the United States. Because of this course, I am now better qualified to explain why the former statement is true using theoretical concepts and why being unapologetically anti-racist is crucial.

West African–descent female student:

This class has been very enlightening to me in numerous ways, as I have been able to reflect on many aspects of my life in a more refined fashion. Many experiences I have gone through that I once had no words for were reexplained to me in sociolinguistic theories. Being so transparent on how I utilize language practices in my everyday life was very relieving to me as I did not feel as though I had to perform to be accepted in the narrative. For once, my experiences became the narrative. What I learned about language is how detailed the reasoning behind some nuances of speech can be. Such as relations of socioeconomic status to pronunciation of words. The bridge that relates language and racism is something that, as a black woman, I am not surprised to. Throughout my life, I understood that certain language practices that I am used to, such as African American Vernacular English or Nigerian pidgin English, would not be marketable amid areas of professionalism. However, I had believed that I would always have to carry that burden and live with that realization to myself. It was empowering that in a space of academia, my experiences outwards from my association to whiteness was truly valued. My grievances to the sides I have always hidden in academic and professional settings have now felt seen. Although, what I have learned more about race is that the structure of it is not as simplistic as I once thought it was. I personally always knew that my race is black and my ethnicity is Nigerian. In the past, when I would meet someone of Hispanic origin that would denounce their blackness, I always simply assumed it was solely out of self-hatred. However, the matter is a lot more complex than that. The understanding of racist and antiracist pathologies is something I have known and engrained through life experiences. In advocation for myself and the people I love, I never could afford to NOT understand the dynamics of racism and how it is characterized by micro-aggressive speech and coded language. In order to combat racism, I must continue to advocate for myself, family, and the various communities that surround me. The progression from equality to liberation is a tedious one but a struggle worth fighting for. What this class has showcased to me is that there is power in my story and that I cannot cease in portraying it as it makes me a holistic human being.

White female student:

This class has really changed my perspective on language, race, racism, and antiracism. Before taking this course, I thought that I knew everything about language and racism, but after learning about the different language ideologies and reading everyone's discussion posts, I realized how ignorant I have been. I thought that I had been a White ally and antiracist, but I did not recognize my White privilege or challenge it in my daily life. I have been taught my whole life that Standard White English was the 'correct' and 'right' way to speak, and that anything other than that was 'bad' or 'informal.' Through what we have talked about in this class, I learned that there is no 'correct' way to speak; the people in power dictate what they think is right and apply that ideology to everyone else. I was also subject to the color-blindness approach to race. I just brushed the racial conversations aside and said that color does not exist or matter. That is what I had been taught by those around me in my predominately white area. After talking about race and how it is a social construct, I realized that this approach to race brings about more bias and does not resolve the issues at hand. It denies the experiences that racialized people have gone through and the systemic racism that exists in our society. Now, I have accepted the social reality of race and how it has real effects on other people.

I am going to use all that we learned about combating racism and apply it to my daily life. To start, I redefined what racism is. Racism is prejudice combined with power to enforce bias. In order to be anti-racist, I must act in a way that resists and erases racism and the ideologies associated with it. In the past four months, I have examined my thoughts and actions, and asked myself how I could do better. I will actively listen to people's experiences with race in our country. I am more aware of what I am saying and what others around me say and am not afraid to call people out when they say or do something racist. By collaborating with people of color to be an active agent of change in our society, I can become a better person and help to dismantle the racism that is entangled in our institutions.

Black/African American male student from the DC-Maryland metro area:

Taking this class has affected my views regarding language's relationship with race and power differences. Before taking this course, I never thought that language had any relation to race or its use in upholding racist systems through power structures. As I reflected on what I have learned throughout the semester, I think back to the concept of language ideologies, linguistic markets, and the differences in language varieties, and what that means for individuals socially, culturally, and politically.

In my personal experience, I have grown up in the US where the standard language is English, specifically Standard American English (SAE). Even though the US does not have an official language, speaking in another variety of English or in a completely different language is usually looked down upon and is seen as un-American and unpatriotic. This prevailing language ideology makes it extremely difficult for African Americans, who usually speak in African American Vernacular English (AAVE), to succeed in education or society. AAVE has little to no overt prestige in the main linguistic market of the US, specifically in the job market or in academia. Both Black people and the language variety they commonly use are demonized and bastardized as a result of centuries of oppression and racism, both individually and systemically. One way to fight and change this reality is by using AAVE in communities that are not familiar or who are opposed to the variety, acknowledging its history and importance for so many people.

In other linguistic markets, AAVE has covert prestige, especially in Black communities where using this language variety is a sign of endearment. It conveys a certain identity about the speaker; however, what that particular identity is and whether that identity has positive or negative connotations is decided by the spectator(s). In hip-hop culture, Black people use AAVE to resist and fight back against the prevailing language ideology that views people who do not speak in SAE as less intelligent and other than.

Going against the stigmas of certain languages and their associations with different groups of people is something vital that I will take away from this course. I always knew it was important to teach anti-racism, but I never knew how to go about it and what specifically should be done. As I reflected on this, I remembered a reading I had done for this class. One of the most memorable and meaningful readings of the semester would be the article by Guillermo Rebollo-Gil and Amanda Moras titled 'Defining an "anti" stance: key pedagogical questions about engaging anti-racism in college classrooms.' The authors do an exceptional job of discussing anti-racism strategies in academia and education, an environment notorious for privileging whiteness and harming students of color, especially for the ways in which they speak.

White male student from Manhattan, New York:

When I entered this class, I had never really considered the language as a concept. I knew that growing up in NYC, there were so many different languages, and I liked the different cultures embodied by them. I never really thought of language further. I held rigid beliefs of language in the sense that language was a concrete way of speaking, and while people may have different dialects in different areas, there was an established 'proper' way of speaking where grammar was non-negotiable. I didn't know what a language ideology was. I learned about the different ways that speaking reflects values, thoughts, and resistance to hegemonic ideas, all things I have never even considered.

Being brought up in a school with no ethnic majority, I came into this class with self-awareness of race that several of my white classmates may have lacked. I do recognize that my awareness is nowhere near what I is for my classmates of color who don't have a choice in engaging with issues regarding race in their day-to-day lives. What I learned was how arbitrary race and self-identification is. An example of this was the Eastern Europeans who came to America being not in the power group and then rejecting their status as white in America. Another example was the Dominicans who identified as being Spanish and not black, while in America they would be considered black. I've lived in America my whole life and hearing how different people in the world approach race in contrast to how we do it here is illuminating.

I knew coming into this class that racism was a core foundation in the creation of this country, but I didn't realize how subtly it is applied in everyday life. Being white, being able to identify these aspects was a challenge. For me, the aspects of racism have been clear and obvious actions to discriminate against people of color. These acts of racism occurring throughout our history include the grandfather clause, the poll tax, and redlining housing. What didn't necessarily occur to me was the subtle racism embodied in educational systems. The determination of what is being taught having racial implications is not something that crossed my mind until this class. History classes neglecting the experiences of non-whites, English classes discriminating against all aspects of grammar except the white, hegemonic variety, and Language classes only teaching the varieties from white countries are aspects of racism in education that I now can identify.

I always opposed and abandoned situations in which people were committing racist acts, saying racist things, or displaying racial prejudice. However, while these things are good, the actions I have taken previously were purely reactive instead of proactive. If I didn't see clear racism occurring, I would tune out. I now realize that my ability to tune out is a result of privilege, and I need to do more. Instead of protesting after a racist event occurs, it is my responsibility to be constantly taking on the system to make sure that the system itself changes, not only the individual acts of racism. I need to be constantly doing this because the moment I switch off, the system gets stronger.

I end this book acknowledging that there is much left to be said. I hope that at least I was able to open up new avenues of inquiry and instruction and that you, the reader, will continue the conversation in many creative ways to end racism. *Se puede.*

Notes

(1) See Magro (2016a) for an in-depth review of the methodology, a more detailed analysis of SPCs' influence on CLA and an analysis of six additional cases.

(2) 'Al menos aquí se reconoce que es una [*sic*] problema, allá se asume esta forma de pensar que el inglés es lo que se habla y ya, ni se plantean la [*sic*] problema, se da por hecho' (Jonatan).

(3) 'Lo que me gusta que es ... es que se habla de esto en una clase de idioma, porque nunca he escuchado de alguien que dice que ha tenido una experiencia así que se habla de los diferentes componentes de un idioma en Estados Unidos, todo el tiempo se dice [cambio de voz imitando a lo que parece una figura de autoridad] "oh, puedes ir a estudiar en otro país y asimilarte a la cultura en el país", pero por primera vez siento que se está poniendo alguna perspectiva de Estados Unidos y estoy en gran favor de esto, y también son temas que se están hablando de bastante en la universidad, manteniéndose con su propia cultura, es una grande cosa que se está hablando ahora en la universidad, yo creo que es una buena cosa que usted quiere continuar y que se está estudiando en esta clase porque ayuda a traer algo nuevo porque siempre se tiene la misma estandarización de clases' (Jonatan).

(4) In US immersion programs, the content of some or most of the classes is taught in an L2. Immersion students are generally native speakers of the majority language. Teaching is carefully structured and tailored to their needs. In contrast, *two-way programs* are those in which two languages are used for approximately the same amount of time in the curriculum. These classes have a mixture of native speakers in both languages (García & Baker, 1995).

Appendices

Appendix A: Questionnaire

Your responses to this questionnaire will remain confidential. Please answer as openly and honestly as you can.

Basic Information

Name:	Age:
Place of birth:	Gender: ( ) M ( ) F
Race: ( ) White or Caucasian ( ) Black or African American ( ) American Indian ( ) Asian ( ) Hispanic or Latino/Latina ( ) Other (specify)_____ _____	( ) Hispanic ( ) Non-Hispanic Total household income before taxes: ( ) Less than $20,000 ( ) $20,000–39,999 ( ) $40,000–59,999 ( ) $60,000–79,999 ( ) $80,000–99,999 ( ) $100,000–149,999 ( ) $150,000–$249,000 ( ) $250,000 or more
High school you attended:	City:
Age of arrival to the US (if you were born in the US, write 'born'):	

How do you consider yourself?
   1 ( ) Very poor
   2 ( ) Poor
   3 ( ) Lower middle-income level
   4 ( ) Middle-income level
   5 ( ) Higher middle-income level
   6 ( ) Rich
   7 ( ) Very rich	

Parents' occupation:	Father: Mother:
Parents' education:	Father: None / Elementary / High school / College / Graduate / PhD _____ Mother: None / Elementary / High school / College / Graduate / PhD

Basic Information

Parents' place of birth or country of origin of their parents if born in the US (do not fill if born in the US):	Father:
	Mother:

First language(s) (if you grew up speaking more than one language or were schooled in more than one language, please list them here):

Second language(s):

Appendix B

https://prezi.com/view/zSwh4rBBRpv7FipDSjgc/

Appendix C: Bullet Points for Goffman's Identity Theory

- The self is constructed entirely through discourse, making our language choices of paramount importance to our identity construction.
- Personal identity is defined by how others identify us, not how we identify ourselves.
- The speaker can attempt to influence how others perceive them, but ultimately it is the hearer who creates the speaker's identity.
- If the speaker is not allowed any influence on their own output, then the hearer is able to construct an identity for the speaker that may be entirely disparate from the speaker's desired identity. This allows the hearer an inordinate amount of power and diminishes the self-sufficiency and independence of the speaker:
  - This is a technique frequently used to control populations in settings as diverse as schools, prisons and workplaces
  - It is also used in national language policies to extinguish the power associated with politically 'subversive' and 'inappropriate' languages, such as Catalan in Spain or Hokkien in Singapore (see Pennycook, 1994).

Appendix D: Excerpts from Bailey (2000) for Unit 9 Final Task

(1) 'Spanish' as identity

BB:	When people ask you what you are, what do you say?
Nanette (recent Central graduate):	I say I'm Spanish. I've had disputes over that one, 'What do you call Spanish, you're not from Spain.' When you're not Spanish, you don't really understand it, and I don't know if I really understand it myself. When people ask me, I'm Spanish. They're like, 'What's Spanish? Where are you from then if you're just Spanish?' Well, there's tons of different Spanish people, but we just come from all different places. But we all speak Spanish, so we're Spanish. And they're like, 'But no we speak English, and we're not all English.' But it's just so different. There's something different. We all say we're Spanish.

(2) Highlighting facets of identity through language

Wilson (DS):	Qué tú vas (a) hacer hoy en tu casa loco?
JB (DS):	Puede ser que vaya a jugar pelota con Tito.
Wilson (DS):	Con?
JB (DS):	Con Tito.
Wilson (AE):	Oh.
JB (DS):	Que si no ibas para /buklin/?
Wilson (SP):	Donde?
JB (HE):	/buklin/
Wilson (AE0DE):	Oh, /bkln/. At what time?
JB (HE):	(five)
Wilson (AAVE):	Oh wor(d)! I'm gonna go break you up.
JB (DS):	No me hagas reir.

(3) Negotiation of phenotype and identity

Wilson: … a lot of people confuse me for an African American most of the time. They ask me, 'Are you Black?' I'm like, 'No, I'm Hispanic.'And they'll be like, 'Oh I thought you were Black or something.' Most of the time I'll be talking with them, chilling, or whatever. They'll be thinking that I'm just African American. Because sometimes the way I talk, my hair, my skin color, it's just that my hair is nappy. I use a lot of slang. You can confuse a lot of Dominicans as African Americans by their color.

(4) 'He is from Haiti'

WR #2, 1:20:07 (Claudia is the Guatemalan American who appeared in the transcript above.)

Wilson:	((singing)) Dame del pollito ['Give me a little bit of that chicken']
Eduardo:	Tú no dique eres de Haití? Tú no eres dominicano, Wilson.
Wilson:	Yo nací en Haití, ((Wilson turns to Eduardo, smiling))
Eduardo:	[( )] ((motions toward camera, Wilson turns to camera))
Wilson:	[pero me] crié en Santo Domingo.
	((Eduardo holds up both hands, palms forward, with middle and ring fingers curled down – the Dominican sign of the cuckold – behind Wilson's head; Wilson turns back toward Eduardo and hits him in the leg with the back of his open hand))
Claudia:	So you're Haitian, huh?
Wilson:	No, I'm Dominican.
Claudia:	You were born in DR?
Wilson:	Yeah.
Eduardo:	Nació en Haití
Wilson:	En Santo Domingo.
Eduardo:	Es haitiano.
Wilson:	Es mentira, ven acá, a quién tú le vas – a quién tú le vas a creer, a mí o a estos dos locos? ((turning his head laterally first to one side then the other, indicating Eduardo and an accomplice on his other side.))
Eduardo:	A mì.
Wilson:	Eh, 'mano ((looking down at magazine)) ['Hey, man']
Wilson:	Azaros(o) ((Hits Eduardo sharply on leg with the back of his hand)) ['Jerk.' literally 'Cursed person.']

(5) 'I never thought you were Spanish'

WR #2, 1:34:57 (Wilson has just finished explaining to JB, in Spanish, the function of the wireless microphone he is wearing.)

Wilson:	((singing)) Angie Pelham is a weird person (2.5)
Wilson:	Me estoy miando yo,'mano. ['I have to piss, man.'] (2.0)
JB:	( ) (2.0)
Pam:	Yo, the first time I saw you, I never thought you were Spanish. (.5)
Wilson:	[Who?]
JB:	[(He's)] Black.
Pam:	I never –

Wilson:	Cause I'm Black.
JB:	( )
Wilson:	Cause I'm Black.
Pam:	No.
JB:	His father [is Black], her mother is − , his mother is uh −
Wilson:	[I'm Black]
Pam:	(Can he) speak Spanish?
JB:	No.
Wilson:	Cause I was − [I was]
Pam:	[Yeah!]
JB:	So why (d − ?)
Wilson:	No, no seriously, I'm Black and I was raised in the Dominican Republic. (.5)
Wilson:	For real.
Pam:	Your mother's Black?
Wilson:	My mom? No, my father.
Pam:	Your father's Black, your [mother's Spanish?]
Wilson:	[My mom's Spanish]
JB:	His mom is Black − and she's Spanish
Wilson:	Is mix(ed)
JB:	His mom was born over here. (2.0) ((Wilson smiles at Pam and throws a piece of paper at her))
JB:	Wilson, don't t(h)row anything to her.
Wilson:	Excúsame, se me olvidó, que es la heva tuya ['Sorry, I forgot that she is your girlfriend.']
JB:	Cállate, todavía no. ['Be quiet, not yet!']
Pam:	English!
JB:	English, yeah!
Wilson:	I said I'm sorry.
JB:	He can't speak Spanish.
Pam:	I saw you were talking to him ( )
Wilson:	I understand, but I don't speak everything. (2.2) ((Wilson smiles broadly at Pam))
JB:	I'm teaching him. (5.5)
Wilson:	Qué tú vas (a) hacer en tu casa hoy, loco? ((slaps JB on the back)) ['What are you going to do at your house today, man?']

(6) 'You don't look like the guy who plays basketball'

1:38:07 (Wilson and JB have been discussing their relative strengths as basketball players, and the previous night's NBA playoff game. They then return to the issue of Pam's perception that JB doesn't look like a basketball player.)

JB:	Why you think I'm not good?
Pam:	You don't look like the guy(s) who plays basketball.
Wilson:	[Him? Huh?] He don't. ((gesturing toward JB))
JB:	[How do I −]
JB:	How do I look? (.5)
Wilson:	Him, huh, like nothing! He just −
Pam:	Yes! ((laughter from at least Pam and Wilson))
JB:	( )
Wilson:	He can be like a, like a lawyer or something, that's what he looks like, for real.
JB:	What about you?
Pam:	Yeah.
Wilson:	I look like a straight basketball player
JB:	Like a
Wilson:	or football player.
Wilson:	For real baseball player and shit.
JB:	Who?
Wilson:	Me.
Pam:	I hate baseball, it's so boring.

Appendix E: Language Control Stratagems Employed by Whites

(1) Silencing Spanish speakers

I had a really bad experience at Disneyworld ... My son at the time was ... three ... He jumped the line and went straight to where there was Pluto or Mickey Mouse or something and I said, '[Son's name], come back,' in Spanish and ... ran after him. And I heard behind me somebody say, 'It would be a fucking spic that would cut the line.' Now my wife saw who said it, and I said, 'Who said that?' in English and nobody said a word. And I said [to my wife], 'Point him out, I want to know who said that,' and she refused. I was like, 'Who was the motherfucker who said that?' I said, 'Be brave enough to say it to my face because I'm going to kill you.' You can see me, I'm 6'3', 275 [pounds]. Nobody volunteered ... So nobody stepped up? No, no and there was a bunch of guys there, and I would have thrown down two or three of them; I wouldn't have had a problem.

(2) Voicing suspicion: Fears of Spanish-speaking Americans

-On one occasion we were at a Bank of ... branch ... We were talking [in Spanish] and all of a sudden this [white] lady comes and asks us [in English] what we were talking about.

-What did you reply?

-We told her we were talking about our business.

(3) Doubting English proficiency of Latinos

-[A professor] in college refused to believe that I had written an essay ... because she assumed that Mexicans don't write very well and so therefore I couldn't have written this paper.

-Did she tell you that?

-Yes she did ... And so she asked that I write it over again ...

-So what did you do?

-I rewrote the assignment and she still didn't believe that it was my own ... She still refused to believe that it was my handwriting or my writing because she still felt that Mexicans could not express themselves well in English ...

-Did she use those words?

-Yes she did.

(4) Denigrating the accent

There was one time that I answered [the telephone] at my work currently, I had this lady ... and she goes, 'I don't want to talk to you, you have an accent!' I was like, 'you don't want to talk to me?' she goes, 'yeah, I want to talk to an American.' I was like 'ok, well I'm sorry you're gonna have to redial to speak to someone that you want.' She goes, 'well go ahead and transfer me over.' I was like, 'I'm sorry, I'm not going to be able to transfer you over. I have to take the call. I'm here to help you if you need anything.' She goes, 'well I don't understand you'. And I just kept going, 'well if there's anything I can do for you, I'm here.' So she finally gave me her number and we went over the account and at the end she goes, 'I'm really sorry that I was too rude to you at the beginning.'

(5) Ignoring Spanish speakers

-In the last five years have you been mistreated in restaurants by whites because of your race, ethnicity, speaking Spanish or accent?

-Yeah, we went to [resort restaurant] and we tried to order some drinks, but the lady kept passing and passing and said that she would come, but never came to ask what we want to drink I think because she heard us speaking Spanish ...

-And was the server, the person white?

-She was white and we told her, we called her and told her if she wasn't going to take our order or what because why that discrimination? We asked her a few times to come nicely and she kept saying, 'I will be back, I will be back' and so she apologized and excused herself of course 'cause if not we were going to make a problem.

-Then you told her that you felt discriminated?

-Yeah.

-And you say 'we', with whom were you at the hotel?

-My mom and her husband and other friends.

-And you were speaking Spanish?

-Yeah. And so the lady then came and ... ? And she kind of apologized and we said 'if not we want to talk to your managers'.

-Did she change her attitude?

-Yeah.

Appendix F

Final Team Project

Weight: 40% of your grade.
In groups of two students.

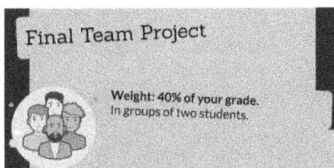

Step 1. Select one of your language courses (if you are not currently teaching or enrolled in a language class, choose any available syllabus for a language class). The syllabus must be recent (being currently taught, has been taught within the last 3 years, or will be taught within the next year), at any level.
Step 2. Identify at least one language ideology and the discourse associated with it in the approach and materials of this course (including, but not limited to, textbooks, readings, films, music, type of assessments). Write a report.
Step 3. Analyze the sociopolitical alignments and affinities of this language ideology with different social groups and how these may promote asymmetric power relationships.
Step 4. Interpret in which way (social, psychological, political, economic) this ideology (or ideologies) identified in your selected course may affect your students in relationship to their diverse identities.
Step 5. While attending to this ideology (or ideologies) and your students' diverse racial backgrounds, develop and implement pedagogical strategies and content that tackle this ideology (or ideologies) and help raise linguistic awareness among your students.
Step 6. Structure of your manuscript (APA style, maximum 5000 words):
o Introduction: Who are your students? Why did you select this course? What are you planning to do with it? Why? ... (length: 1 page)
o Report of step 2 (length: 2-3 pages)
o Analysis and interpretation (step 3 and 4: length: 2-3 pages)
o Final syllabus including footnotes explaining how your strategies and content attend the ideology(s) identified, your students' diverse racial backgrounds, and critical linguistic awareness
o Conclusion: Synthesis. What could be improved? What next? (length: 1 page)
o References
The Final Project will have these detailed instructions in the Canvas course space and will be scored using the associated rubric.

Final project in-class presentation
Weight: 10% of your grade
During the last session, you will present your final project in a short 5-minute presentation focusing on how your own critical linguistic awareness influenced your decisions in the development of your pedagogical strategies to raise linguistic awareness among your students. You will articulate theory and practice and explain the fundamental key points of your project.
The Final Project Presentation will have detailed instructions in the Canvas course space and will be scored using the associated rubric.

Appendix G: Glossary of Terms

AAVE: African American Vernacular English
ABD: all but dissertation
ACTFL: American Council on the Teaching of Foreign Languages
CALx: critical applied linguistics
CBI: content-based instruction
CLA: critical linguistic awareness
CLAp: critical linguistic awareness pedagogies
CRT: critical race theory

HL: heritage language
HLS: heritage language speaker
IPA: integrated performance assessments
L2:   second language
MLA: Modern Language Association
SLA: second language acquisition
SPCs: sociopolitical contents/content related to the sociopolitical dimension of language

References

Ade-ojo, G. (2021) Bourdieu's capitals and the socio-cultural perspective of literacy frameworks: A ready-made vessel for decolonising the curriculum. *Academia Letters*. https://doi.org/10.20935/AL173

Adichie, C.N. (2013) *Americanah: A Novel*. New York, NY: Alfred A. Knopf.

Alim, H.S. (2004) Hip hop nation language. In E. Finegan and J.R. Rickford (eds) *Language in the USA: Themes for the Twenty-First Century* (pp. 387–409). Cambridge: Cambridge University Press.

Alim, H.S. (2007) Critical hip-hop language pedagogies: Combat, consciousness, and the cultural politics of communication. *Journal of Language, Identity & Education* 6 (2), 161–176. https://doi.org/10.1080/15348450701341378

Alim, H.S. (2009) Translocal style communities: Hip Hop youth as theorists of style, language, and globalization. *Pragmatics: Quarterly Publication of the International Pragmatics Association (IPrA)* 19 (1), 111–135. https://doi.org/10.1075/prag.19.1.06ali

Alim, H.S. and Baugh, J. (2007) *Talkin Black Talk: Language, Education, and Social Change*. New York, NY: Teachers College Press.

Alim, H.S., Rickford, J.R. and Ball, A.F. (eds) (2016) *Raciolinguistics: How Language Shapes Our Ideas about Race*. New York: Oxford University Press.

Allan, K. (2016) Contextual determinants on the meaning of the N word. *SpringerPlus* 5 (1), 1141. https://doi.org/10.1186/s40064-016-2813-1

Almoayidi, K.A. (2018) The effectiveness of using L1 in second language classrooms: A controversial issue. *Theory and Practice in Language Studies* 8 (4), 375. https://doi.org/10.17507/tpls.0804.02

Androutsopoulos, J. (2009) Language and the three spheres of hip hop. In H.S Alim, A. Ibrahim and A. Pennycook (eds) *Global Linguistic Flows: Hip Hop Cultures, Youth Identities, and the Politics of Language*. (pp. 43–62). New York: Routledge.

Androutsopoulos, J. (2010) Ideologizing ethnolectal German. In S. Johnson and T.M. Milani (eds) *Language Ideologies and Media Discourse: Texts, Practices, Politics* (pp. 182–202). London: Continuum.

Ansari, A. and Yang, A. (2015) *Master of None*. Netflix.

Apple, M.W. (2004) *Ideology and Curriculum* (3rd edn). New York: RoutledgeFalmer.

Asim, J. (2008) *The N Word: Who Can Say It, Who Shouldn't, and Why*. Boston: HMH.

Asturiano, P. (2005) '¡Jau, rostro pálido!' Análisis sociolingüístico del discurso etno-racial en el Western. *Tonos digital: Revista electrónica de estudios filológicos*, 10.

Attinasi, J.J. (1983) Language attitudes and working class ideology in a Puerto Rican barrio of New York. *Ethnic Groups* 5, 55–78.

Autman, H.K. (2021) My nigga: The potential acceptability of an N-word derivative in hip-hop based education and university educational contexts (Order No. 28866384). Available from ProQuest Dissertations and Theses Global. (2619546104). Accessed May 2021 from https://www.proquest.com/dissertations-theses/my-nigga-potential-acceptability-n-word/docview/2619546104/se-2?accountid=14696

Bailey, B. (2000) Language and negotiation of ethnic/racial identity among Dominican Americans. *Language in Society* 29 (4), 555–582. https://doi.org/10.1017/s0047404500004036

Bakhtin, M.M. (1981) *The Dialogic Imagination: Four Essays*. (C. Emerson, trans., M. Holquist, ed.). Austin: University of Texas Press.

Bañón Hernández, A.M. (1996) *Racismo, discurso periodístico y didáctica de la lengua*. Almería: Servicio de Publicaciones de la Universidad de Almería.

Barrett, R. (2009) Language ideology and racial inequality: Competing functions of Spanish in an Anglo-owned Mexican restaurant. In S. Blum (ed.) *Making Sense of Language* (pp. 285–304). New York: Oxford University Press.

Barthes, R. (1975) *The Pleasure of the Text*. New York : Hill and Wang.

Baugh, J. (1992) El lenguaje: contexto sociocultural. Panorama de la lingüística moderna de la Universidad de Cambridge. Coord. por Frederick J. Newmeyer, Vol. 4, 87–98. Madrid: Visor.

Beaudrie, S., Amezcua, A. and Loza, S. (2021) Critical language awareness in the heritage language classroom: Design, implementation, and evaluation of a curricular intervention. *International Multilingual Research Journal* 15 (1), 61–81.

Bidol, P.A. (1972) *Developing New Perspectives on Race: An Innovative Multi-Media Social Studies Curriculum in Race Relations for the Secondary Level*. Detroit: New Detroit.

Bissainthe, J.G. (2003) Migración transnacional: Dominicanos en New York City. *Ciencia y Sociedad* 28 (1), 128–160. https://doi.org/10.22206/cys.2003.v28i1.pp128-160

Blommaert, J. (2005) *Discourse: A Critical Introduction*. Cambridge: Cambridge University Press.

Blommaert, J. (2020a) Jan Blommaert on homogeneism. YouTube. Accessed May 2021, from https://www.youtube.com/watch?v=kOVuW2VCGSw

Blommaert, J. (2020b) Looking back: What was important? *Ctrl+Alt+Dem*, July 18. Accessed January 20, 2020, from https://alternative-democracy-research.org/2020/04/20/what-was-important

Blommaert, J. and Verschueren, J. (1998) *Debating Diversity: Analysing the Discourse of Tolerance*. New York: Routledge.

Blum, S.D. (2017) The significant learning benefits of getting rid of grades. *Inside Higher Ed*, 14 November. Accessed May 2022 from https://www.insidehighered.com/advice/2017/11/14/significant-learning-benefits-getting-rid-grades-essay

Blum, S.D. (ed.) (2020) *Ungrading: Why Rating Students Undermines Learning (and What to Do Instead)*. Morgantown, WV: West Virginia University Press.

Bonilla-Silva, E. (2003) *Racism Without Racists: Color-Blind Racism and the Persistence of Racial Inequality in the United States*. Lanham, MD: Rowman and Littlefield.

Boswell, M. (2019) MLK and Marxism. *Progressive Southern Theologians*. Accessed January 2021 from https://progressivesoutherntheologians.com/news/2019/4/7/mlk-and-marxism

Bourdieu, P. (1991) *Language and Symbolic Power*. Cambridge, MA: Harvard University Press.

Breed, B. (2016) Exploring a co-operative learning approach to improve self-directed learning in higher education. *Journal for New Generation Sciences* 14 (3), 1–21.

Brodkin, K. (1999) How Jews became white folks and what that says about race in America. *Choice Reviews Online* 36 (08), 36–47.

Brown, R.M. (1984) *Unexpected News: Reading the Bible with Third World Eyes*. Philadelphia: Westminster John Knox Press.

Brinton, D., Snow, M.A. and Wesche, M.B. (1989) *Content-Based Second Language Instruction*. New York: Heinle and Heinle Publishers.

Bucholtz, M. and Hall, K. (2004) Language and identity. In A. Duranti (ed.) *A Companion to Linguistic Anthropology* (pp. 268–294). Malden, MA: Basil Blackwell.

Burch, A.D. and Ploeg, L.V. (2022) Buffalo shooting highlights rise of hate crimes against Black Americans. *The New York Times*, May 16. See http://www.nytimes.com/

Buyssens, E. (1970) *Linguistique contemporaine: hommage à Eric Buyssens.* (J. Dierickx and Y. Lebrun, eds). Bruxelles: Éditions de l'Institut de Sociologie.

Cabrera, N.L. (2019) *White Guys on Campus: Racism, White Immunity, and the Myth of 'Post-Racial' Higher Education.* New Brunswick, NJ: Rutgers University Press.

Cabrera, N.L., Franklin, J.D. and Watson, J.S. (2017) *Whiteness in Higher Education: The Invisible Missing Link in Diversity and Racial Analyses.* Chichester: Wiley Subscription Services.

Cameron, D. (1995) *Verbal Hygiene.* New York: Routledge.

Canagarajah, S. (2011) Codemeshing in academic writing: Identifying teachable strategies of translanguaging. *The Modern Language Journal* 95 (3), 401–417. https://doi.org/10.1111/j.1540-4781.2011.01207.x

Carreira, M. (2007) Spanish-for-native-speaker matters: Narrowing the Latino achievement gap through Spanish language instruction. *Heritage Language Journal* 5, 147–171.

Castagno, A.E. (2014) *Educated in Whiteness: Good Intentions and Diversity in Schools.* Minneapolis: University of Minnesota Press.

Ceo-DiFrancesco, D. (2013) Instructor target language use in today's world language classrooms. In S. Dhonau (ed.) *Multitasks, Multiskills, Multiconnection: Selected Papers from the 2013 Central States Conference on the Teaching of Foreign Languages* (pp. 1–20). Central States Conference on the Teaching of Foreign Languages.

Chavez, L.R. (2008) *The Latino Threat: Constructing Immigrants, Citizens, and the Nation.* Stanford, CA: Stanford University Press.

Chun, E.B. and Feagin, J.R. (2020) *Rethinking Diversity Frameworks in Higher Education.* New York: Routledge.

Ciller, J. and Ortín, R. (2019) Evaluación de programas de lengua: Perspectivas profesionales E investigadoras. *Revista Internacional de Lenguas Extranjeras / International Journal of Foreign Languages* 2 (12). https://doi.org/10.17345/rile12.2759

Cobas, J.A. and Feagin, J.R. (2008) Language oppression and resistance: The case of middle class Latinos in the United States. *Ethnic and Racial Studies* 31 (2), 390–410. https://doi.org/10.1080/01419870701491945

Colburn, H.L. (2017) Not what it used to be: The future of Spanish language teaching. *Hispania* 100 (5), 87–92. https://doi.org/10.1353/hpn.2018.0021

Coseriu, E. (1981) Los conceptos de dialecto, nivel y estilo de lengua y el sentido propio de la dialectología. *LEA: Lingüística Española Actual* 3 (1), 1–32.

Crawford, J. (1992) Editor's Introduction. In J. Crawford (ed.) *Language Loyalties: A Source Book on the Official English Controversy.* Chicago: University of Chicago Press.

Cutler, C. (2008) Brooklyn style: Hip-hop markers and racial affiliation among European immigrants in New York City. *International Journal of Bilingualism* 12 (1–2), 7–24. https://doi.org/10.1177/13670069080120010201

Cutler, C. and Røyneland, U. (2015) Where the fuck am I from? Hip Hop youth and the (re)negotiation of language and identity in Norway and the US. In J. Nortier and B.A. Svendsen (eds) *Language, Youth and Identity in the 21st Century* (pp. 139–163). Cambridge: Cambridge University Press.

Damen, L. (1987) *Culture Learning: The Fifth Dimension in the Language Classroom.* Reading, MA: Addison-Wesley.

Daniels, M. (2019) The largest vocabulary in Hip Hop. Rappers ranked by the number of unique words used in their lyrics. *The Pudding.* Accessed July 2020, from https://rappers.mdaniels.com.s3-website-us-east-1.amazonaws.com/

Darder, A. (1991) *Culture and Power in the Classroom: A Critical Foundation for Bicultural Education.* Westport, CT: Greenwood Publishing Group.

Dávila, A.M. (2012) *Latinos, Inc: The Marketing and Making of a People.* Berkeley, CA: University of California Press.

Davila, D. (2011) 'White people don't work at McDonald's' and other shadow stories from the field: Analyzing preservice teachers' use of Obama's race speech to teach for social. *English Education* 44 (1), 13–50.

Del Valle, J. (2005) La lengua, patria común: Política lingüística, política exterior y post-nacionalismo hispánico. In R. Wright, R. Peter and P.T. Ricketts (eds) *Studies on Ibero-Romance Linguistics: Dedicated to Ralph Penny* (pp. 391–416). Newark, DE: Juan de la Cuesta-Hispanic Monographs.

Del Valle, J. (2007a) *La lengua, ¿patria común?* Frankfurt am Main: Vervuert/Iberoamericana.

Del Valle, J. (2007b) Las variedades del español en Nueva York. *El Castellano*, July. https://www.elcastellano.org/ns/edicion/2007/julio/ny3.html

Del Valle, J. (ed.) (2013) *A Political History of Spanish: The Making of a Language.* Cambridge: Cambridge University Press.

Del Valle, J. (2014) The politics of normativity and globalization: Which Spanish in the classroom? *The Modern Language Journal* 98 (1), 358–372. https://doi.org/10.1111/j .1540-4781.2014.12066.x

Del Valle, J. (2019) Lengua y democracia. *Confabulario.* Accessed March 2020, from https://confabulario.eluniversal.com.mx/lengua-y-democracia/?fbclid=IwAR1NV iTJWoKNejeph3-0ly5b9eWPEm3HYfA_JzaJByqDM7XdOTreqhs9vfI

DiAngelo, R. (2011) White fragility. *International Journal of Critical Pedagogy* 3 (3), 54–70.

Dixson, A., Gillborn, D., Ladson-Billings, G., Parker, L., Rollock, N. and Warmington, P. (eds) (2018) *Critical Race Theory in Education: Off-Shoot Movements.* New York: Routledge.

Dörnyei, Z. (2003) *Attitudes, Orientations, and Motivations in Language Learning: Advances in Theory, Research, and Applications.* Oxford: Blackwell.

Dörnyei, Z. and Ushioda, E. (2013) *Teaching and Researching: Motivation.* New York: Routledge.

Dufeu, B. (1994) *Teaching Myself.* Oxford: Oxford University Press.

Duff, P. (2012) Identity, agency, and second language acquisition. In S. Gass and A. Mackey (eds) *Handbook of Second Language Acquisition* (pp. 410–426). New York: Routledge.

Ehrman, M.E. (1996) *Understanding Second Language Learning Difficulties.* Thousand Oaks, CA: SAGE Publications.

Fairclough, A. (1983) Was Martin Luther King a Marxist? *History Workshop Journal* 15 (1), 117–125. https://doi.org/10.1093/hwi/15.1.117

Fairclough, N. (1992) *Critical Language Awareness.* New York: Longman.

Fairclough, N. (1995) *Critical Discourse Analysis: The Critical Study of Language.* New York: Longman.

Feagin, J. and Vera, H. (2002) Confronting one's own racism. In P.S. Rothenberg (ed.) *White Privilege* (pp. 121–125). New York, NY: Worth Publishers.

Feinberg, A., Branton, R. and Martinez-Ebers, V. (2019) Counties that hosted a 2016 Trump rally saw a 226 percent increase in hate crimes. *The Washington Post,* 22 March. Accessed August 2019 from https://www.washingtonpost.com /politics/2019/03/22/trumps-rhetoric-does-inspire-more-hate-crimes/?utm_term= .008d6325785b

Feldman, G. (2011) Right versus right: how neoliberals and neo-nationalists dominate migration policy in Europe. In *The Migration Apparatus: Security, Labor, and Policy-making in the European Union* (pp. 25–55). Redwood City: Stanford University Press. https://doi.org/10.1515/9780804779128-005

Fishman, J. (1967) Bilingualism with and without diglossia; diglossia with and without bilingualism. *Journal of Social Issues* 23 (2), 29–38.

Flores, J. (2000) Puerto rocks: Rap, roots and amnesia. In J. Flores (ed.) *From Bomba to Hip-Hop: Puerto Rican Culture and Latino Identity* (pp. 115–140). New York: Columbia University Press.

Flores, N. (2017) From language-as-resource to language-as-struggle: Resisting the Coke-ification of bilingual education. In M.-C. Flubacher and A. Del Percio (eds) *Language, Education and Neoliberalism: Critical Studies in Sociolinguistics* (pp. 62–81). Bristol: Multilingual Matters. https://doi.org/10.21832/9781783098699-006

Flores, N. and Rosa, J. (2015) Undoing appropriateness: Raciolinguistic ideologies and language diversity in education. *Harvard Educational Review* 85 (2), 149–171. https://doi.org/10.17763/0017-8055.85.2.149

Flores-Ohlson, L. (2011) El cambio de código en la producción musical del grupo domin-icano-americano Aventura: Funciones pragmáticas y estilísticas. *Actas del XVI Congreso internacional de la ALFAL, Dialectología y Sociolingüística.*

Flubacher, M.-C. and Del Percio, A. (2017) Language, education and neoliberalism. In M.-C. Flubacher and A. Del Percio (eds) *Language, Education and Neoliberalism: Critical Studies in Sociolinguistics* (pp. 1–18). Bristol: Multilingual Matters. https://doi.org/10.21832/9781783098699-003

Fong, M. and McEwen, K.D. (2004) Cultural and intercultural speech uses and meanings of the Term Nigga. *Communicating Ethnic and Cultural Identity*, 165–178.

Ford, K.A. and Orlandella, J. (2015) The 'not-so-Final remark'. *Sociology of Race and Ethnicity* 1 (2), 287–301. https://doi.org/10.1177/2332649214559286

Freire, P. (1970) *Pedagogy of the Oppressed.* New York: Seabury Press.

Gallagher, C.A. (2011) *Defining Race and Ethnicity. Rethinking the Color Line: Readings in Race and Ethnicity.* New York, NY: McGraw-Hill Education.

Gándara, P. (2012) From González to Flores: A return to the Mexican room? In O. Santa Ana and C. Bustamante (eds) *Arizona Frestorm* (pp. 121–144). Lanham, MD: Rowman & Littlefield.

García, O. and Baker, C. (1995) *Policy and Practice in Bilingual Education: A Reader Extending the Foundations.* Clevedon: Multilingual Matters.

García, O. and Otheguy, R. (2015) Spanish and Hispanic bilingualism. In M. Lacorte (ed.) *The Routledge Handbook of Hispanic Applied Linguistics* (pp. 639–658). New York: Routledge.

García, O. and Tupas, R. (2019) Doing and undoing bilingualism in education. In A. De Houwer and L. Ortega (eds) *The Cambridge Handbook of Bilingualism* (pp. 390–407). Cambridge: Cambridge University Press.

García, O. and Li, W. (2014) *Translanguaging: Language, Bilingualism and Education.* New York: Palgrave Macmillan.

Gardner, R.C. and Lambert, W.E. (1972) *Attitudes and Motivation in Second Language Learning.* Rowley, MA: Newbury House Publishers.

Garrett, P.D. (2001) Language attitudes and sociolinguistics. *Journal of Sociolinguistics* 5 (4), 626–631. https://doi.org/10.1111/1467-9481.00171

Geiger, R.L. (2005) Ten generations of American higher education. In P.G. Altbach, R.O. Berdahl and P.J. Gumport (eds) *American Higher Education in the Twenty-First Century: Social, Political, and Economic Challenges* (2nd edn, pp. 38–70). Baltimore, MD: Johns Hopkins University Press.

Gibson, K. (2004) English Only court cases involving the U.S. Workplace: The myths of language use and the homogenization of bilingual workers' identities. *Second Language Studies* 22 (2), 1–60.

Gironzetti, E., Lacorte, M., Merediz, E. and Bartis, S. (2020) Evaluación y rediseño curricular para la integración de lengua, cultura y literatura en programas de español como L2. *Revista Nebrija De Lingüística Aplicada a La Enseñanza De Lenguas* 14 (28), 12–35. https://doi.org/10.26378/rnlael1428401

Giroux, H. (1983) Theories of reproduction and resistance in the new sociology of education: A critical analysis. *Harvard Educational Review* 53 (3), 257–293.

Goffman, E. (1956) *The Presentation of Self in Everyday Life.* New York: Overlook Press.

Goffman, E. (1963) *Stigma: Notes on the Management of Spoiled Identity.* Englewood Cliffs, NJ: Prentice-Hall.

Gooden, M.A., Davis, B.W., Spikes, D.D., Hall, D.L. and Lee, L. (2018) Leaders changing how they act by changing how they think: Applying principles of an anti-racist principal preparation program. *Teachers College Record* 120 (14), 1–26.

Griva, E., Chostelidou, D. and Tsakiridou, E. (2011) Assessment of metalinguistic awareness and strategy use of young EFL learners. *Journal of Communications Research* 3 (2/3), 203.

Guevara Urbina, M. and Álvarez Espinoza, S. (2018) *Hispanics in the U.S. Criminal Justice System* (2nd edn). Springfield, IL: Charles C Thomas.

Gusa, D.L. (2010) White institutional presence: The impact of whiteness on campus climate. *Harvard Educational Review* 80 (4), 464–490. https://doi.org/10.17763/haer.80 .4.p5j483825u110002

Gutierrez, R.A. and Zavella, P. (eds) (2009) *Mexicans in California: Transformations and Challenges.* Urbana, IL: University of Illinois Press.

Haugen, E. (1966) Dialect, language, nation. *American Anthropologist* 68 (4), 922–935. https://doi.org/10.1525/aa.1966.68.4.02a00040

Holguín Mendoza, C. (2018) Critical language awareness (CLA) for Spanish heritage language programs: Implementing a complete curriculum. *International Multilingual Research Journal* 12 (2), 65–79. https://doi.org/10.1080/19313152.2017.1401445

hooks, b. (1994) *Teaching to Transgress: Education as the Practice of Freedom.* New York: Routledge.

Hualde, J.I., Olarrea, A., Escobar, A.M. and Travis, C.E. (2010) *Introducción a la lingüística hispánica.* New York: Cambridge University Press.

Ibrahim, A. el K.M. (1998) Hey, whassup homeboy? Becoming Black: Race, language, culture, and the politics of identity: African students in a Franco-Ontarian high school. Dissertation, National Library of Canada.

Inoue, A.B. (2015) *Antiracist Writing Assessment Ecologies: Teaching and Assessing Writing for a Socially Just Future.* Fort Collins, CO: WAC Clearinghouse.

Irvine, J. and Gal, S. (2000) Language ideology and linguistic differentiation. In P.V. Kroskrity (ed.) *Regimes of Language: Ideologies, Polities, and Identities* (pp. 35–84). School of American Research Press.

Jackman, M. (1994) *The Velvet Glove: Paternalism and Conflict in Gender, Class, and Race Relations.* Berkeley, CA: University of California Press.

Johnson, F.L. (2000) *Speaking Culturally: Language Diversity in the United States.* Thousand Oaks, CA: SAGE Publications.

Kalantzis, M., Cope, B. and the Learning by Design Project Group (2005) *Learning by Design.* Champaign, IL: Victorian Schools Innovation Commission and Common Ground Publishing.

Karabel, J. (2005) *The Chosen: The Hidden History of Admission and Exclusion at Harvard, Yale, and Princeton.* Boston: Houghton Mifflin.

Kendi, I.X. (2019) *How to Be an Antiracist.* New York: One World.

Kennedy, R. (2002) *Nigger: The Strange Career of a Troublesome Word* (1st edn). New York: Pantheon Books.

King, W., Emanuel, R., Brown, X., Dingle, N., Lucas, V., Perkins, A. and Witherspoon, Q.D. (2018) Who has the 'right' to use the n-word? A survey of attitudes about the acceptability of using the n-word and its derivatives. *International Journal of Society, Culture & Language* 6 (2), 47–58.

Klee, C.A. (2015) Content-based programs and Spanish for the professions. In M. Lacorte (ed.) *The Routledge Handbook of Hispanic Applied Linguistics* (pp. 639–658). New York: Routledge.

Krashen, S. (1981) *Second Language Acquisition and Second Language Learning.* Oxford: Pergamon Press.

Kubota, R. (2020) Toward a performative commitment to heterogeneity. In T.J. Silva and Z. Wang (eds) *Reconciling Translingualism and Second Language Writing* (pp. 163–171). New York: Routledge.

Labov, W. (1966) *The Social Stratification of English in New York City.* Washington, DC: Center for Applied Linguistics.

Labov, W. (1972) The study of language in its social context. In J.B. Pride and J. Holmes (eds) *Sociolinguistics* (pp. 180–202). Harmondsworth: Penguin.

Lacorte, M. (2007) Interacción y contexto en el aprendizaje y enseñanza de español como L2. *Spanish in Context* 4 (1), 73–98.

Lacorte, M. (2017) Spanish and Portuguese programs in higher education institutions in the United States: Perspectives and possibilities. *Hispania* 100 (5), 185–191. https://doi .org/10.1353/hpn.2018.0046

Lacorte, M. and Magro, J.L. (2022) Foundations for critical and antiracist heritage language teaching. In S. Loza and S. Beaudrie (eds) *Heritage Language Teaching and Research: Perspectives from Critical Language Awareness.* New York: Routledge.

Lado, B. and Quijano, C. (2020) Ideologies, identity, capital, and investment in a critical multilingual Spanish classroom. *Critical Multilingualism Studies: An Interdisciplinary Journal* 8 (1), 141–175.

Ladson-Billings, G. (2000) *Racialized Disclosures and Ethnic Epistemologies.* Thousand Oaks, CA: Sage.

Lanehart, S.L. (1998) African American Vernacular English and education: The dynamics of pedagogy, ideology, and identity. *Journal of English Linguistics* 26 (2), 122–136. https://doi.org/10.1177/007542429802600204

Larson, C.L. and Ovando, C.J. (2001) *The Color of Bureaucracy: The Politics of Equity in Mulicultural School Communities.* Belmont, CA: Wadsworth Publishing Company.

Lee, C. (2017) *Multilingualism Online.* New York: Routledge.

Lee, E., Menkart, D. and Okazawa-Rey, M. (eds) (1998) *Beyond Heroes and Holidays: A Practical Guide to K–12 Anti-Racist, Multicultural Education and Staff Development.* Teaching for Change.

Leeman, J. (2005) Engaging critical pedagogy: Spanish for native speakers. *Foreign Language Annals* 38 (1), 35–45. https://doi.org/10.1111/j.1944-9720.2005.tb02451.x

Leeman, J. (2015) Critical approaches to the teaching of Spanish as a local-foreign language. In M. Lacorte (ed.) *The Handbook of Hispanic Applied Linguistics* (pp. 275–292). New York: Routledge.

Leeman, J. (2018) Critical language awareness and Spanish as a heritage language: Challenging the linguistic subordination of US Latinxs. In K. Potowski (ed.) *The Routledge Handbook of Spanish as a Minority/Heritage Language* (pp. 345–358). Abingdon: Routledge.

Leeman, J. and Serafini, E.J. (2016) Sociolinguistics for heritage language educators and students: A model for critical translingual competence. In M. Fairclough and S.M. Beaudrie (eds) *Innovative Strategies for Heritage Language Teaching: A Practical Guide for the Classroom* (pp. 56–79). Washington, DC: Georgetown University Press.

Leeman, J., Rabin, L. and Román-Mendoza, E. (2011) Identity and activism in heritage language education. *Modern Language Journal* (95) 4, 481–495.

Lewis, A.E. and Diamond, J.B. (2015) *Despite the Best Intentions: How Racial Inequality Thrives in Good Schools.* Oxford: Oxford University Press.

Lippi-Green, R. (1997) *English with an Accent: Language, Ideology and Discrimination in the United States* (pp. 79–103). New York: Routledge.

Lipski, J.M. (2006) Hispanic linguistics: In a glass house or a glass box? *HIOL: Hispanic Issues Series,* 107–114.

Looney, D. and Lusin, N. (2019) Modern Language Association of America: *Enrollments in Languages Other than English in United States Institutions of Higher Education,* Summer 2016 and Fall 2016: Final Report. https://umaryland.on.worldcat.org/oclc/8514715896

Lorenzo, F. (2006) *Motivación y segundas lenguas*. Madrid: Arco libros.

Macat (2016) An introduction to Antonio Gramsci's *The Prison Notebooks* – A Macat politics analysis. YouTube. https://youtu.be/XMSlgrgmmTs

Macedo, D. (1997) English only: The tongue-tying of America. In A. Darder, R.D. Torres and H. Gutierrez (eds) *Latinos and Education: A Critical Reader* (pp. 269–278). New York: Routledge.

Magro, J.L. (2016a) Lengua y racismo-motivación, competencia y conciencia lingüística en la clase de español como segunda lengua: Integración de contenidos relacionados con la dimensión socio-política del lenguaje en un acercamiento content-based. CUNY Academic Works. http://academicworks.cuny.edu/gc_etds/1568

Magro, J.L. (2016b) Talking Hip-Hop: When stigmatized language varieties become prestige varieties. *Linguistics and Education* 36, 16–26. https://doi.org/10.1016/j .linged.2016.06.002

Magro, J.L. (2020) 'Dope!! *Puta vergona*': Identity 'en el middle' and language choice in Instagram among urban music affiliated male Spanish legacy speakers from da DMV. In F. Salgado-Robles and E.M. Lamboy (eds) *Spanish Across Domains in the United States: Education, Public Space, and Social Media* (pp. 333–363). Boston: Brill.

Mar-Molinero, C. (2000) *The Politics of Language in the Spanish-Speaking World: From Colonisation to Globalisation*. New York: Routledge.

Marshall, D.F. (1986) The question of an official language: Language rights and the English Language Amendment. *International Journal of the Sociology of Language* 1986 (60), 7–76. https://doi.org/10.1515/ijsl.1986.60.7

Martínez, G.A. (2003) Classroom based dialect awareness in heritage language instruction: A critical applied linguistic approach. *Heritage Language Journal* 1 (1), 44–57. https:// doi.org/10.46538/hlj.1.1.3

Martínez-Avila, D., Ferreira, M. and Magro, J.L. (2015) Aplicación de la Teoría Crítica de Raza en la organización y representación del conocimiento. *SCIRE: Representación organización del conocimineto* 21 (2), 27–33.

Marx, K. and Engels, F. (1972) *The German Ideology*. C. Arthur (ed.). International.

Masgoret, A.M. and Gardner, R.C. (2003) Attitudes, motivation, and second language learning: A meta-analysis of studies conducted by Gardner and Associates. *Language Learning* 53, 123–163.

Massey, D.S. and Pren, K.A. (2012) Unintended consequences of US immigration policy: Explaining the post-1965 surge from Latin America. *Population and Development Review* 38 (1), 1–29. https://doi.org/10.1111/j.1728-4457.2012.00470.x

McCroskey, J.C. (1977) Oral communication apprehension: A summary of recent theory and research. *Human Communication & Search* 4, 78–96.

McWhorter, J.H. (2010) Let's make a deal on the N-word. *The Root*. https://www.theroot .com/lets-make-a-deal-on-the-n-word-1790880617

McWhorter, J.H. (2021) *Woke Racism: How a New Religion Has Betrayed Black America*. New York, NY: Portfolio/Penguin.

Memmi, A. (2000) *Racism*. (S. Martinot, trans). Minneapolis: University of Minnesota Press.

Montagu, A. (1976) *The Nature of Human Aggression*. Oxford: Oxford University Press.

Morales, E. (2002) *Living in Spanglish: The Search for Latino Identity in America*. New York: St. Martin's Press.

Moreno-Fernández, F. (2007) Anglicismos en el léxico disponible de los adolescentes de Chicago. In K. Potowski and R. Cameron (eds) *Spanish in Contact: Policy, Social and Linguistic Inquiries* (pp. 41–60). Amsterdam: John Benjamins.

Muñoz, C. (2012) *Intensive Exposure Experiences in Second Language Learning*. Bristol: Multilingual Matters.

National Center for Education Statistics. (2020) Washington, DC: NCES.

National Education Association of the United States. Human Relations Section. (1973) *Education and Racism: An Action Manual*. Washington, DC: National Education Association.

Nguyen, P. and Sanchez, J. (2001) *Ethnic Communities in New York City: Dominicans in Washington Heights*. NYU. Accessed September 2001, from https://www.nyu.edu/classes/blake.map2001/dominican2.html

Nieto, S. (2009) *Language, Culture, and Teaching: Critical Perspectives*. New York: Routledge.

Nortier, J. and Svendsen, B.A. (eds) (2015) *Language, Youth and Identity in the 21st Century*. Cambridge: Cambridge University Press.

Norton, B. (2012) Identity and second language acquisition. In C. Chapelle (ed.) *The Encyclopedia of Applied Linguistics*. https://doi.org/10.1002/9781405198431.wbeal0521

Ochoa, A.M. (1995) Language policy and social implications for addressing the bicultural immigrant experience in the United States. In A. Darder (ed.) *Culture and Difference: Critical Perspectives on the Bicultural Experience in the United States* (pp. 227–253). Westport, CT: Bergin & Garvey.

Ochoa de Michelena, F.J. (2007) La europeización de España desde la cultura y las categorías del juicio. Reflexiones en torno a Ganivet, Unamuno y Ortega. *Barataria. Revista Castellano-Manchega de Ciencias Sociales* (8), 193–213. https://doi.org/10.20932/barataria.v0i8.220

Omi, M. and Winant, H. (1994) *Racial Formation in the United States: From the 1960s to the 1990s* (2nd edn). New York: Routledge.

Ortega, L. (2019) SLA and the study of equitable multilingualism. *The Modern Language Journal* 103, 23–38. https://doi.org/10.1111/modl.12525

Otheguy, R. and Zentella, A.C. (2008) Language and dialect contact in Spanish in New York: Toward the formation of a speech community. *Language* 83 (4), 770–802. https://doi.org/10.1353/lan.2008.0019

Otheguy, R. and Stern, N. (2011) On so-called Spanglish. *International Journal of Bilingualism* 15 (1), 85–100. https://doi.org/10.1177/1367006910379298

Paris, D. and Alim, H.S. (2017) *Culturally Sustaining Pedagogies: Teaching and Learning for Justice in a Changing World*. New York: Teachers College Press.

Paulino, E. (2016) *Dividing Hispaniola: The Dominican Republic's Border Campaign Against Haiti, 1930–1961*. Pittsburgh: University of Pittsburgh Press.

Penny, R.J. (2000) *Variation and Change in Spanish*. Cambridge: Cambridge University Press.

Pennycook, A. (1994) *The Cultural Politics of English As an International Language*. London: Longman.

Pennycook, A. (2001) *Critical Applied Linguistics: A Critical Introduction*. Mahwah, NJ: Lawrence Erlbaum.

Pennycook, A. (2007) *Global Englishes and Transcultural Flows*. New York: Routledge.

Pérez-Peña, R. (2015) Black or white? Woman's story stirs up a furor. *The New York Times*, June 12. Accessed April 2020, from https://www.nytimes.com/2015/06/13/us/rachel-dolezal-naacp-president-accused-of-lying-about-her-race.html

Pew Research Center (2018) *An Examination of the 2016 Electorate, Based on Validated Voters*. Pew Research Center – U.S. Politics and Policy. Accessed April 2020, from https://www.people-press.org/2018/08/09/an-examination-of-the-2016-electorate-based-on-validated-voters/

Pew Research Center (2020) *What the 2020 Electorate Looks Like by Party, Race and Ethnicity, Age, Education and Religion*. Accessed November 2020, from https://www.pewresearch.org/fact-tank/2020/10/26/what-the-2020-electorate-looks-like-by-party-race-and-ethnicity-age-education-and-religion/

Potowski, K. (2005) *Fundamentos de la enseñanza del español a hispanohablantes en los EE.UU*. Madrid: Arco/Libros.

Potter, R. A. (1995) *Spectacular Vernaculars: Hip-Hop and the Politics of Postmodernism*. Albany: State University of New York Press.

Rahman, J. (2008) Middle-class African Americans: Reactions and attitudes toward African American English. *American Speech* 83 (2), 141–176. https://doi.org/10.1215/00031283-2008-009

Ramjattan, V.A. (2019) Raciolinguistics and the aesthetic labourer. *Journal of Industrial Relations* 61 (5), 726–738. https://doi.org/10.1177/0022185618792990

Rampton, B. (2009) Social class and sociolinguistics. *Applied Linguistics Review* 1, 1–22.

Ray, S. (2007) Politics over official language in the United States: Aspects of constitutional silence on the status of English. *International Studies* 44 (3), 235–252. https://doi.org /10.1177/002088170704400303.

Rebollo-Gil, G. and Moras, A. (2006) Defining an 'anti' stance: Key pedagogical questions about engaging anti-racism in college classrooms. *Race Ethnicity and Education* 9 (4), 381–394. https://doi.org/10.1080/13613320600957702

Rodríguez-Iglesias, I. (2016) Ideologías lingüísticas: Descapitalización fanoniana de los andaluces. *Nueva revista del Pacífico* (65), 105–136. https://doi.org/10.4067/s0719 -51762016000200005

Rosa, J. (2019) *Looking Like a Language, Sounding Like a Race: Raciolinguistic Ideologies and the Learning of Latinidad.* Oxford: Oxford University Press.

Rothenberg, P.S. (2005) *White Privilege: Essential Readings on the Other Side of Racism* (2nd edn). New York: Worth.

Ryan, E.B. (1979) Why do low prestige language varieties persist? In H. Giles and R.N. St. Clair (eds) *Language and Social Psychology* (pp. 145–157). Oxford: Basil Blackwell.

Sackstein, S. (2015) *Hacking Assessment: 10 Ways to Go Gradeless in a Traditional Grades School.* Cleveland, OH: Times 10 Publications.

Schaffner, B.F., Nteta, T. and Macwilliams, M.C. (2018) Understanding white polarization in the 2016 vote for president: the sobering role of racism and sexism. *Political Science Quarterly* 133 (1), 9–34. https://doi.org/10.1002/polq.12737

Schwartz, A. (2014) Third border talk: Intersubjectivity, power negotiation and the making of race in Spanish language classrooms. *International Journal of the Sociology of Language* 2014 (227), 157–173. https://doi.org/10.1515/ijsl-2013-0093

Silverstein, M. (1996) Encountering language and languages of encounter in North American ethnohistory. *Journal of Linguistic Anthropology* 6 (2), 126–144.

Sisneros, J., Stakeman, C., Joiner, M.C. and Schmitz, C.L. (2008) *Critical Multicultural Social Work.* New York: Oxford University Press.

Smith, H.L. (2019) Has nigga been reappropriated as a term of endearment? A qualitative and quantitative analysis. *American Speech* 94 (4), 420–477.

Solórzano, D.G. and Yosso, T.J. (2002) Critical race methodology: Counter-storytelling as an analytical framework for education research. *Qualitative Inquiry* 8 (1), 23–44. https://doi.org/10.1177/107780040200800103

Spolsky, B. (1999) Second-language learning. In J. Fishman (ed.) *Handbook of Language and Ethnic Identity* (pp. 181–192). Oxford: Oxford University Press.

Squire, D., Williams, B.C. and Tuitt, F. (2018) Plantation politics and neoliberal racism in higher education: A framework for reconstructing anti-racist institutions. *Teachers College Record: The Voice of Scholarship in Education* 120 (14), 1–20. https://doi.org /10.1177/016146811812001412

Stanley, S. (2017) From a whisper to a voice: Sociocultural style and anti-racist pedagogy. *Journal of Basic Writing* 36 (2), 5–25. https://doi.org/10.37514/jbw-j.2017.36.2.02

Stengel, B. (2008) Facing fear, releasing resistance, enabling education. *Philosophical Studies in Education* 39, 66–75.

Stevick, E.W. (1980) *Teaching Languages: A Way and Ways.* Rowley, MA: Newbury House.

Stewart, D. (2018) Minding the gap between diversity and institutional transformation: Eight proposals for enacting institutional change. *Teachers College Record* 120 (14), 1–16.

Strasser, N. (2014) Using Prezi in higher education. *Journal of College Teaching & Learning (TLC)* 11 (2), 95–98. https://doi.org/10.19030/tlc.v11i2.8547

Talmy, S. (2010) Critical research in applied linguistics. In B. Paltridge and A. Phakiti (eds) *Continuum Companion to Research Methods in Applied Linguistics* (pp. 127–142). London: Continuum.

Terkourafi, M. (2010) *The Languages of Global Hip-Hop.* London: Continuum.

Thelin, J.R. (2004) *A History of American Higher Education.* Baltimore, MD: Johns Hopkins University Press.

Toasijé, A. (2009) The Africanity of Spain: Identity and Problematization. *Journal of Black Studies* 39 (3), 348–355. https://doi.org/10.1177/0021934706297563

Torres-Saillant, S. (1998) The tribulations of Blackness: Stages in Dominican racial identity. *Latin American Perspectives* 25 (3), 126–146.

Urciuoli, B. (1996) *Exposing Prejudice.* Boulder: Westview Press.

Urciuoli, B. (2008) Whose Spanish? The tension between linguistic correctness and cultural identity. In M. Niño-Murcia and J. Rothman (eds) *Bilingualism and Identity: Spanish at the Crossroads with Other Languages* (pp. 257–278). Amsterdam: John Benjamins.

Valdés, G. (1995) The teaching of minority languages as academic subjects: Pedagogical and theoretical challenges. *The Modern Language Journal* 79 (3), 299–328.

Valdés, G. (2000) The teaching of heritage languages: An introduction for Slavic teaching professionals. In O. Kagan and B. Rifkin (eds) *The Learning and Teaching of Slavic Languages and Cultures* (pp. 375–403). Bloomington, IN: Slavica.

Valenzuela, A. (1999) *Subtractive Schooling: U.S.-Mexican Youth and the Politics of Caring.* Albany, NY: SUNY Press.

Vygotsky, L.S. (1980) *Mind in Society: The Development of Higher Psychological Processes.* Cambridge, MA: Harvard University Press.

Wagner, J.K., Yu, J., Ifekwunigwe, J.O., Harrell, T.M., Bamshad, M.J. and Royal, C.D. (2016) Anthropologists' views on race, ancestry, and genetics. *American Journal of Physical Anthropology* 162 (2), 318–327. https://doi.org/10.1002/ajpa.23120

Weiner, B. (1992) *Encyclopedia of Educational Research* (6th edn, vol. 3). New York: Macmillan.

Welton, A.D., Owens, D.R. and Zamani-Gallaher, E.M. (2018) Anti-racist change: A conceptual framework for educational institutions to take systemic action. *Teachers College Record* 120 (14), 1–22.

Wilder, C.S. (2013) *Ebony and Ivy: Race, Slavery, and the Troubled History of America's Universities* (1st US edn). New York: Bloomsbury Press.

Willis, P.E. (2004) Twenty-five years on: Old books, new times. In N. Dolby and G. Dimitriadis (eds) *Learning to Labor in New Times* (pp. 167–196). New York: Routledge.

Wills, D. (2009) Ben Stiller Biography. *Talktalk.* http://www.talktalk.co.uk/entertainment/film/biography/artist/ben-stiller/biography/7. 2009

Wise, T. (2002) Membership has its privileges: Thoughts on acknowledging and challenging whiteness. In P.S. Rothenberg (ed.) *White Privilege: Essential Readings of the Other Side of Racism* (pp. 107/–110). New York: Worth Publishers.

Wodak, R. (2012) Language, power and identity. *Language Teaching* 45, 215–233. doi:10.1017/S0261444811000048.

X, M. (1966) *The Autobiography of Malcolm X: With the Assistance of Alex Haley.* New York: Hutchinson.

Zapata, G.C. and Lacorte, M. (2018) *Multiliteracies Pedagogy and Language Learning: Teaching Spanish to Heritage Speakers.* Cham: Palgrave Macmillan.

Zentella, A.C. (1981) Language variety among Puerto Ricans. In C. Ferguson (ed.) *Language in the USA* (pp. 219–238). New York: Cambridge University Press.

Zentella, A.C. (1990) Lexical levelling in four New York City Spanish dialects: Linguistic and social factors. *Hispania* 73, 1094–1105.

Zentella, A.C. (1997) Spanish in New York. In O. García and J.A. Fishman (eds) *The Multilingual Apple: Languages in New York City* (pp. 3–50). Berlín/NY: Mouton de Gruyter.

Zentella, A.C. (2016) 'Socials,' 'poch@s,' 'normals' y los demás: School networks and linguistic capital of high school students on the Tijuana–San Diego border. In H.S. Alim, J.R. Rickford and A.F. Ball (eds) *Raciolinguistics: How Language Shapes Our Ideas About Race* (pp. 327–346). Oxford: Oxford University Press. https://doi.org/10.1093/acprof:oso/9780190625696.003.0019

Index

For Product Safety Concerns and Information please contact our EU Authorised Representative:

Easy Access System Europe

Mustamäe tee 50

10621 Tallinn

Estonia

gpsr.requests@easproject.com

www.ingramcontent.com/pod-product-compliance
Lightning Source LLC
Chambersburg PA
CBHW071849270326
41929CB00013B/2151